ARTIFICIAL INTELLIGENCE:
AN INTRODUCTORY COURSE

ARTIFICIAL INTELLIGENCE:

AN INTRODUCTORY COURSE

A.Bundy
R.M.Burstall
S.Weir
R.M.Young

EDINBURGH
University Press

© 1978
Edinburgh University Press
22 George Square, Edinburgh
ISBN 0 85224 340 5
Printed in Great Britain by
R. & R. Clark Ltd, Edinburgh

CONTENTS

PREFACE

These are the collected lecture notes of the course, Artificial Intelligence 2, given at the University of Edinburgh in the academic year 1976-77 by the staff of the Department of Artificial Intelligence. Despite its title the course was introductory, requiring no previous knowledge of AI or Computer Science (the "2" is a code meaning "not for first years"). The course attracted students from psychology, linguistics, philosophy, computer-science, mathematics, and other disciplines. It has now run for three years.

Teaching a new and multi-disciplinary course, like AI, is very hard. Even though we put a lot of work into it, we are still conscious of the need for improvement, especially in the teaching of programming to social science and arts students. By binding our notes into this volume we hope both to promote feedback and perhaps to save others some work.

Rather than attempt a broad survey of the field we have tried to show how AI programs are built. This was done by taking a series of tasks, proposing and discussing ways of modelling them, then extending and debugging these models. Students eventually tried this for themselves in their projects. A lot of emphasis was placed on the acquisition of skills e.g. programming, writing robot operators, writing a context-free grammar, line labelling polyhedral scenes, etc. General issues were delayed until the students had acquired some grasp of the subject. Most discussion of these issues took place in class sessions and student presentations and so is not recorded in the notes.

The notes are divided into six sections: Representation of Knowledge; Natural Language; Question Answering and Inference; Visual Perception; Learning; and Programming. The lectures were not given in this order; in particular, the Representation of Knowledge and Programming lectures were closely integrated. The actual sequence of lectures is given in appendix 2.

The programming section is a guide to the programming language LOGO, which was especially developed for non-numerical work and for teaching to young students. It has also been used successfully to teach people without a strong mathematical background and so is particularly good for a course like ours. LOGO programs have been used to illustrate ideas in other sections of the book. In order to make the book suitable for a wider audience, LISP translations of most of these programs are provided.

The book is concluded with a number of useful appendixes for those planning a similar course to ours. These include details of the way in which the course was given and a discussion of the difficulties inherent in a course of this nature.

vii

ACKNOWLEDGEMENTS

During the three years the course has been running, a tremendous number of people have had a hand in it. We would like to thank the various demonstrators, tutors, project supervisors, lecturers and examiners, without whom it would not have been possible. Although it is not possible to mention everyone, we would like to single out: Peter Buneman, the original organiser; Colin McArthur and Rosemary Robinson, who kept LOGO running; Aaron Sloman, our external examiner; Mark Adler, who carefully translated many of our LOGO programs into LISP; and last, but certainly not least, the secretaries, Jean, both Margarets, Peggy and Eleanor, who tirelessly typed the original huge volume of notes.

1.   PROBLEM SOLVING

1.1   GEOMETRIC ANALOGY PROBLEMS

1.1.1   Introduction

Pick some task that involves intelligence and try to give a precise "recipe" for doing task, e.g. the analogy test in example 1:

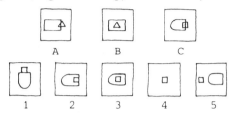

Instructions. Find the rule by which A has been changed to make B. Apply the rule to C.
Select the result from 1 — 5.

Questions to ask yourself. Can I do it? Is intelligence needed? Could I explain to someone how to do it? Could I write an instruction booklet? Would a machine be intelligent if it could do the task, or if it could do some such tasks, but not all?

1.1.2   First Recipe

Consider the original instructions and focus on the imprecise parts of them: finding the rule (a creative act?); applying the rule (probably straightforward); selecting the best answer (either straightforward or go back to the beginning).

Finding the Rule. Because the problem is solved "in the head" the rule must apply to some description of A and produce a description of B.
1. Make a description of A in English.
2. Make a description of B in English.
3. Compare descriptions to find what must be done to one to produce the other.

Thus, for example 1 we could have:

      A is "a rectangle with a triangle on its perimeter"
      B is "a rectangle with a triangle inside it"
      rule is change "on its perimeter" to "inside it"
      C is "arch with a square on its perimeter"

Therefore, applying the rule to C, the answer should be

      "Arch with a square inside it"

which corresponds to answer 3.

1.1.3   Debugging the Rule Finder — Symbolic Descriptions

If we had described B as "a triangle inside a rectangle", or "a rectangle

1

surrounding a triangle", we would not have found this simple rule. We need some unique form for the description of a figure, e.g. [inside triangle rectangle], where:

1. We drop all superfluous words e.g. "a" and limit ourselves to the objects mentioned (triangle, rectangle) and the relationship between them (inside).
2. We decide always to replace all descriptions using "outside", "surrounding" etc. with the equivalent description using "inside".
3. The objects are put in some fixed (but arbitrary) order. In our case the inside object (triangle) always comes first.

The description [inside triangle rectangle] will be called a *symbolic description*. The first word (inside) is sometimes called the *predicate* and the remainder (triangle, rectangle) its *arguments*. The brackets are currently just for punctuation. However, when we come to represent these symbolic descriptions in the computer we will see that the brackets are part of the syntax of the data-structure called *lists*.

The descriptions in example 1 become:
> A: [on triangle rectangle]
> B: [inside triangle rectangle]
> rule: change "on" to "inside"
> C: [on square arch]
> new description: [inside square arch]

1.1.4 More Debugging — More Complete Descriptions
Let us try this on another example, example 2:

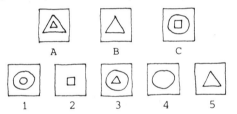

Descriptions. Because we must distinguish different objects, these become:
> A: [inside triangle1 triangle2]
> B: ?
> rule: delete everything?

It would be a good idea to add a list of objects in the figure to our description, or we will not be able to separate answers 2, 4 and 5. It would also be a good idea to allow several relationships in a description. So our general description becomes:
> [objects in the figure] [relationships in the figure]

Try the example again:
> A: [triangle1 triangle2] [inside triangle1 triangle2]
> B: [triangle2]

2

rule: remove "inside" object and any relationships it is involved in
C: [circle square] [inside square circle]
new description: [circle]
Which answer is this a description of?

1.1.5   Even More Debugging — Similarity Descriptions

When we gave the triangle in B (example 2) the same name as one of the triangles in A we were begging the question. These two triangles are matched because the similarity between them is most direct. Suppose, however, that answer 4 was not available, but that there *was* a large square, as in example 3:

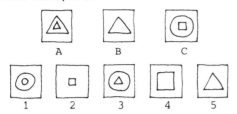

Then we might extract the rule "remove outside object and blow up inside object by a factor of 2", i.e. there are two different correspondences between objects in A and B. From each correspondence we get a different rule, yielding a different answer. We must therefore distinguish objects in A from objects in B, and then make any correspondences explicit. Thus the descriptions become:

    A: [triangle1 triangle2] [inside triangle1 triangle2]
    B: [triangle3]
    similarity 1: [sim triangle2 triangle3 direct]   (for example 2)
    similarity 2: [sim triangle1 triangle3 [scale 2]]   (for example 3)
where, in similarity 2, triangle1 and triangle3 are identical if we apply the [scale 2] transformation to the first. Each of the correspondences between objects in A and B gives rise to a different rule.

1.1.6   Making the Rule Precise

Can we now be more precise in our definition of a rule? One thing a rule must do is to say which objects in A correspond to objects in B, and which objects in A are just removed. For instance in our previous example the rules must say:

    rule 1: [remove triangle1] [match triangle2 triangle3]
    rule 2: [remove triangle2] [match triangle1 triangle3]

Remove Part. Consider the first rule. [Remove triangle1] really means, "remove 'triangle1' from the list of objects in the description of A and also remove any relationships it is involved in". But, of course, triangle1 is not mentioned in the description of C, so how will we know which object to remove from the description? We will have to give sufficient information to identify the object in C that corresponds to triangle1 in A, namely "square". Why do triangle1 and square correspond? Because they both

3

bear similar relationships to the other objects in their figures, i.e. they are both "inside" the other object. So if we say what relationships the object to be removed takes part in, this should be sufficient information to identify the correct object in C:

    [remove x [inside x y]]

where x and y are some arbitrary names that will be associated with square, etc., when we apply the rule.

Match Part. [Match triangle2 triangle3] means "replace triangle2 by triangle3 in the list of objects in the description of A and replace all relations involving triangle2 with the relations involving triangle3".

To make this a rule that can be applied to C we will again have to replace triangle2, triangle3, etc., with some arbitrary name that can be associated with any object.

We will have to add the relations that triangle2 is involved in so that the appropriate association is made.

We will have to add the relations that triangle3 is involved in so that we know what relationships the "new" object is to have.

We will also have to say what transformation must be applied to triangle2 to make it into triangle 3.

So the rule becomes:

    [match   y   [inside x y]   []   direct]

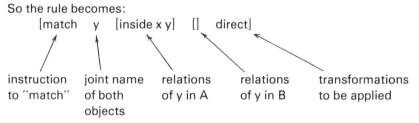

instruction to "match"	joint name of both objects	relations of y in A	relations of y in B	transformations to be applied

Does this rule totally describe the changes?

Previous Examples Revisited. The rule in example 3 is now:

    [remove y [inside x y]]
    [match x [inside x y] [] [scale 2]]

Does the rule totally describe changes?

Let us try to formalise the rule in example 1. Our descriptions are now:

    A: [triangle1 rectangle1] [on triangle1 rectangle1]
    B: [triangle2 rectangle2] [inside triangle2 rectangle2]
    C: [square arch] [on square arch]

Correspondences are:

    [sim triangle1 triangle2 direct]
    [sim rectangle1 rectangle2 direct]

The rule is:

    [match x [on x y] [inside x y] direct]
    [match y [on x y] [inside x y] direct]

Let us try this on another example.

4

1.1.7 Debugging the Rule — Add Part

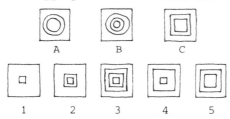

A   B   C

1   2   3   4   5

We see that as well as Remove rules we need Addition rules.

[add object [relations it is in involved in in B]]

Are we now in a position to give a precise recipe for doing geometric analogy problems? Consider the task of finding the rule given the symbolic descriptions of A and B and similarities between objects in them, i.e. given:

a description of A in the form

[objects in A] [relationships between objects in A]

a description of B in the form

[objects in B] [relationships between objects in B]

and various similarities in the form

[sim objA objB transformation]

obtain a symbolic description of a rule that transforms A into B.

Describing how to form the rule from these symbolic descriptions is not a deep task, but it is tricky and involved. The English language does not lend itself to the task of making clear and precise instructions. Later you will see how to use programming languages, like LOGO, for such tasks. In the meantime we will use English for what it is good for — giving hints and clues as to how a precise recipe might be put together.

Clue 1. The rule will be composed of a series of:

"Match" descriptions, one for each object in A that appears (possibly transformed) in B.

"Remove" descriptions, one for each object in A that does not appear in B.

"Add" descriptions, one for each object in B that does not appear in A.

Clue 2. Each similarity description will give rise to a match description, e.g.

[Sim triangle1 triangle2 direct]

gives rise to

[Match x [on x y] [inside x y] direct]

Clue 3. The candidates for "removing" are those objects in A that are not involved in a similarity description with an object from B. Similarly with "adding" and left-over objects from B.

Clue 4. The names of actual objects, e.g. triangle1, square2, etc., are always replaced with a variable, e.g. x, y, z, etc., and by a symbolic description that will enable the appropriate actual object to be identified in A and C, e.g. [on x y], [inside u v], etc.

5

Clue 5. Some of the similarity descriptions are incompatible, e.g.
    (i) [Sim triangle2 triangle3 direct]
    (ii) [Sim triangle1 triangle3 [scale 2]]
We can form several sets of compatible similarities ((i) will be in one set and (ii) in another). Each set will give rise to a different rule. Which rule is finally used will depend on the answer figures available.

*Exercise 1.1.1. Using the above clues, try to describe in English how rule descriptions could be formed from the description of A and B and the similarity descriptions.

1.1.8   Questions and Answers on Computers
We have made instructions more and more precise — how do we know when to stop? When we can express instructions in the form of a computer program that works. How close are we to that?

Can we represent descriptions of figures and rules in the computer? Yes, using list data-structures. We will see how in the programming chapter.

Can we automatically form descriptions of figures from, say, input from a TV camera? Yes. This problem will be addressed in the chapter on visual perception. The impatient can read the recommended paper by Evans (see below).

Can we write a computer program that can carry out the English recipe described in the last section? That is, can we form the descriptions of the rule given the descriptions of the figures? Yes, using simple list manipulation programs — breaking down, copying and building up lists.

Can we automatically apply rules to description of figures? Yes, but using rather harder list manipulation involving pattern matching.

1.1.9   Recommended Reading
T.G. Evans (1964) A heuristic program to solve geometric analogy problems. Spring *J.S.C.C.* (April). This section is based on Evans' work but is not an exact description of it. Evans' program chooses the answer figure by building rules to take A to B and C to each of 1 — 5. It then compares these rules to see which are the most similar. He also describes how the symbolic descriptions can be formed from a Cartesian description of the figures.

M. Minsky & S. Papert (1972) *Artificial Intelligence Progress Report*, section 1.1. AI Memo No. 252, MIT. This is a condensed version of Evans' work.

1.1.10   Exercises
1.1.2.

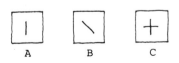

(a) Give a symbolic description of A, B and C and the similarities between objects in A and B.

(b) Give a symbolic description of the rule that transforms A to B.

(c) If this rule were applied to your description of C what would be the resulting description, and what would the answer figure look like?

*1.1.3.

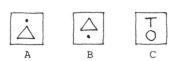

(a) Repeat 2(a), (b) and (c) with the above figure.

(b) Suppose C had been

What goes wrong when we try to apply the description of the rule to the description of D? How might we amend the rule description so that it applies to the description of D and produces a description of E?

[Discussion point: Does the new kind of rule description create problems for the rule-finding and rule-applying recipes?]

*1.1.4. Discuss briefly the statement "Since a computer program can now do analogy problems it makes no sense to use them as human intelligence tests."

*1.1.5. Design a geometric analogy problem that the recipes we have been building could not cope with. Explain why they could not cope. If possible, suggest ways of amending the recipes to deal with the new situation.

1.2 MISSIONARIES AND CANNIBALS: THE PROBLEM AND THE APPROACH

1.2.1 The Problem

Three missionaries and three cannibals seek to cross a river from the left bank to the right bank. A boat is available, which will hold two people and which can be navigated by any combination of missionaries and cannibals involving one or two people. If the missionaries on either bank of the river are outnumbered at any time by cannibals, the cannibals will indulge in their anthropophagic tendencies and do away with the missionaries. When the boat is moored at a bank, it is counted as part of the bank for these purposes.

Find the simplest schedule of crossings that will permit all the missionaries and cannibals to cross the river safely.

1.2.2 The Approach

Consider the missionaries and cannibals (M & C) problem. Do it yourself and note the following points:

1. You will have to develop a more precise statement of the problem in terms of initial and goal states and legal moves.
2. You will have to develop a symbolic description of states of the river banks e.g. something like M M C C/BOAT M C
3. Note the method you use to describe a move. Is it a verbal description like "move a missionary and a cannibal from left to right"?
4. Note whether your attempts to solve the problem can be described by a path through a tree of bank states and moves.

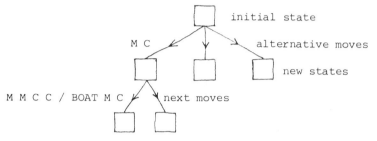

5. In such a tree a solution is represented by a path from the initial state to the goal state.
6. The solution can be found by exhaustively searching the tree.
7. If the real missionaries and cannibals try to solve the problem by actually trying out sequences of crossings, their behaviour can be described by a "depth first" search through the tree.
8. If the real missionaries and cannibals try this method someone might get eaten. It is best to plan in advance.

Precise Recipe. Can we design a "precise recipe" for finding a solution to this problem? In order to guarantee the precision of our recipe let us aim at making it a computer program from the start. Let us weaken the task, initially, to that of writing a computer program that will merely check our solution, and then develop it into a program that finds the solution itself. On the way we will introduce numerous ideas about programming and problem solving.

What Will We Need? A formalisation of the problem, e.g. in terms of states and moves. How to get from the natural language input to this formalisation is an issue we delay tackling until we get to the Natural Language chapter.

We need to represent "states" inside the computer. We will also need to be able to apply moves to these states to produce new states. It seems natural to represent the states and the objects to be moved as data structures, for instance lists, and to represent the move-maker as a procedure to manipulate these lists.

For example, *States* represent M M C C BOAT/M C as
    a list called leftbank = [M M C C BOAT]
    a list called rightbank = [M C]

Moves represent "move a missionary and a cannibal from left to right" in two parts: (a) as a list of things to be moved, e.g. [M C BOAT], called the "movelist", (b) as a program to transfer these things from one bank to the other, called the "move-left-to-right" procedure. For example:

    To Move-left-to-right the movelist
    Make new leftbank, old leftbank without the movelist
    Make new rightbank, old rightbank with the movelist
    End

(Note that the boat is moved automatically by including it in the movelist.)

Solution Checker. If we could turn our English version of the move-left-to-right procedure into a computer program, together with a move-right-to-left procedure, and if we could make leftbank and rightbank take their initial values, then we could use the computer to check potential solutions. We need a procedure

    To Start-Missionary-and-Cannibal
    Make leftbank be [M M M C C C BOAT]
    Make rightbank be the empty list
    End

In order to be able to do these things, we are going to have to learn something about programming. [Read sections 6.1-3.]

1.3   MISSIONARIES AND CANNIBALS: BUILDING THE PROGRAM
1.3.1   A Solution-Checking Program

Armed with our knowledge of programming we can now try to make our recipe for a solution checker more precise. LEFTBANK and RIGHTBANK will be variables. Their values at any one time will be the current states of the left and right banks. These variables cannot be local to any of our procedures or their values would be lost when the procedures were exited. Therefore we will not declare them as new and they will become *global variables*, i.e. always accessible. The procedures translate fairly directly, i.e.

    TO MOVELTOR 'MOVELIST
    10 MAKE 'LEFTBANK WITHOUT :MOVELIST :LEFTBANK
    20 MAKE 'RIGHTBANK WITH :MOVELIST :RIGHTBANK
    END

similarly

    TO MOVERTOL 'MOVELIST
    10 MAKE 'RIGHTBANK WITHOUT :MOVELIST :RIGHTBANK
    20 MAKE 'LEFTBANK WITH :MOVELIST :LEFTBANK
    END

```
TO  STARTMANDC
10  MAKE  'LEFTBANK  [M  M  M  C  C  C  BOAT]
20  MAKE  'RIGHTBANK  [ ]
END
```

It is necessary to define the subprocedures WITH and WITHOUT. WITH is relatively easy, but WITHOUT is much harder and needs concepts we have not yet introduced, so we delay consideration of it until later in the course.

Let us also define a procedure to tell us the current state. Otherwise we will find it difficult to remember how we are doing.

```
TO  PRINTSTATE
10  PRINTLEFTBANK
20  PRINTRIGHTBANK
END

TO  PRINTLEFTBANK
10  TYPE  'LEFTBANK
20  TYPE  SPACE
30  TYPE  'IS
40  TYPE  SPACE
50  TYPE  :LEFTBANK
60  TYPE  NL
END

TO  PRINTRIGHTBANK
10  TYPE  'RIGHTBANK
20  TYPE  SPACE
30  TYPE  'IS
40  TYPE  SPACE
50  TYPE  :RIGHTBANK
60  TYPE  NL
END
```

Exercise 1.3.1. PRINTLEFTBANK and PRINTRIGHTBANK are very similar. Can you write a procedure with one argument that can do the work of both?

Solution Checking. Using the procedures introduced, we can try solving the problem "by hand", but using the computer to keep track of where we are. We use the procedures STARTMANDC, MOVELTOR, MOVERTOL and PRINTSTATE. For example:

```
1:STARTMANDC
1:PRINTSTATE
```

LEFTBANK IS [M M M C C C BOAT]   starting position
RIGHTBANK IS [ ]

```
1:MOVELTOR  [M  C  BOAT]
1:PRINTSTATE
```

10

```
LEFTBANK IS [M M C C]
RIGHTBANK IS [M C BOAT]
```

1:MOVERTOL [M BOAT]
1:PRINTSTATE

```
LEFTBANK IS [M M C C M BOAT]
RIGHTBANK IS [C]
```

1:MOVELTOR [M C BOAT]
1:PRINTSTATE

```
LEFTBANK IS [M C M]           after these moves, Missionary
RIGHTBANK IS [C M C BOAT]      on rightbank gets eaten
```

1:STARTMANDC   start over again
1:MOVELTOR [C C BOAT]   try a different first move
1:PRINTSTATE

```
LEFTBANK IS [M M M C]
RIGHTBANK IS [C C BOAT]
```

1.3.2 APPLYMOVE

It seems a bit clumsy to have to specify MOVELTOR or MOVERTOL each time, and also unnecessary. The computer itself ought to be able to figure out which way to move next. How? Suppose, for instance, we are in this situation:

1:PRINTSTATE

```
LEFTBANK IS [M C BOAT]
RIGHTBANK IS [M C M C]
```

which way should we move next? Obviously, since the boat is on the LEFTBANK, we have to MOVELTOR. So if we could get the computer to see which bank the boat is on, we ought to be able to write a *single* procedure APPLYMOVE, which can decide to MOVELTOR or MOVERTOL as appropriate.

Writing APPLYMOVE. We now try to write the procedure APPLYMOVE. Like MOVELTOR and MOVERTOL it takes a single argument, a list of what is to be moved across the river. Let us call it MOVELIST, so we can type in

1:TO APPLYMOVE 'MOVELIST

What do we want APPLYMOVE to do? Well, if the BOAT is at LEFTBANK, we want it to MOVELTOR the MOVELIST and that's all, so we type:

&:10 IF AMONGQ 'BOAT :LEFTBANK THEN RESULT MOVELTOR
:MOVELIST AND STOP

AND STOP causes procedure to exit.

We need a procedure called AMONGQ, whose arguments are an item and a list of items, which looks to see whether the item appears in the list. If it does, the procedure returns TRUE; if not, FALSE:

'BOAT [M M C BOAT] → AMONGQ → TRUE

So we have:

    1:<u>PRINT AMONGQ 'BOAT [M M C BOAT]</u>
    TRUE
    1:<u>PRINT AMONGQ 'CAT [BOY GIRL CAT DOG]</u>
    TRUE
    1:<u>PRINT AMONGQ 15 [21 12 212]</u>
    FALSE
    1:<u>PRINT AMONGQ FIRST [MAN HUMAN CHILD]</u>
      <u>[CHIMPANZEE MAN ELEPHANT]</u>
    TRUE

In programming lectures we will see how to write AMONGQ. Go back to writing APPLYMOVE

    &:<u>20 IF AMONGQ 'BOAT :RIGHTBANK THEN RESULT</u>
    <u>MOVERTOL :MOVELIST AND STOP</u>

and that's it:

    &:<u>END</u>

Now, if we SHOW APPLYMOVE, we have

    TO APPLYMOVE 'MOVELIST
    10 IF AMONGQ 'BOAT :LEFTBANK THEN RESULT
      MOVELTOR :MOVELIST AND STOP
    20 IF AMONGQ 'BOAT :RIGHTBANK THEN RESULT
      MOVERTOL :MOVELIST AND STOP
    END

That looks OK, so let us try using it in our instructions to the computer:

    1:<u>STARTMANDC</u>
    1:<u>PRINTSTATE</u>

    LEFTBANK IS [M M M C C C BOAT]
    RIGHTBANK IS [ ]

    1:<u>APPLYMOVE [C BOAT]</u>
    1:<u>PRINTSTATE</u>

    LEFTBANK IS [M M M C C]
    RIGHTBANK IS [C BOAT]

    1:<u>APPLYMOVE [C BOAT]</u>
    1:<u>PRINTSTATE</u>

    LEFTBANK IS [M M M C C C BOAT]
    RIGHTBANK IS [ ]

12

```
1:APPLYMOVE [C  C  BOAT]
1:PRINTSTATE

LEFTBANK  IS  [M  M  M  C]
RIGHTBANK  IS  [C  C  BOAT]
```

1.3.3   Simple Interaction

Even with APPLYMOVE we still have to do a lot of unnecessary typing. Why not write a simple program that *knows* that we want to STARTMANDC and then specify a sequence of moves, with a PRINTSTATE to be done after each?

Let's try:

```
        TO  MANDC
        10  STARTMANDC
        20  MAKEMOVES
        END
```

and

```
        TO  MAKEMOVES
        10  REQUESTAMOVE
        20  APPLYMOVE IT              IT returns the result of line 10
        30  MAKEMOVES
        END
```

where we use

```
        TO  REQUESTAMOVE
        10  PRINTSTATE                        ⎰  This line reads in a
        20  PRINT [TYPE A MOVELIST]      ⎬  movelist and makes a
        30  GETLIST                            ⎱         list out of it

        40  IF AMONGQ 'BOAT IT THEN RETURN IT  ←⎰which is then
                                                ⎱  returned
        50  PRINT [YOU FORGOT THE BOAT, DUMMY: TRY AGAIN]
        60  REQUESTAMOVE
        END
```

This makes things much easier. For example:

```
        1:MANDC

LEFTBANK  IS  [M  M  C  C  C  BOAT]
RIGHTBANK  IS  [ ]

[TYPE  A  MOVELIST]
DATA:C  C  BOAT

LEFTBANK  IS  [M  M  M  C]
RIGHTBANK  IS  [C  C  BOAT]

[TYPE  A  MOVELIST]
DATA:C  BOAT

LEFTBANK  IS  [M  M  M  C  C  BOAT]
RIGHTBANK  IS  [C]
```

13

[TYPE A MOVELIST]
DATA:<u>C C</u>
[YOU FORGOT THE BOAT, DUMMY: TRY AGAIN]

LEFTBANK IS [M M M C C BOAT]
RIGHTBANK IS [C]

[TYPE A MOVELIST]
DATA:<u>C C BOAT</u>

LEFTBANK IS [M M M]
RIGHTBANK IS [C C C BOAT]

1.3.4   Towards an M & C Solver

Although so far *we* have been doing all the problem solving, remember that our goal is to write a LOGO program that can solve the M & C problem by itself. We try gradually working towards such a program.

Backup. We have

    TO MAKEMOVES
    10 REQUESTAMOVE
    20 APPLYMOVE IT
    30 MAKEMOVES
    END

But what happens if we make a mistake? We have to start again from the beginning. It would be nice to be able to "back-up", i.e. to reverse the last move and try again. We recognise that we are really searching a tree

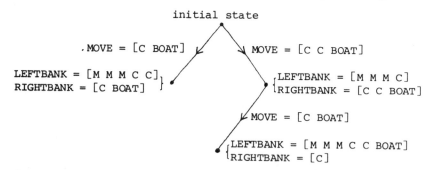

Suppose we decide that we are in a blind alley and we want to "back-up" and try again?

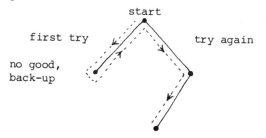

We must remember the previous states!!

TRYMOVES. Change MAKEMOVES so that instead of just applying the move at step 20 it also explores all the consequences of applying the move, i.e. it tries further moves. If these consequences are not to our liking we can decide to terminate step 20 and go on with step 30, which tries alternative moves, i.e.

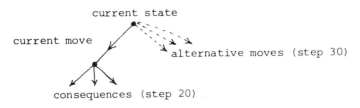

```
TO TRYMOVES
10 REQUESTAMOVE                                     ⎧ totally explores
20 EXPLOREASTATE :LEFTBANK :RIGHTBANK IT ⎨ consequences
                                                    ⎩ of current move
30 TRYMOVES                          ⎧ restores previous state
                                     ⎩ and requests another move
END
```

Specifying :LEFTBANK and :RIGHTBANK ensures that the present context of TRYMOVES is not sullied by EXPLOREASTATE.

```
TO EXPLOREASTATE 'LEFTBANK 'RIGHTBANK 'MOVELIST
50 APPLYMOVE :MOVELIST              makes move
100 TRYMOVES                 makes consequent moves
END
```

```
TO MANDC
10 STARTMANDC
20 TRYMOVES
END
```

REQUESTAMOVE. How do we tell the program we have made a mistake and wish to back-up? Just type BACKUP when it asks for our next move, i.e. after REQUESTAMOVE.

```
TO REQUESTAMOVE
10 PRINTSTATE
20 PRINT [TYPE A MOVE OR BACKUP]
30 GETLIST
40 IF EITHER AMONGQ BOAT IT OR EQUALQ IT [BACKUP]
     THEN RESULT IT
50 PRINT [YOU FORGOT THE BOAT, DUMMY: TRY AGAIN]
60 REQUESTAMOVE
END
```

How do we make use of this information when we get it? By altering

TRYMOVES so that it does not continue if it is told to back-up.

```
    TO TRYMOVES
    10 REQUESTAMOVE
→  20 IF EQUALQ IT [BACKUP] THEN STOP
       ELSE EXPLOREASTATE :LEFTBANK :RIGHTBANK IT
    30 TRYMOVES
    END
```

Now try it on the computer.

    1:<u>MANDC</u>

LEFTBANK IS [M M M C C C BOAT] RIGHTBANK IS [ ]	initial node1
[TYPE A MOVE OR BACKUP] DATA:<u>C C BOAT</u>	first move
LEFTBANK IS [M M M C] RIGHTBANK IS [C C BOAT]	gives a new node2
[TYPE A MOVE OR BACKUP] DATA:<u>C BOAT</u>	second move from there
LEFTBANK IS [M M M C C BOAT] RIGHTBANK IS [C]	gives a new node3
[TYPE A MOVE OR BACKUP] DATA:<u>M C BOAT</u>	third move
LEFTBANK IS [M M C] RIGHTBANK IS [C M C BOAT]	gives a state where the Cs eat a M
[TYPE A MOVE OR BACKUP] DATA:<u>BACKUP</u>	so backup
LEFTBANK IS [M M M C C BOAT] RIGHTBANK IS [C]	to node3
[TYPE A MOVE OR BACKUP] DATA:<u>M BOAT</u>	and try a different move
LEFTBANK IS [M M C C] RIGHTBANK IS [C M BOAT]	

Checking for Solution. In exploring a new state we ought at least to notice when we have solved the problem. This is easily done, by adding a new line (line 80) to EXPLOREASTATE:

```
    TO EXPLOREASTATE 'LEFTBANK 'RIGHTBANK 'MOVELIST
    50 APPLYMOVE :MOVELIST
→  80 IF SUCCEEDEDQ THEN PRINT 'SUCCESS AND QUIT
    100 TRYMOVES
    END
```

16

QUIT stops all procedures.

Here we have assumed the existence of a predicate, SUCCEEDEDQ, which outputs TRUE when the M & C problem is solved. How could we write such a predicate? One simple way is to notice that there is somebody on the LEFTBANK until the problem is solved, so we could check for that condition:

```
TO SUCCEEDEDQ
10 RESULT EMPTYQ :LEFTBANK
END
```

Checking for Cannibalism. In a similar way we can arrange for EXPLOREASTATE to check whether the cannabalism condition is violated. Adding an appropriate command to EXPLOREASTATE is straightforward:

```
     TO EXPLOREASTATE 'LEFTBANK 'RIGHTBANK 'MOVELIST
     50 APPLYMOVE :MOVELIST
 ——▶ 60 IF MISSIONARIESEATENQ THEN STOP
     80 IF SUCCEEDEDQ THEN PRINT 'SUCCESS AND QUIT
     100 TRYMOVES
     END
```

But then we have to spell out the predicate MISSIONARIESEATENQ. Missionaries get eaten if they get eaten either on the LEFTBANK or on the RIGHTBANK, so if we invent a subsidiary predicate MEATENQ that worries only about one bank at a time, then we can write:

```
TO MISSIONARIESEATENQ
10 RESULT EITHER MEATENQ :LEFTBANK OR MEATENQ
   :RIGHTBANK
END
```

So under what conditions *do* the missionaries on a bank get eaten? Clearly if there are more cannibals there than missionaries. But this means that we need to be able to *count* the number of missionaries (or cannibals) on a bank. How do we do this? By our favourite trick of simply supposing a suitable procedure to exist, and then worrying about how to define it later. So let us assume that we have available a procedure NUMBEROF, which takes two arguments, an item and a list of items, and returns the number of times the item occurs in the list:

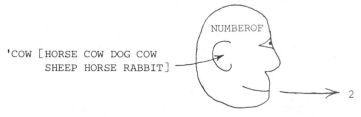

```
'COW [HORSE COW DOG COW
      SHEEP HORSE RABBIT]
```

So NUMBEROF is in several ways analogous to AMONGQ, but whereas AMONGQ merely tells whether or not an item occurs at all, NUMBEROF tells *how many times* it occurs:

17

```
1:PRINT NUMBEROF 'COW [HORSE COW DOG COW SHEEP
  RABBIT]
2
1:PRINT NUMBEROF 'M [M C M BOAT]
2
1:PRINT NUMBEROF 'M [C C C]
0
```

So now we can write MEATENQ. The condition that there are more cannibals than missionaries on some BANK becomes just:

GRTRQ (NUMBEROF 'C :BANK) (NUMBEROF 'M :BANK)

But this can't be quite right, since when the number of missionaries is zero it doesn't matter *how* many cannibals there are. In other words, there have to be some missionaries present if any are to be eaten. This gives us:

```
TO MEATENQ 'BANK
10 BOTH GRTRQ (NUMBEROF 'C :BANK) (NUMBEROF 'M
   :BANK) ANDALSO GRTRQ (NUMBEROF 'M :BANK) 0
END
```

Exercise 1.3.2. Add all the changes made so far to the original program. Try running MANDC. You may find it more helpful to make line 60 of EXPLOREASTATE print out an informative message, perhaps:

$\longrightarrow$ 60 IF MISSIONARIESEATENQ THEN PRINT
   [MISSIONARIES EATEN, MOVE REJECTED] AND STOP

1.3.5 Generating Applicable Moves

By now the program is doing all the work except for the actual selection of moves, so the last step is to have it do this as well. How can it? What basis is there for choosing moves? One way is to simply let it try all the possible moves in turn. This is perfectly reasonable, since there are only five of them. So let us begin by making sure that some list contains all five of these possible moves:

```
TO STARTMANDC
10 MAKE 'LEFTBANK [M M M C C C BOAT]
20 MAKE 'RIGHTBANK [ ]
```
$\longrightarrow$
```
40 MAKE 'POSSIBLEMOVES [[C C BOAT] [C BOAT]
   [M C BOAT] [M M BOAT] [M BOAT]]
END
```

Then in EXPLOREASTATE, we replace the line telling it to TRYMOVES typed in by us, by a line telling it to TRYALL :POSSIBLEMOVES (see line 100, below). And how should it TRYALL? Simply by trying one at a time:

```
TO TRYALL 'SETOFMOVES
10 IF EMPTYQ :SETOFMOVES THEN STOP
20 EXPLOREASTATE :LEFTBANK :RIGHTBANK FIRST
   :SETOFMOVES
30 TRYALL BUTFIRST :SETOFMOVES
END
```

We have to change MANDC in the same way:

```
    TO MANDC
    10 STARTMANDC
──▶ 20 TRYALL :POSSIBLEMOVES
──▶ 30 PRINT [NO SOLUTION FOUND]
    END
```

(Line 30 is justified because if the program does try all possible moves without meeting success, it will indeed have failed.)

There is only one snag left now, which is that not all moves are necessarily applicable to a particular state. For example, if we have LEFTBANK IS [M C BOAT], it is impossible to move two cannibals across! What should we do about this? One possibility would be to modify TRYALL so that it tries only applicable moves, but it seems simpler to add a further test to EXPLOREASTATE, this time *before* the move:

```
    TO EXPLOREASTATE 'LEFTBANK 'RIGHTBANK 'MOVELIST
──▶ 40 IF NOT APPLICABLEQ :MOVELIST THEN STOP
    50 APPLYMOVE :MOVELIST
    60 IF MISSIONARIESEATENQ THEN STOP
    80 IF SUCCEEDEDQ THEN PRINT 'SUCCESS AND QUIT
──▶ 100 TRYALL :POSSIBLEMOVES
```

What decides whether a move is applicable? Clearly there must be at least as many missionaries on the bank as are specified in the move, and similarly for cannibals:

```
    TO APPLICABLEQ 'MOVE
    10 BOTH LESSEQUALQ (NUMBER OF 'M :MOVE)
       (NUMBEROF 'M FROMSIDE)
       ANDALSO LESSEQUALQ (NUMBEROF 'C :MOVE)
       (NUMBEROF 'C FROMSIDE)
    END
```

FROMSIDE is a function that returns the bank that the BOAT will be leaving from. Could you write it?

Looping. Try out the above procedure pretending to be the computer.

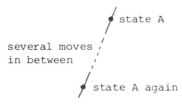

```
        {:LEFTBANK = [M M M C C C BOAT]
         :RIGHTBANK = [ ]

        [C C BOAT]

        {:LEFTBANK = [M M M C]
         :RIGHTBANK = [C C BOAT]

        [C C BOAT]

        {:LEFTBANK = [M M M C C C BOAT]
         :RIGHTBANK = [ ]

    etc.
```

We are in a loop!

We could avoid this particular loop by ensuring that we do not immediately reverse a step we have just made. Unfortunately there are more subtle loops.

```
                        state A

    several moves
    in between

                        state A again
```

Note that if we have a solution with repeated states, we can modify it to get a simpler solution without repeated states. Therefore a solution with repeated states is not the simplest solution, which is what is required. To avoid loops we need to keep track of which states we have seen before and avoid repeatedly exploring them. How shall we do this?

As always, the appropriate changes to EXPLOREASTATE are easy to make. We just need to reject a state if we have seen it before (line 70, see below), but if it is a genuinely new state then we must record the fact that we have seen it (line 90):

```
      TO EXPLOREASTATE 'LEFTBANK 'RIGHTBANK 'MOVELIST
      40 IF NOT APPLICABLE :MOVELIST THEN STOP
      50 APPLYMOVE :MOVELIST
      60 IF MISSIONARIESEATENQ THEN STOP
  ──→ 70 IF SEENSTATEBEFOREQ THEN STOP
      80 IF SUCCEEDEDQ THEN PRINT 'SUCCESS AND QUIT
  ──→ 90 RECORDNEWSTATE
      100 TRYALL :POSSIBLEMOVES
      END
```

How are we to remember which states we have seen before? One way

20

would be to keep a list of all the LEFTBANKs and RIGHTBANKs we have seen, and then, when we have a possibly new state, check whether we have seen this particular combination before. But that would be a bit complicated, and we can simplify it in two ways: (a) We don't need to record both the LEFTBANKs *and* the RIGHTBANKs, since given one we know what the other must be. For example, if LEFTBANK is [M C BOAT] then we know that the RIGHTBANK must be [M C M C]. So it would be sufficient to remember just, say, the LEFTBANKs. (b) We still must be careful over what it is about the LEFTBANKs that we remember. Suppose that we have previously seen a LEFTBANK of [M C BOAT], and that it is now [C M BOAT] then they are really the *same* LEFTBANK even though they are not "equal":

    1:PRINT EQUALQ [M C BOAT] [C M BOAT]
    FALSE

What is really important about the LEFTBANK is the *number* of missionaries and cannibals (and boat) there, not the order in which they appear in the list. This suggests remembering the LEFTBANK as a group of three numbers — (number-of-boat-on-leftbank, number-of-missionaries-on-leftbank, number-of-cannibals-on-leftbank) — so that, for example, [M C BOAT] corresponds to [1 1 1], one boat, one missionary, one cannibal.

Let us define a procedure to construct these triples:

    TO STATETRIPLE
    10 《 NUMBEROF 'BOAT :LEFTBANK
    NUMBEROF 'M :LEFTBANK
    NUMBEROF 'C :LEFTBANK 》
    END

(The list brackets 《 ... 》 allow elements to be results of procedure calls.) So that we have, for example:

    1:PRINTSTATE

    LEFTBANK IS [M M M]
    RIGHTBANK IS [C C C BOAT]

    1:PRINT STATETRIPLE
    [0 3 0]

If we have a list, STATESEEN, which holds all the state triples we have seen, it is easy to write our procedures to examine or update it:

    TO SEENSTATEBEFOREQ
    10 RESULT AMONGQ STATETRIPLE :STATESEEN
    END

    TO RECORDNEWSTATE
    10 MAKE 'STATESEEN FIRSTPUT STATETRIPLE :STATESEEN
    END

And we should remember to start STATESEEN off with the initial

```
LEFTBANK:
        TO  STARTMANDC
        10 MAKE 'LEFTBANK [M M M C C C BOAT]
        20 MAKE 'RIGHTBANK [ ]
───►30 MAKE 'STATESEEN [[1 3 3]]
        40 MAKE 'POSSIBLEMOVES [[C C BOAT] [C BOAT]
           [M C BOAT] [M M BOAT] [M BOAT]]
        END
```

1.3.6. Exercises

1.3.3. Make these additions and try using them. As before, you will find it more helpful if line 70 of EXPLOREASTATE prints out an appropriate message.

1.3.4. Edit STARTMANDC and change the order of POSSIBLEMOVES. Describe the effect this has.

1.3.5. The representation of states by LEFTBANK and RIGHTBANK is redundant. Modify the M & C program so that only LEFTBANK is explicitly represented.

*1.3.6. The STATETRIPLES we invented, to record states already reached, suggest an alternative way of representing states. Modify the M & C program so that it uses this representation.

1.4   MISSIONARIES AND CANNIBALS: SEARCH TECHNIQUES

1.4.1   Analysis of Search Strategy

We can represent all possible sequences of moves in the missionaries and cannibals problem by a tree:

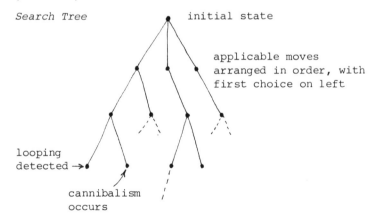

We can regard the program as growing some of this tree as it runs, and thus exploring it. In what order does it grow the tree? What was our *search strategy*?

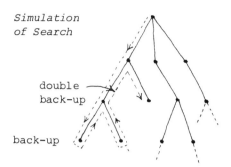

Simulation of Search

double back-up

back-up

This is called *depth first search*. That is, we keep going down, taking the left-most branch at every choice point, until we have to back-up. Then we go back one place and take the next choice.

Simplest Solutions. Unfortunately this does not necessarily give us the simplest solution.

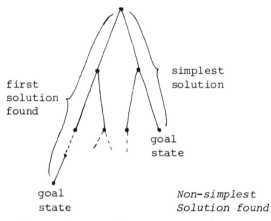

first solution found

simplest solution

goal state

goal state

Non-simplest Solution found

We may find a complicated solution on the left-hand side, before a simple one on the right-hand side. We could search the whole tree then choose the simplest solution from among all the solutions found. Alternatively we could explore all solutions *in parallel* so that the first found was bound to be the simplest.

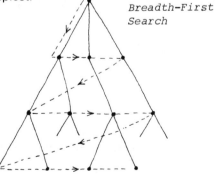

Breadth-First Search

23

Suppose that *simplest* means the smallest number of moves, then we can advance each branch of the tree one step, then go back and do it again. This is called *breadth first search*. If our definition of simplest was a bit more subtle, the search would not be so easy, but we could still do basically the same thing.

Exercise 1.4.1. How would you implement the M & C program so that it did a breadth first search?

1.4.2 Guidance

The search tree for the M & C problem is fairly small, and we are able to find a solution by a brute-force search (straight down, keep to the left). Many search trees in AI problems are very large (e.g. draughts) and programs to search them need to be guided, if they are not to become bogged down. Typically one would want to choose the most promising looking move, at any choice point, instead of choosing the next one on some fixed list. One might want to temporarily stop exploring some particular state and move on to another, while reserving the right to come back.

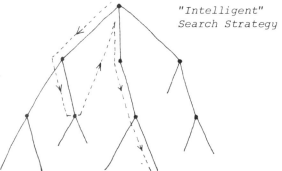

"Intelligent"
Search Strategy

Graph Traverser. Many AI programs *can* be regarded as involving some search through a search tree. These trees are typically large (especially if the problem domain is not well understood) and the search through one needs to be guided if the program is not to become bogged down. Attempts have been made to write general purpose tree-searching programs that only need to be fed particular details about the state descriptions and legal moves. Having such a program available makes it easier to formalise problems like the missionaries and cannibals. This is important when it comes to designing a program to solve problems from their verbal statement. One such general search program is the *Graph Traverser* of Doran and Michie (see recommended reading). Their program searches graphs instead of trees, but the difference is slight. In a tree, if we have two identical states on different branches, we record them separately; in a graph we use one node to record them both. When we say we are searching a graph, rather than a tree, we imply that the test for looping is built-in to our program.

24

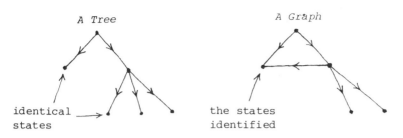

A Tree

A Graph

identical states →

the states identified

Evaluation Functions. The Graph Traverser provides a general mechanism for guiding search. The user is expected to provide a procedure which takes a state and calculates a numerical score which measures how close the present state is to the goal state. Such a procedure is called a Heuristic Evaluation Function. The graph traverser always chooses to explore next the unexplored state with the highest score.

1.4.3   Exercises

1.4.2. Write an evaluation function for the missionaries and cannibals problem.

1.4.3. The "Eight-Puzzle" is played on the 3 x 3 tray illustrated below:

A	B	C
D	▨	E
F	G	H

Mounted in the tray are eight 1 x 1 square pieces, which are free to slide left, right, up or down into an empty square. The standard position is illustrated, in which the centre square is empty and the letters are arranged in order. The puzzle is played by initialising the pieces in some other order and then trying to get them back into the standard position.

(a) Explain how a course of play can be represented as a search through a tree or graph.

(b) How would this representation help you to design a computer program to solve eight-puzzle problems?

(c) Suppose you were writing such a program. How could you represent in LOGO: states of the tray and moves. Explain in English (or LOGO) how you would apply moves to states to produce new states.

1.4.4   Recommended Reading

J. Doran (1971) An approach to problem solving, in *Machine Intelligence 1* (eds N. L. Collins & D. Michie) pp. 105-23. Edinburgh: University Press. This paper describes the Graph Traverser program, which embodies an heuristic search strategy. It can solve any puzzle input to it in the form of states and legal moves plus an evaluation function for assigning a numeric score to states.

1.5 MISSIONARIES AND CANNIBALS: THE COMPLETE LOGO PROGRAM

```
TO MOVELTOR 'MOVELIST
10 MAKE 'LEFTBANK WITHOUT :MOVELIST :LEFTBANK
20 MAKE 'RIGHTBANK JOIN :RIGHTBANK :MOVELIST
END

TO MOVERTOL 'MOVELIST
10 MAKE 'RIGHTBANK WITHOUT :MOVELIST :RIGHTBANK
20 MAKE 'LEFTBANK JOIN :LEFTBANK :MOVELIST
END

TO APPLYMOVE 'MOVELIST
10 IF AMONGQ 'BOAT :LEFTBANK THEN RESULT MOVELTOR
   :MOVELIST
20 IF AMONGQ 'BOAT :RIGHTBANK THEN RESULT MOVERTOL
   :MOVELIST
30 BREAK ERROR IN APPLYMOVE
END

TO WITHOUT 'DELETIONS 'ORIGINAL
10 APPLIST :DELETIONS [MAKE 'ORIGINAL WITHOUT1 EACH
   :ORIGINAL]
20 RESULT :ORIGINAL
END

TO WITHOUT1 'DELETION 'ORIGINAL
10 IF EMPTYQ :ORIGINAL THEN SAY JOIN [CANNOT REMOVE]
   FIRSTPUT :DELETION [FROM GIVEN LIST] AND BREAK ERROR
20 IF EQUALQ :DELETION FIRST :ORIGINAL THEN RESULT
   BUTFIRST :ORIGINAL
30 RESULT FIRSTPUT FIRST :ORIGINAL WITHOUT1 :DELETION
   BUTFIRST :ORIGINAL
END

TO MANDC
10 STARTMANDC
20 TRYALL :POSSIBLEMOVES
30 PRINT [NO SOLUTION FOUND]
END

TO EXPLOREASTATE 'LEFTBANK 'RIGHTBANK 'MOVELIST
40 IF NOT APPLICABLEQ :MOVELIST THEN STOP
50 APPLYMOVE :MOVELIST
60 IF MISSIONARIESEATENQ THEN STOP
70 IF SEENSTATEBEFOREQ THEN STOP
80 IF SUCCEEDEDQ THEN PRINT 'SUCCESS AND QUIT
90 RECORDNEWSTATE
```

26

```
100 TRYALL :POSSIBLEMOVES
END

TO PRINTSTATE
 5 TYPE NL
10 TYPE 'LEFTBANK AND TYPE SPACE AND TYPE 'IS AND TYPE
   SPACE
20 TYPE :LEFTBANK AND TYPE NL
30 TYPE 'RIGHTBANK AND TYPE SPACE AND TYPE 'IS AND
   TYPE SPACE
40 TYPE :RIGHTBANK AND TYPE NL
50 TYPE NL
END

TO STARTMANDC
10 MAKE 'LEFTBANK [M M M C C C BOAT]
20 MAKE 'RIGHTBANK []
30 MAKE 'STATESEEN [[1 3 3 ]]
40 MAKE 'POSSIBLEMOVES [[C C BOAT] [C BOAT] [M C BOAT]
   [M M BOAT] [M BOAT]]
50 PRINTSTATE
END

TO NUMBEROF 'ITEM 'LIST
10 IF EMPTYQ :LIST THEN RESULT 0
20 IF EQUALQ :ITEM FIRST :LIST THEN RESULT 1+NUMBEROF
   :ITEM BUTFIRST :LIST
30 RESULT NUMBEROF :ITEM BUTFIRST :LIST
END

TO TRYALL 'SETOFMOVES
10 IF EMPTYQ :SETOFMOVES THEN STOP
20 PEXPLOREASTATE :LEFTBANK :RIGHTBANK FIRST
   :SETOFMOVES
30 TRYALL BUTFIRST :SETOFMOVES
END

TO FROMSIDE
10 IF AMONGQ 'BOAT :LEFTBANK THEN RESULT :LEFTBANK
20 IF AMONGQ 'BOAT :RIGHTBANK THEN RESULT :RIGHTBANK
30 BREAK ERROR IN FROMSIDE
END

TO APPLICABLEQ 'MOVE
10 BOTH LESSEQUALQ (NUMBEROF 'M :MOVE)
   (NUMBEROF 'M FROMSIDE)
   ANDALSO LESSEQUALQ (NUMBEROF 'C :MOVE)
   (NUMBEROF 'C FROMSIDE)
END
27
```

```
TO RECORDNEWSTATE
10 MAKE 'STATESEEN FIRSTPUT STATETRIPLE :STATESEEN
END

TO SEENSTATEBEFOREQ
10 RESULT AMONGQ STATETRIPLE :STATESEEN
END

TO MISSIONARIESEATENQ
10 RESULT EITHER MEATENQ :LEFTBANK MEATENQ :RIGHTBANK
END

TO MEATENQ 'BANK
10 BOTH GRTRQ (NUMBEROF 'C :BANK) (NUMBEROF 'M :BANK)
   ANDALSO GRTRQ (NUMBEROF 'M :BANK)  O
END

TO SUCCEEDEDQ
10 RESULT EMPTYQ :LEFTBANK
END

TO STATETRIPLE
10  《 (NUMBEROF 'BOAT :LEFTBANK) (NUMBEROF 'M
   :LEFTBANK) (NUMBEROF 'C :LEFTBANK)》
END

TO PEXPLOREASTATE 'LEFTBANK 'RIGHTBANK 'MOVELIST
40 IF NOT APPLICABLEQ :MOVELIST THEN STOP
50 APPLYMOVE :MOVELIST
55 TYPE 'APPLIEDMOVE AND TYPE SPACE AND PRINT
   :MOVELIST
60 IF MISSIONARIESEATENQ THEN PRINT 'MISSIONARIESEATEN
   AND STOP
70 IF SEENSTATEBEFOREQ THEN PRINT 'SEENSTATEBEFORE
   AND STOP
75 PRINT 'NEWSTATE AND PRINTSTATE
80 IF SUCCEEDEDQ THEN PRINT 'SUCCESS AND QUIT
90 RECORDNEWSTATE
100 TRYALL :POSSIBLEMOVES
105 PRINT 'BACKUP
END
```

1.6   MISSIONARIES AND CANNIBALS: THE COMPLETE LISP PROGRAM

```
(DEFUN QUIT () (IOC G))

(DEFUN MOVELTOR (MOVELIST)
    (SETQ LEFTBANK (WITHOUT MOVELIST LEFTBANK))
    (SETQ RIGHTBANK (APPEND RIGHTBANK MOVELIST)))
```

```
(DEFUN MOVERTOL (MOVELIST)
     (SETQ RIGHTBANK (WITHOUT MOVELIST RIGHTBANK))
     (SETQ LEFTBANK (APPEND LEFTBANK MOVELIST)))

(DEFUN APPLYMOVE (MOVELIST)
     (COND ((MEMBER 'BOAT LEFTBANK) (MOVELTOR MOVELIST))
           ((MEMBER 'BOAT RIGHTBANK) (MOVERTOL (MOVELIST))
           (T (BREAK (ERROR IN APPLYMOVE) T))))

(DEFUN WITHOUT (DELETIONS ORIGINAL)
     (MAPC '(LAMBDA (EACH) (SETQ ORIGINAL (WITHOUT1 EACH
           ORIGINAL))) DELETIONS)
     ORIGINAL)

(DEFUN WITHOUT1 (DELETION ORIGINAL)
     COND ((NULL ORIGINAL)
           (PRINT
                 (APPEND '(CANNOT REMOVE) (CONS DELETION
                                       '(FROM GIVEN LIST))))
           (BREAK ERROR T))
          ((EQ DELETION (CAR ORIGINAL))
          (CDR ORIGINAL))
          (T (CONS (CAR ORIGINAL) (WITHOUT1 DELETION
                                       (CDR ORIGINAL))))))

(DEFUN MANDC ( )
     (STARTMANDC)
     (TRYALL POSSIBLEMOVES)
     (PRINT '(NO SOLUTION FOUND)))

(DEFUN EXPLOREASTATE (LEFTBANK RIGHTBANK MOVELIST)
   (PROG ( )
     (COND ((NOT (APPLICABLEQ MOVELIST)) (RETURN NIL)))
     (APPLYMOVE MOVELIST)
     (COND ((MISSIONARIESEATENQ) (RETURN NIL))
           ((SEENSTATEBEFOREQ) (RETURN NIL))
           ((SUCCEEDEDQ) (PRINT 'SUCCESS) (QUIT)))
     (RECORDNEWSTATE)
     (TRYALL POSSIBLEMOVES)))

(DEFUN PRINTSTATE ( )
     (TERPRI)
     (PRIN1 'LEFTBANK) (TYO 40) (PRIN1 'IS) (TYO 40)
     (PRIN1 LEFTBANK) (TERPRI)
     (PRIN1 'RIGHTBANK) (TYO 40) (PRIN1 'IS) (TYO 40)
     (PRIN1 RIGHTBANK) (TERPRI)
     (TERPRI))
```

```
(DEFUN STARTMANDC ( )
    (SETQ LEFTBANK '(M M M C C C BOAT))
    (SETQ RIGHTBANK NIL)
    (SETQ STATESEEN '((1 3 3)))
    (SETQ POSSIBLEMOVES '((C C BOAT) (C BOAT) (M C BOAT)
                                    (M M BOAT) (M BOAT)))
    (PRINTSTATE))

(DEFUN NUMBEROF (ITEM LIST)
    (COND ((NULL LIST) 0)
          ((EQ ITEM (CAR LIST)) (1+ (NUMBEROF ITEM (CDR
                                                    LIST))))
          (T (NUMBEROF ITEM (CDR LIST)))))

(DEFUN TRYALL (SETOFMOVES)
    (COND ((NULL SETOFMOVES))
          (T (PEXPLOREASTATE LEFTBANK RIGHTBANK (CAR
              SETOFMOVES)) (TRYALL (CDR SETOFMOVES)))))

(DEFUN FROMSIDE ()
    (COND ((MEMBER 'BOAT LEFTBANK) LEFTBANK)
          ((MEMBER 'BOAT RIGHTBANK) RIGHTBANK)
          (T (BREAK (ERROR IN FROMSIDE) T))))

(DEFUN APPLICABLEQ (MOVE)
    (AND (NOT (>(NUMBEROF 'M MOVE) (NUMBEROF 'M
                                        (FROMSIDE))))
         (NOT (>(NUMBEROF 'C MOVE) (NUMBEROF 'C
                                        (FROMSIDE))))))

(DEFUN RECORDNEWSTATE ()
    (SETQ STATESEEN (CONS (STATETRIPLE) STATESEEN)))

(DEFUN SEENSTATEBEFOREQ ()
    (MEMBER (STATETRIPLE) STATESEEN))

(DEFUN MISSIONARIESEATENQ ()
    (OR (MEATENQ LEFTBANK) (MEATENQ RIGHTBANK)))

(DEFUN MEATENQ (BANK)
    (AND (>(NUMBEROF 'C BANK) (NUMBEROF 'M BANK))
         (>(NUMBEROF 'M BANK) 0)))

(DEFUN SUCCEEDEDQ ()
    (NULL LEFTBANK))

(DEFUN STATETRIPLE ()
    (LIST (NUMBEROF 'BOAT LEFTBANK)
          (NUMBEROF 'M LEFTBANK)
          (NUMBEROF 'C LEFTBANK)))
```

```
(DEFUN PEXPLOREASTATE (LEFTBANK RIGHTBANK MOVELIST)
    (PROG ()
        (COND ((NOT (APPLICABLEQ MOVELIST)) (RETURN)))
        (APPLYMOVE MOVELIST)
        (PRIN1 'APPLIEDMOVE) (TYO 40) (PRIN1 MOVELIST)
        COND ((MISSIONARIESEATENQ) (PRINT 'MISSIONARIESEATEN)
                                            (TERPRI) (RETURN))
             ((SEENSTATEBEFOREQ) (PRINT 'SEENSTATEBEFORE)
                                            (TERPRI) (RETURN)))
        (PRINT 'NEWSTATE) (PRINTSTATE)
        (COND ((SUCCEEDEDQ) (PRINT 'SUCCESS) (QUIT)))
        (RECORDNEWSTATE)
        (TRYALL POSSIBLEMOVES)
        (PRINT 'BACKUP)))
```

1.7 DRAUGHTS

1.7.1 Introduction

In many ways M & C was a toy problem. For instance, the search tree was
very small and we did not need to exercise much intelligence in searching
it (once we had arrived at the formal representation). We now turn our
attention to a problem area where it is perhaps easier to see how to
represent the problem as searching a tree, but where the search raises
formidable problems. The problem area is draughts. Can we give a precise
recipe for playing a good game of draughts?

1.7.2 Complete Analysis (and the search tree)

One way to guarantee a good game would be to analyse completely the
game, i.e. to explore, once and for all, all the possible games. Maybe this is
possible using modern high-speed computers? Let us draw a picture of
such a complete analysis:

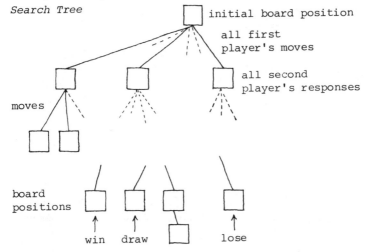

31

It has been estimated that this tree contains 10^{40} nodes. If we make the (very optimistic) assumption that we can consider 3 nodes per milli-microsecond, it would take 10^{21} centuries to explore the whole tree. Clearly this is out of the question (regardless of whether we search the tree depth first, breadth first, etc.)

1.7.3   Look-Ahead

An alternative to searching the whole tree is to search some way ahead, whenever we have a choice, to see what is locally the best choice.

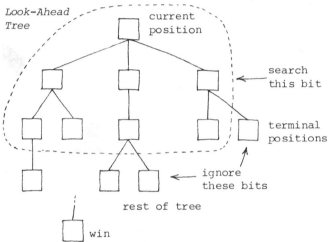

In order to analyse completely the look-ahead tree we must be able to assign some value to the terminal nodes (previously they were all wins, draws or losses). As a first step let us decide to award a numerical score to each terminal position:

a win for first player gets the biggest positive number
a lose for first player gets the biggest negative number
a draw gets zero
other scores will be in between, as we decide

1.7.4   Mini-Maxing

Having fixed scores for the terminal positions how do we analyse the board? (Assume that the first player is to choose throughout.)

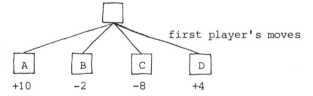

Clearly, in this case, the first player will choose move A. However, if we look further ahead, the tree may look like this (note that this is a different tree):

32

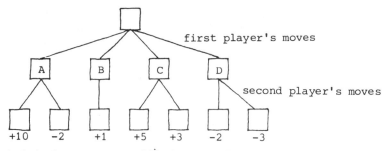

first player's moves

second player's moves

Is A the best move now? No, because the second player can be assumed to take the −2 branch to maximise his chances; so move B, for instance, would be better. In fact C is best, because the second player can only take the +3 branch at best. Can we formalise this procedure?

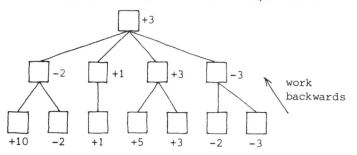

work
backwards

Starting with the scores of the terminal positions we work backwards up the tree, labelling the nodes as follows. If the second player has the choice of move we label the node with the *lowest* possible score from the available alternatives. If the first player has the choice, we label the node with the *highest* possible score. We can carry out the process to any depth, and this technique is called mini-maxing.

1.7.5 Choosing the Score

How do we decide what score to give a board position? Could we decide in advance on a score for each individual position? No, because there are too many ($\sim 10^{40}$). We must use some high-level classification of board positions, e.g. we must look for features. What is a feature? Some examples are:

Who has the most pieces?
Is anybody in a position to fork?
Is anybody in a position to gain a king?
Who controls the centre?

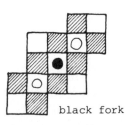

black fork

We can look for features and award points for each, e.g. so many points for each potential king, etc. Then we can add up all the points to get a total score for the board, advantages for the first player being scored positive, and advantages for the second player being scored negative.

How do we decide relative values between different features? Usually by experimentation and practice. Therefore it is useful to be able to adjust relative values easily. The way to do this is to score each feature separately, without regard to relative values, and to weight each score before adding them together, i.e.

$$\text{Total Score} = w_1 s_1 + w_2 s_2 + \ldots + w_n s_n$$

where w is the weight allocated to each feature score s.

1.7.6 Factors Affecting Look-Ahead

How do we decide how far ahead to look, and where to stop? We must take into account: (a) The limited capacity of the machine. The number of nodes increases exponentially with depth, which means that typically we can only search 3-4 moves deep. (This phenomenon is called the *Combinatorial Explosion*.) (b) The principle of hot pursuit, i.e. we want to pursue further those branches that are not stable. For instance, if the next move is a jump, keep looking unless we are nearly exceeding the capacity of machine. (c) The fact that we may waste time considering branches that cannot be any good, e.g.

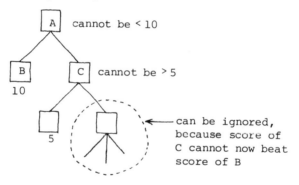

This refinement is called α - β search.

Exercise 1.7.1. Consider the following look-ahead tree, where the scores for the terminal positions have been filled in. Using the mini-max procedure, determine which move the first player should make.

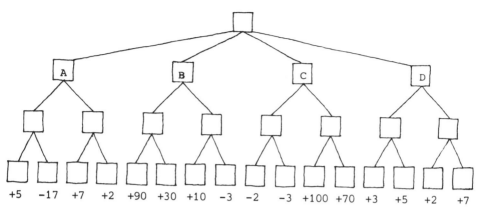

+5   −17   +7   +2   +90   +30   +10   −3   −2   −3   +100   +70   +3   +5   +2   +7

1.7.7   Conclusion

Samuel's checkers (American for draughts) program, which is based on these principles, beats all but the very best players. Chess-playing programs have also been written along the same lines. Here the situation is not so healthy. They can play only as well as the best amateurs, and there is no hope of a radical improvement in their performance. Their play can only be improved by searching deeper or increasing the effort involved in calculating the score of a position. Both of these involve an increase in the time spent choosing moves, and the existing programs already use all the time allocated to them under tournament rules.

The whole area of chess-playing programs is currently undergoing a revolution, and new techniques are being explored. For instance, using high-level descriptions of board positions to carry out a strategic search, before unpacking this into a more detailed, deep but narrow search. For a good account of the problems of the old approach and some of the new techniques, see the paper by Berliner.

1.7.8   Recommended Reading

A. L. Samuel, (1963) Some studies in machine learning using the game of checkers, in *Computers and Thought* (eds F. A. Feigenbaum & J. Feldman). McGraw-Hill. This paper describes Samuel's highly successful draughts-playing program, including a discussion of how it was able to learn from experience. (See also section 4.1.)

If this area particularly interests you, see H. Berliner, (1973) Some necessary conditions of a master chess program, in *Proceedings of the 3rd IJCAI*, pp 77–85. Stanford. Berliner describes the limitations of the mini-max techniques and suggests ways of overcoming these limitations.

1.8   THE GENERAL PROBLEM SOLVER

1.8.1   Introduction

So far we have constructed or discussed computational models for particular tasks (IQ tests, the M & C problem, and draughts), but humans have the ability to solve problems in a wide variety of domains, including areas they have not encountered before. What does this general problem-solving ability consist of? Can we construct a program with this capability? In the late 'fifties and early 'sixties a lot of energy was devoted to this question, the most famous program being the General Problem Solver (GPS) of Newell, Simon & Shaw.

Naturally it is necessary to explain a particular problem to GPS, and this is done by giving descriptions of the initial and goal states of the world (called *objects*) and *operators* to transform these objects. Thus, just as in the M & C problem, GPS has to search for a sequence of operators that transform the initial object into the final object. To help it with this search GPS must also be given a procedure for finding differences between objects, and a way of relating these differences to operators relevant to reducing such differences. The central contribution of GPS is a *general search technique* called *means-ends analysis*.

1.8.2 Means-Ends Analysis

Consider the problem of getting from my home in Edinburgh to Trafalgar Square, London. GPS would go through a process of reasoning like the following:

"My *goal* or *end* is to transform 'me at home' into 'me in Trafalgar Square'. The first task is to compare these two *states* and find the *difference*. I find the difference to be one of location. The *means* I have of reducing differences of location are *operators* like 'walk' or 'travel by train'. Some operators, like 'walk', can be rejected as infeasible, but 'travel by train' is feasible, so my next task is to apply this operator to the *initial state*, 'me at home'. Unfortunately the operator will not apply immediately because the conditions are not right; I am not at the station. So I set up a new sub-goal to transform 'me at home' into 'me at the station'. Again the difference is one of location and again I find the 'travel' operators. I can reject 'walk' as infeasible (I am lazy) and 'go by train' as a potential loop and select 'go by taxi'. This cannot be applied because the conditions are wrong; the taxi driver does not know I need him. The difference is one of information, so I look for an operator that can reduce differences of information and find the communication operators like 'use the telephone' . . .".

This kind of analysis can be carried on to any required depth and will eventually produce a plan consisting of a sequence of operators.

Methods. Means-ends analysis is embodied in GPS as a series of procedures called *methods*. These are usually explained by the following *flowcharts*.

Method 1. Goal: Transform object A into object B.

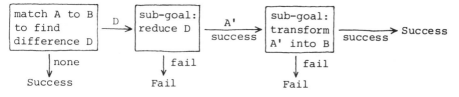

Method 2. Goal: Reduce difference D between objects A and B.

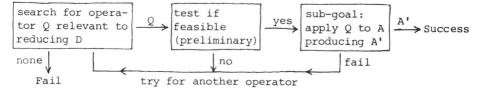

Method 3. Goal: Apply operator Q to object A.

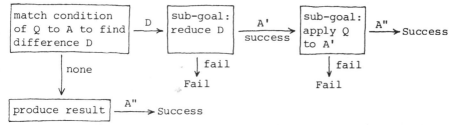

GPS can achieve *goals* of three different types:
1. Transforming one object into another.
2. Reducing a difference.
3. Applying an operator.

For each type of goal there is a method. These methods generate *sub-goals* and call the appropriate methods to achieve these sub-goals. Thus each method can call itself and the others in a highly recursive way.

Exercise 1.8.1. Using the above flowcharts, trace the behaviour of GPS on the Trafalgar Square example.

1.8.3 Defining the Problem

How can we describe a problem to GPS? We must choose a way of describing states of the world. A good way might be lists of symbolic descriptions like:

[[at me home] [near me telephone] [has me £29]]

We must also tell it what operators are available, what preconditions they have, and how to apply them to one object to produce another. For instance, we could describe the operator "go by train" as

provided the object contains [at me station1]

form a new object by deleting [at me station1]

and adding [at me station2]

(in a suitable procedural form of course).

37

Unfortunately, this is not all we have to do. We must also give GPS a procedure for picking the most significant differences between objects. For example, location is the most significant difference between the initial state above and [[at me Trafalgar Square]]. Then it must be able to use these differences to extract relevant operators. This is usually done by feeding GPS a *difference/operator table*, e.g.

difference \ operator	walk	train	taxi	phone	cable	write
location	X	X	X			
information				X	X	X
...						
...						

A cross in the table indicates that the operator in this column is useful for reducing the difference in this row. These differences must also be ordered by the difficulty of reducing them. The most difficult is always selected as the most significant between objects, and there is a check to see that we never try to reduce a hard difference as a subgoal of an easier one.

GPS also requires us to supply a procedure for testing the feasibility of an operator in some particular situation. For instance, we might reject "walk" if the difference in location is more than a mile, or reject "write a letter" if the demand for information exchange is pressing. This feasibility test is a *hack*, enabling us to include ad-hoc, unsystematised knowledge that supplements the distance/operator table. If we succeeded in systematising this knowledge we might prefer to include it in the table, e.g.

location difference in miles	walk	taxi	train	plane
0-1	X			
1-10		X	X	
10-100			X	
> 100				X

This is rather a lot of information to have to give for a particular problem, and the question arises whether GPS succeeds as a *general* problem solver. We will return to this later.

1.8.4   The Search
When GPS is set loose on a problem it becomes involved in a complicated series of recursive calls to the three methods. It is useful to have a neat way of describing the search behaviour, and we present such a way here.

Another description for the GPS search strategy is *problem reduction*. Problem reduction is the strategy of exchanging your current goal for a series of simpler sub-goals, and then exchanging these for even simpler sub-goals, until all the sub-goals are trivial. Problem reduction searches can always be represented as *and-or search trees*. These are like ordinary search trees, except that the sub-nodes of a particular node can be grouped into *and bundles*, e.g.

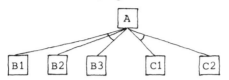

The three Bs are one and bundle. The two Cs are another. The interpretation is that sub-goals B1, B2 and B3 together establish A, and that sub-goals C1 and C2 together establish A.

The search for a solution to the "Trafalgar Square" example can be illustrated by the following and-or search tree. This tree is grown in a depth-first manner.

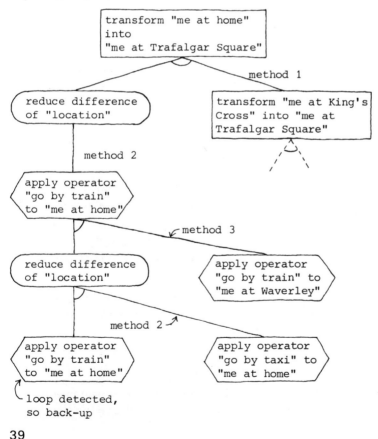

Exercise 1.8.2. Explain how the look-ahead tree used in draughts can be regarded as a type of and-or search tree.

1.8.5   Psychological Validity

GPS was claimed to be not only a general problem solver, but also to have psychological validity, i.e. it was supposed to solve problems in a similar way to humans. How could we test this claim? First we have to choose a *level* at which to make the comparison. For instance, at a very basic level, that of the excitation of neurones and of currents passing through transistors, the human and the computer are obviously behaving differently. On the other hand, at the gross level of whether they both solve the problem the similarity can be trivial. Newell's contribution was to define an intermediate level of comparison, that of the programs running in each. Even this is not quite right. It would clearly be silly to claim that people are programmed in LOGO or any other computer language. What Newell does claim is that people are programmed in *some* language and that the GPS program is similar to the human program but in a different language, just as a programmer will often claim that some ALGOL program, say, is similar to some FORTRAN program. This level of comparison is called the *Information Processing Level*.

This claim is tested by comparing the *trace* of both programs. The GPS trace is easy to obtain, by getting the program to print out messages as it proceeds. The human trace is obtained by getting the subject to "think aloud" while he is doing the problem. The result is tape recorded and is called a *protocol*. Newell et al. claim that this protocol is not introspection but behaviour.

However, the traces still cannot be compared directly, since the computer trace is not in English. Instead the human is assumed to be searching the same and-or tree as the computer and his protocol is examined for evidence as to *how he searched this tree*. The computer and the human are said to be behaving similarly if they searched the tree in the same way.

How successful was this attempt at psychological simulation? In the example in the recommended reading the correlation was fairly good. There are, however, some aspects of behaviour that GPS finds difficult to simulate:

(a) The program makes no distinction between searches conducted in memory and searches conducted in the world, e.g. between remembering a telephone number or looking it up in the directory.

(b) The program does not handle meta-remarks (i.e. reflections about the task) like "this is difficult" or "I am lost", etc.

(c) Subjects sometimes handle similar goals in parallel, which the program could not do. For example, the subject might consider, and reject, several modes of transport (aircraft, ship, hovercraft) at a stroke, whereas the program would have to consider each possibility individually.

(d) Subjects sometimes indulge in a more complex kind of back-up than the depth-first search that GPS is capable of. For example, when planning how to get from King's Cross to Trafalgar Square, you may realise that you will not have enough money for a taxi unless you decide to walk from home to Waverley Station after all.

1.8.6   Conclusions

As a general problem solver, GPS was not an unqualified success. Its main shortcoming was the tremendous amount of information that had to be input about each particular problem and the small contribution made by GPS. Few people in AI now believe that it is possible to construct a general problem solver that does make a large contribution, and the effort is now directed to building systems with expertise in areas of commonsense reasoning (like visual perception). The role of GPS is now filled by new, high-level programming languages (like CONNIVER and PLANNER), which we will hear more about later. Judged as a programming language GPS's shortcoming is that information about particular problems has to be fed in in a highly stylised, awkward way. Some of its applications seem rather forced. Newell et al. have now dropped GPS in favour of a type of programming language called Production Systems, which we will discuss in the chapter on learning. The new high-level programming languages are designed to make the programming of task-specific information easier.

Despite its shortcomings, GPS has been highly influential in AI. Many of the ideas embodied in it have been adopted in later programs, sometimes to better effect. For instance, compare GPS differences with the Geometric Analogy problem rules, which really describe differences between figure descriptions.

1.8.7   Exercises

1.8.3. Suppose you were trying to get GPS to solve the M & C problem. What would you choose as the objects, operators and differences?
**1.8.4.* We can express each of the GPS methods as a LOGO procedure. For instance, method 1, for transforming one object into another, can be written:

```
TO TRANSFORM 'A 'B
10 NEW [D A1]
20 MAKE 'D FINDDIFF :A :B
30 IF EQ :D 'NONE THEN RESULT 'SUCCESS
40 MAKE 'A1 REDUCEDIFF :D :A
50 IF EQ :A1 'FAIL THEN RESULT 'FAIL
60 RESULT TRANSFORM :A1 :B
END
```

Express the other two methods as LOGO procedures, (Hint: method 2 is more difficult because of the loop. Make a list of all relevant operators, then work down this list.) Each of the methods call sub-procedures like FINDDIFF. Write these using CALLUSER, then run your program on the "Trafalgar Square" example.

*1.8.5. There is a deep bug in the GPS flowcharts associated with back-up. What is it?

1.8.8   Recommended Reading
A. Newell & H.A. Simon (1963) GPS, a program that simulates human thought, in *Computers and Thought* (eds E.A. Feigenbaum & J. Feldman) pp.279-93. McGraw-Hill. GPS is described using an example from propositional logic as a vehicle. The trace of GPS and the protocol of a human subject are compared.

If you are particularly interested in the computer simulation of human behaviour (i.e. in information processing models) then another good reference is
A. Newell, H.A. Simon, & J.C. Shaw. Elements of a theory of human problem solving, in *Readings in the Psychology of Cognition* (eds Anderson & Austel).

1.9   ROBOT PLAN FORMATION: THE BACKGROUND

1.9.1   The Problem
Suppose we had a robot janitor, looking after a suite of rooms. We want to give him a series of tasks to perform each day, then leave him to it. We do not want to have to give a separate program for every conceivable task. Rather we would like to give him a few basic programs (called operators), and have him put them together into a big program to perform whatever task we give him. The task will usually be explained by giving a description of the desired state of the rooms.

Example: Collecting Boxes. Suppose the initial state of one of room A is:

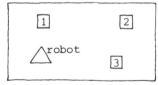

We might ask that all the boxes be put in the same place, i.e. that the final state of room A is:

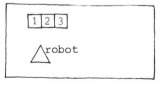

where the robot has available two operators: (a) he can go from one place to another; or (b) he can push something from one place to another.

He might devise the plan:
1. go to box 2
2. push it to box 1
3. go to box 3
4. push it to box 1

It will be no use him just performing various operations at random, until he chances upon some combination that works. This would take far too long, and might cause irreparable damage to the rooms. Rather, he must form a plan. To form a plan he must perform a GPS-like means-ends analysis, i.e. he must find the difference between his current description of the rooms, and the description of the desired state, then pick an operator relevant to reducing that difference. This implies that he must know something about his basic operators, e.g. under what conditions they can be run, and what their effects are.

1.9.2 Automatic Programming
This problem is analogous to the problem of getting computers to write their own procedures. That is, instead of writing a procedure to do a task, we would like to be able to specify the task, and to have a computer program put together its existing procedures into a procedure to achieve this task. This is called *Automatic Programming*. The operators here will be the procedures that have already been written. The task will be described by making statements about the values various variables should have before and after the procedure is run.

Example: Reversing a List. Given the procedures EMPTYQ, NOT, FIRST, BUTFIRST and FIRSTPUT, write a procedure to reverse a list.

We might explain the task by giving some example input/output pairs, e.g.
    input is [A B C D]
    output is [D C B A]
or by giving a mathematical definition of REVERSE, e.g.
    REVERSE of [] is []
    otherwise
    REVERSE of :LIST is LASTPUT (FIRST :LIST) (REVERSE BUTFIRST :LIST)
We would expect the program to write a procedure like

```
TO  REVERSE  'LIST
10 NEW  'ANS
20 MAKE  'ANS  []
30 WHILE  NOT  EMPTYQ  :LIST
      THEN  FPUT  F  :LIST  :ANS
      AND  MAKE  'LIST  BF  :LIST
40 RESULT  :ANS
END
```

1.9.3 Comparison

Work is going on in both domains, robot planning and automatic programming, and there has been useful interaction between the fields. We will be mainly concerned with the former in these sections. The work on robot planning has tended to concentrate on searching for so-called *simple plans*, i.e. a sequence of operators, as in the collecting boxes example. On the other hand, people in automatic programming have been unable to ignore the need for conditionals, loops and recursion, as in our list-reversing example. Consequently they have made less progress (this work is still in its infancy), but results in this domain should have repercussions in robot planning, since plans for everyday tasks need conditionals, loops and recursion too, as the following example shows.

Example: Cigarette Lighting.

> To light-a-cigarette
> Put cigarette in your mouth
> get a flame
> hold flame against end of cigarette
> inhale until cigarette lights
> end

> To get-a-flame
> If you have matches then
> Take a match out of box
> Strike match against box repeatedly, until it lights
> else ask someone else for a light
> end

Each of the lines with "until" in them implies repeating some action until some predicate is true, i.e. looping. Compare the use of WHILE in the list-reversing example (section 1.9.2).

1.9.4 Describing the Task

How can we describe the task of "collecting three boxes" to a computer program? By giving symbolic descriptions of the initial state of the room and the final goal, e.g.

> Initial state: [AT ROBOT A] [AT BOX1 B] [AT BOX2 C]
> [AT BOX3 D]
> Final goal: [AT BOX1 ?X] [AT BOX2 ?X] [AT BOX3 ?X]

A, B, C and D are constants representing *places*. ?X is a variable that may be assigned a place as its value during the construction of the plan. In what follows it will not always be possible to say, in advance, which variables are to be assigned values (denoted 'X) and which are to be replaced by their values (denoted :X). We will therefore drop the prefixes ' and :, and write ?X instead. When the inference system meets ?X, it will first check to see whether X has been assigned a value. If X has a value, ?X will mean :X. Otherwise, if X has no value, ?X will mean 'X.

When we search for a plan we will need to represent intermediate states. These can also be represented as a set of facts. Note that a fact, like [AT ROBOT A], may be true at one time and false at another. We can deal with this in at least two ways:

(a) We can give each fact an extra argument, stating at *what time* or in *what situation* the fact is true (called the situation calculus), e.g.

time $\left\{ \begin{array}{l} \text{[AT ROBOT A1]} \\ \text{[AT ROBOT C2]} \end{array} \right.$

situation $\left\{ \begin{array}{l} \text{[AT ROBOT A INITIALLY]} \\ \text{[AT ROBOT C [DO [GO A C] INITIALLY]]} \end{array} \right.$

(b) We can have a sequence of databases, each one labelled with a particular time or situation.

(a) and (b) are essentially (logically) the same, but (b) is more suggestive when it comes to designing an efficient computer program to do planning, so we will adopt it here. In fact what we will really need when we are searching for a plan is not a sequence of databases, but a search tree of databases, where the links are operators:

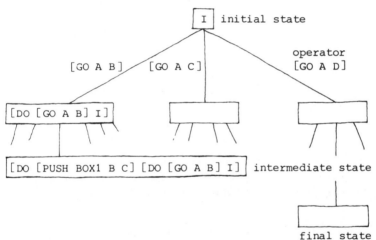

Clearly simple times will not do to label these states (why?); we must use situations.

1.9.5 Representing the Operators

How can we describe the operators to the computer program? It is easy to represent the two operators "robot go from x to y" and "push z from x to y" as [GO ?X ?Y] and [PUSH ?Z ?X ?Y], but in order to construct sensible plans we must also know (a) when the operators can be applied, and (b) what effect they have on databases.

We deal with (a) first. In our planning model we must say what properties the database must have for an operator to be applicable to it. For instance,

45

for the robot to go from x to y, he must first be at x. So we can say that [AT ROBOT ?X] is a *precondition* of [GO ?X ?Y], i.e. [AT ROBOT ?X] must be true in a database (s, say) before we can apply [GO ?X ?Y] to produce a new database, [DO [GO ?X ?Y] S]. Similarly the preconditions of [PUSH ?Z ?X ?Y] are [AT ROBOT ?X] and [AT ?Z ?X]. Thus each operator will have associated with it a pattern called its precondition, and this precondition must be true in a database if the operator is to apply to it.

We now turn to (b), representing the effects of the operator. These effects are represented in our planning model by instructions about how to modify a database when an operator is applied to it. For instance, when the robot goes from x to y, we should delete the fact [AT ROBOT ?X] and add the fact [AT ROBOT ?Y]. Similarly when the robot pushes z from x to y, we should delete [AT ROBOT ?X] and [AT ?Z ?X] and add [AT ROBOT ?Y] and [AT ?Z ?Y].

In general most facts remain true when an operator is applied, e.g. the pictures stay on the wall when I pour the tea. (Explosions are a notable exception.) Therefore it is most convenient to list what old facts become false (or unknown) and what new facts become true. So each operator has associated with it two patterns, called the *add* and *delete* lists. The new database is formed by taking the old database and first subtracting the delete list, then adding the add list.

The Frame Problem(s). Unfortunately, representing the effects of an operator is not as easy as this. The problems are collectively referred to as the *frame problem* (the name comes from an early proposed solution to them). We discuss these problems in the order of their increasing difficulty.

The first problem we have already dealt with, namely, we overcome the tedium of listing all the facts that remain true when an operator is applied, by only mentioning (in the delete list) those that become false (or unknown).

The second problem is one of computational efficiency. In a realistic planning situation, any one of the databases will be very large, containing perhaps thousands of facts. The search tree similarly may contain thousands of databases, each of which will be very similar. Storing all these facts in the computer will use up lots of space. Every time a new database is created we will have to spend lots of computer time copying facts into it. The solution is to store only the initial database and the add and delete lists every time an operator is applied. To decide whether a fact is true in a database we apply the following procedure:

    To lsq fact database
    10 If the database is the initial one, access as normal
    20 Else if the fact is in the add list of the last operator then true
    30 Else if the fact is in the delete list of the last operator then false

46

40 Else call procedure recursively on the previous database
end

This procedure can be supplemented by (a) earmarking various facts that are always true (true initially, and cannot be changed by available operators) and adding line 5:

5 If fact always true then true

and (b) checking if the fact was in the precondition of the last operator, in which case it must have been true then and has not been deleted since, i.e.

35 Else if the fact is in the precondition of the last operator then true.

There is no reason why these solutions cannot be adopted in the situation calculus formalism, but they are suggested by the sequence of databases.

The last problem is the most serious and is still an open one, namely, that the effects of an operator may be more subtle than can be represented by simple add and delete lists. We delay further discussion of it until later.

1.10   ROBOT PLAN FORMATION: MAKING PLANS

1.10.1 Collecting Boxes Again

We now turn our attention to the problem of actually making a plan, given a description of the task and the operators. We will work through the "collecting three boxes" example in detail. The initial state is:

[AT ROBOT A] [AT BOX1 B] [AT BOX2 C] [AT BOX3 D]

and we call this state S_1. The final state must satisfy the pattern:

[AT BOX1 ?X] [AT BOX2 ?X] [AT BOX3 ?X]

The operators are described in the following *operator table*:

Operator	Preconditions	Delete List	Add List
[GO ?X ?Y]	[AT ROBOT ?X]	[AT ROBOT ?X]	[AT ROBOT ?Y]
[PUSH ?Z ?X ?Y]	[AT ?Z ?X]	[AT ROBOT ?X]	[AT ROBOT ?Y]
	[AT ROBOT ?X]	[AT ?Z ?X]	[AT ?Z ?Y]

The plan we will build up is:

[GO A C] [PUSH BOX2 C B] [GO B D] [PUSH BOX3 D B]

As we build this plan up, we will need to refer to the intermediate states, so it will be helpful to define them now. They are defined by the following *planned state sequence*:

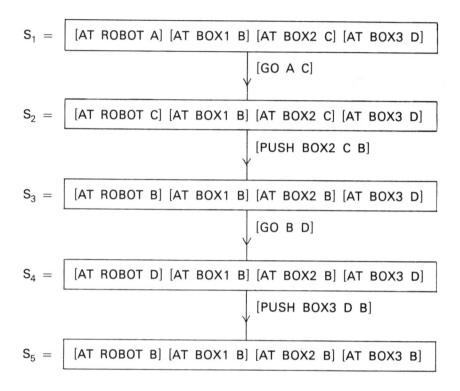

1.10.2 The Plan

At each stage of building the plan we consider the current state and plan, and the goals we have still to achieve. Initially we are in state S_1 with the goal [AT BOX1 ?X] [AT BOX2 ?X] [AT BOX3 ?X] and no plan. Our first step is to see whether we can satisfy this goal in the current state. We can satisfy [AT BOX1 ?X] by assigning B to ?X. This leaves us with the goal [AT BOX2 B] [AT BOX3 B], which is not satisfied in S_1 and becomes our first *difference*. We concentrate on trying to achieve one of the facts, say the first [AT BOX2 B], and look for a *means* of *reducing the difference*. A means would be any operator that contains in its add list a pattern that matches [AT BOX2 B]. The only such operator is [PUSH ?Z ?X ?Y], which contains [AT ?Z ?Y] in its add list. We assign BOX2 to ?Z and B to ?Y, and decide to try to apply [PUSH BOX2 ?X B]. But for an operator to be applicable to a state, its preconditions must be satisfied, so we must check [AT BOX2 ?X] [AT ROBOT ?X] in S_1. We can satisfy [AT BOX2 ?X] if we assign C to ?X, but then [AT ROBOT C] is not true and becomes our second difference. Again we look for an operator with a matching pattern in its add list, and first find [GO ?X ?Y] with pattern [AT ROBOT ?Y]. We match C to Y, and try to apply [GO ?X C]. The preconditions of the operator are satisfied in S_1, if we assign A to X. Now the preconditions of [GO A C] are satisfied, and we apply it to create state

S_2. Similarly the preconditions of [PUSH BOX2 C B] are satisfied, so we apply it to create state S_3.

We are now left with the task of achieving [AT BOX3 B], in the current state S_3. This is done in a very similar way to the achievement of [AT BOX2 B].

We can sum up the above argument by listing the stages of *development of the plan* together with a note about the reason for the change.

Current Plan	Reason for Change
[PUSH BOX2 ?X B]	to achieve [AT BOX2 B]
[PUSH BOX2 C B]	to make precondition match [AT BOX2 C]
[GO ?X C] [PUSH BOX2 C B]	to achieve [AT ROBOT C]
[GO A C] [PUSH BOX2 C B]	to make precondition match [AT ROBOT A]

These two operators can now be applied to S_1 to produce S_3 and the first goal is achieved. S_3 is now used for checking preconditions.

[GO A C] [PUSH BOX2 C B] [PUSH BOX3 ?X B]	to achieve [AT BOX3 B]
[GO A C] [PUSH BOX2 C B] [PUSH BOX3 D B]	to make precondition match [AT BOX3 D]
[GO A C] [PUSH BOX2 C B] [GO ?X D] [PUSH BOX3 D B]	to achieve [AT ROBOT D]
[GO A C] [PUSH BOX2 C B] [GO B D] [PUSH BOX3 D B]	to make precondition match [AT ROBOT B]

The remaining two operators can now be applied to produce S_5 and the second goal is achieved.

1.10.3 Search

The process of making a plan described above really involves search. At any stage there may be several preconditions or goals (e.g. [AT ?Z ?X] and [AT ROBOT ?X]) remaining to be satisfied and we must attempt them in some order. There may also be several operators applicable (e.g. GO and PUSH), and these must be attempted in some order. In each case we have chosen to use the order in which they appear in our operator table.

This order was carefully chosen. We never had to remake a choice. We could have got stuck in all the normal ways. We might have got in a loop. We might have got into a situation where no operator was applicable. We might have produced a non-optimal plan. We could recover from these situations by remaking one of our choices.

Note that the search space was not as big as it would have been if we had just tried putting together operators in random order. For instance every attempted plan must include the PUSH operator. The search tree is made smaller by the use of GPS-like means-ends analysis.

Exercise 1.10.1. Think of a non-optimal plan for the collecting three boxes example. At what points must we exercise different choices to get this plan rather than the previous one?

1.10.4 Protection
Note that all the conjuncts of the final goal must be simultaneously true at the end, and that all the preconditions of an operator must be true just before the operator is applied. Unfortunately, a goal, once achieved, can be deleted later by the effect of a subsequent operator. In our example [AT BOX1 B] was true initially, but it could have been inadvertently deleted during the course of achieving [AT BOX2 B] or [AT BOX3 B]. Suppose we have reached the state:

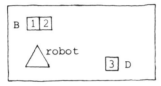

The robot must go to D to collect BOX3. Suppose it (stupidly) tried to get there by applying [PUSH BOX1 B D]. The resulting situation would be

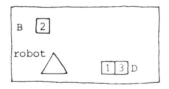

[AT BOX1 B] would be deleted — a retrograde step.

How can we prevent this happening? We could insist that PUSH is not used to achieve goals like [AT ROBOT D]. Unfortunately there are situations in which we prefer PUSH to GO, e.g., achieve [AT ROBOT D] [AT BOX1 D]. In any case this is an example of a wider problem — how not to destroy an achieved goal during the achievement of a subsequent one. People sometimes have trouble with this, e.g. "How can you take your car to the garage, then come home but leave it there?".

Another solution is to *protect* achieved goals and preconditions, until they are no longer needed, i.e. to mark them in some way and arrange that any operator that tries to delete a marked fact is not incorporated in the plan. Thus, once we had achieved [AT CAR GARAGE], no operator that deleted this would be considered, and we would have to go home by bus. Of course, when we have achieved [SERVICED CAR], this mark would be removed.

1.10.5 Stacking Boxes

We now further debug our plan formation recipe, by considering a new example. We will consider a robot with a single ability, that of stacking and unstacking boxes. We will express this by a single operator [MOVE ?X ?Y ?Z], which means "move box X from place Y to place Z". A place can be another box or the floor. In our very simple world all boxes are assumed to be the same size, so in order for the operator to be applicable place Z must be "clear" — i.e. if it is a box there must be no other boxes on it. To simplify matters further, we will assume that there is always room on the floor, by asserting that the floor is always "clear". To make box X easier to manipulate we will further insist that it must be "clear" before it can be moved. We can sum all this up by the following table and diagrams.

Operator	Preconditions	Delete List	Add List
[MOVE ?X ?Y ?Z]	[DIFF ?X ?Z]	[ON ?X ?Y]	[ON ?X ?Z]
	[DIFF ?Y ?Z]	[CLEAR ?Z]	[CLEAR ?Y]
	[ON ?X ?Y]		[CLEAR FLOOR]
	[CLEAR ?X]		
	[CLEAR ?Z]		

There are three cases to consider.

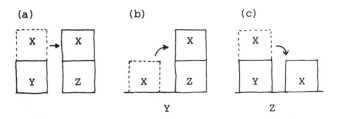

Note [CLEAR FLOOR] is needed in the add list because it is inadvertently deleted in case (c). This begins to show the inadequacy of add and delete lists for dealing with the effects of operators.

1.10.6 A Three Box Problem

Consider the problem defined by the following diagram:

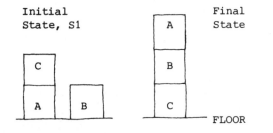

We can describe the initial state by
    [ON C A] [ON A FLOOR] [ON B FLOOR]
    [CLEAR C] [CLEAR B] [CLEAR FLOOR]
    [DIFF A B] [DIFF B C], etc.
We can describe the final goal by
    [ON A B] [ON B C]
Suppose we decide to work on [ON A B] first. We pick the only relevant application of an operator [MOVE A ?Y B]. We can satisfy all but one of the preconditions of this by choosing Y to be FLOOR. We are left with the precondition [CLEAR A]. The only relevant operator application for reducing this is [MOVE ?X A ?Z], and the preconditions of this are all satisfied if we let X be C and Z be FLOOR, so the plan is now
    [MOVE C A FLOOR] [MOVE A FLOOR B]
This partial plan can now be executed and achieves [ON A B]. It creates the state

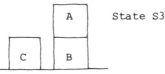

State S3

So we protect [ON A B] and proceed with proving [ON B C]. The only relevant operator application is [MOVE B FLOOR C]. Unfortunately a precondition of this is [CLEAR B] and the achievement of this would undo [ON A B], which is protected.

This difficulty arises because we tried to achieve the two goals independently with two plans, and then put these plans one after the other, i.e. [MOVE C A FLOOR] [MOVE A FLOOR B] followed by [MOVE B FLOOR C]. In fact the two goals interact, and their plans have to be intermingled in order to achieve both goals at the same time. (Trying the plans in reverse order results in a similar difficulty.) So we try inserting the new operator [MOVE B FLOOR C] in different places in the previous plan. It turns out that the sequence
    [MOVE C A FLOOR] [MOVE B FLOOR C] [MOVE A FLOOR B]
works.

1.10.7 Exercises

1.10.2. Consider the problem defined by the following diagram.

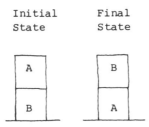

(a) Give a description of the initial state.
(b) Give a description of the final goal.
(c) Give a plan using the MOVE operator.
(d) Draw a diagram of the planned state sequence.
*(e) Show how your plan could have been discovered by a planning program by listing the stages of its development, giving reasons for each change.

1.10.3. Design a set of robot operators that will enable the robot to turn a light switch on, i.e. starting from the initial state

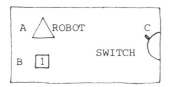

achieve the goal [STATUS SWITCH ON]

Describe the initial state with the facts:
[AT ROBOT A] [AT BOX1 B] [AT SWITCH C]
[STATUS SWITCH OFF] [ON ROBOT FLOOR] [TYPE BOX1 BOX]
Give the robot the two operators GO and PUSH described earlier. In addition, give him an operator [TURNON ?X], which is applicable provided that X, the switch, is initially off, the *robot is standing on a box* and the box, robot and switch are at the same place. This operator changes the status of the switch from off to on. To get on the box the robot will need an additional operator [CLIMBON ?X], which is applicable provided X is a box, the robot is initially on the floor and both are at the same place. You will need to alter PUSH so that it can only push boxes, and both GO and PUSH to make sure the robot is on the floor before they are applied.

(a) Describe the four operators by drawing an operator table giving their preconditions, delete lists and add lists.
(b) Describe a plan for achieving the task and draw a planned state sequence diagram.

1.11   ROBOT PLAN FORMATION: ASSORTED ISSUES

1.11.1 Controlling Search
During a process of making a plan we have to exercise various choices, i.e. we have to choose
(a) Which unachieved goal or precondition (hereafter, collectively called sub-goals) to work on next.
(b) Which fact from the database to try to match the subgoal against.
(c) Which relevant operator to try to apply.

Making these choices badly can cause us to:

(a) go into a loop

(b) work on a branch containing an unachievable subgoal.

(c) Find a non-optimal plan.

It is obviously of crucial importance to make these choices sensibly.

The following diagram illustrates a stage of the development of the plan to collect three boxes:

Current Database

[AT ROBOT A] [AT BOX1 B] [AT BOX2 C] [AT BOX3 D]

Current Sub-goals

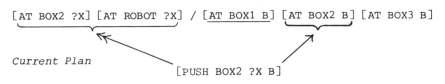

The top line is a description of the current (and initial) state. The second line lists the various goals and preconditions that have yet to be satisfied. The three goals on the right of the stroke are the original three goals. The underlined goal has already been satisfied. We are working on the next one, [AT BOX2 B]. The bottom line lists the partial plan, containing one operator [PUSH BOX2 ?X B]. The operator is pointing, with a single-headed arrow, at the goal it is meant to achieve. It is pointing with a double-headed arrow at its preconditions.

To continue with building up the plan we must choose one of these preconditions to work on next. If we choose to work on [AT ROBOT ?X] next, something silly happens. [AT ROBOT ?X] is matched against [AT ROBOT A], i.e. A is assigned to X. We next try to satisfy [AT BOX2 A]. Even if we are very sensible (or lucky) with the remaining choices, we are now bound to get a non-optimal plan, e.g. [GO ROBOT C] [PUSH BOX2 C A] [PUSH BOX2 A B]... etc. What kind of control mechanism would choose to work on [AT BOX2 ?X] first?

The area is still controversial, but one method is to arrange the sub-goals into a *hierarchy*, according to how difficult they are to satisfy, and always work on the hardest sub-goal first (c.f. GPS ordering of differences and difficulty of goals). According to this method [AT BOX2 ?X] is tackled before [AT ROBOT ?X] because it is more difficult to get a box to a place than the robot to a place. At the top of the hierarchy are the sub-goals that are impossible to change, unless they are already true, i.e. those like [TYPE ?X BOX] and [AT SWITCH ?X], which no available operator can effect.

A hierarchy for the "switch on the light" example is:

```
top      [TYPE ?X ?Y]
         [AT SWITCH ?X]
         [STATUS ?X ON]
         [ON ROBOT ?X]
         [AT BOX ?X]
bottom  [AT ROBOT ?X]
```

At present, these hierarchies have to be provided by the human programmer for each new domain. Work is proceeding on the problem of having the planning program work them out for itself, by examining the operators that achieve each sub-goal.

If we correctly choose [AT BOX2 ?X], and satisfy it by assigning C to X, we must then work on [AT ROBOT C]. Since this fact is not in the database, we must find a relevant operator to apply. Both GO and PUSH have patterns in their add lists of the form [AT ROBOT ?Y], so both are relevant. We can choose either but would clearly prefer GO. Choosing PUSH would lead to a non-optimal plan.

How can we express or characterise our preference, in order to get a general solution to the problem? Notice that if one choice of operator works, we do not need to try another. This is different from the situation with sub-goals, where all sub-goals need to be satisfied for a successful conclusion. So the sensible choice is to choose the *easiest* operator first. The easiest operator means the one with the easiest preconditions. We can see that GO is easier than PUSH, since the preconditions of GO are a subset of those of PUSH.

1.11.2 Macro Operators
It is possible for our robot to indulge in an elementary form of learning by remembering the plans he constructs. In effect a plan, properly remembered, becomes a new ability, i.e. a new operator (sometimes called a *macro operator*). Properly remembered here means, of course, not only remembering the sequence of operators that constitute the plan, but also working out under what conditions the plan can be applied and what its effects are, i.e., we need to know the preconditions, add list and delete list of the new operator. These can all be worked out (at the cost of some book-keeping) by studying the derivation of the plan. The preconditions of the new operator are just the sub-goals that were not achieved by an operator, but by direct reference to the initial state. The add and delete lists can be worked out by comparing the initial and final state.

To be useful these macro operators must be generalised before they are stored as new operators. For instance, if we were remembering the plan to switch on the light we would not want to insist that it is BOX1 we climb onto — any box would do. Similarly the precise places involved are not of interest. In practice the operators are generalised before the precondition and add and delete lists are worked out, but the same principles apply.

Even with generalisation the macro operators are still susceptible to slight changes in the initial situation. Suppose that the initial state of the switch on the light example were:

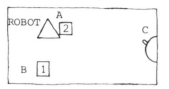

We would like the robot to be able to adapt the plan

[GO ?P1 ?P2] [PUSH ?B ?P2 ?P3] [CLIMBON ?B]
[TURNON ?S]

and only use the last three operators. Otherwise it might pick up **BOX1** and take that to the switch. Therefore the plan is stored in a *triangular table*, with the preconditions and effects of each operator stored separately. This is explained in the reference, and the details are not important. Using this the robot is able to execute subplans of the plan. He is also able to recover to a certain extent when the plan goes wrong during execution (see section 1.11.4).

Great care must be exercised over the formation of macro operators. Properly used the robot can be taught how to achieve a complex task that it previously found too difficult. Suppose that the search tree of a task is so large that the robot cannot find a plan in a reasonable length of time (an all-too-frequent occurrence). By giving it a judicious training sequence of simpler tasks, the robot can be made to learn just those macro operators he needs to solve the original task. Let loose on it again he quickly finds a short plan consisting of these macro operators. However, if we allow the robot to form macro operators for every task he performs, he quickly becomes bogged down with hundreds of operators with long preconditions and add and delete lists. The search trees of all tasks become too large for him to find any plans. Getting the robot to decide for himself what is worth keeping, and what is not, is a long way off.

Exercise 1.11.1. Form a macro operator called [COLLECT ?BOX2 ?PLACE1 ?PLACE2 ?PLACE3] for collecting two boxes.

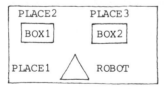

Look at the operator table for GO and PUSH to decide what the preconditions, add list and delete list of the new operator, COLLECT, should be.

1.11.3 The Frame Problem Re-Visited

We now return to the most serious aspect of the frame problem — that the effects of an operator may be more subtle than can be represented by simple add and delete lists. For instance, we may have to refer to the previous state before we can be sure precisely what to add or delete, e.g. (a) how much tea is left in the pot after we have poured one cup? (b) pushing one box may change the position of another if they are joined by a rod or rope, or if one is on top of another.

We can think up situations in which the contents of the add and delete lists depend on an arbitrary amount of deduction. If this deduction is computationally too expensive to perform, e.g. an explosion, or if we have imperfect information about the previous state, then we may be unable to predict the effect of an operator. We may resort to: (a) predicting nothing; (b) predicting the "most likely" event and being prepared to be contradicted; (c) adding or deleting laws instead of facts; or (d) performing the operation and observing the result. Can you think of circumstances under which you would resort to each of the above possibilities? Can you think of any other possibilities?

The plan formation program we discussed in these lectures modelled the effects of operators using the add and delete lists. So it was not able to handle these more subtle effects. What modifications to it are required, and whether these modifications would enable us to preserve our solutions to the other aspects of the frame problem is an open question.

1.11.4 Executing Plans (and the Qualification Problem)

If the plans our robot janitor is to make are ever to be put to use, there must be a procedure associated with each operator that will actually perform the operation, e.g., really make the robot go from a to b. Such a procedure is called the operator's *action routine*. We must be careful to distinguish the operator from the action routine. The operator, with its preconditions and add and delete lists, is only a *model* of the action routine, just as our databases are *models* of states of the real world.

Because our planning program is only a model, it is liable to go wrong due to unforeseen difficulties. For instance, we may make a plan to go to America, by driving to the airport by car, catching the 3.00 p.m. plane, etc., only to find that the car runs out of petrol halfway or the plane's crew are on strike. This problem is called the *Qualification Problem*. Again the problem has been foolishly named after a possible solution, though not one that was ever seriously proposed. The solution is that one could hedge one's plans about with various *qualifications*, about what to do if you ran out of petrol, etc. This may be possible for simple worlds, but it is a well known platitude that one "can't think of everything" for more realistic situations. Note also that we would need plans with conditionals to handle qualifications.

The solution to this problem would seem to be, that one would want to write qualifications into the plan to deal with the most likely difficulties, but that, more importantly, the action routines must have the capacity to fail and pass control back to the planning program, together with a message about what went wrong. Unfortunately, how to provide a measure of what is "most likely", and how to decide what has "gone wrong" with a plan, are not well understood at the moment.

1.11.5 Reference

Several AI groups have written robot plan formation programs. The best known program is probably STRIPS — the Stanford Research Institute Problem-Solver. This program is used by SHAKEY, the Stanford Research Institute robot, to form plans for the tasks he is given. You can read more about the program, and possible extensions of it, in R.E. Fikes, P.E. Hart & N.J. Nilsson (1972) Some new directions in robot problem solving, in *Machine Intelligence 7* (eds. B. Meltzer, & D. Michie) p.405-30. Edinburgh: University Press. STRIPS is briefly described, then various possible extensions of it are discussed, including how it might deal with unexpected changes to its environment during the execution of a plan.

2. NATURAL LANGUAGE

2.1 SENTENCE GENERATION

2.1.1 Introduction

Some of the reasons for studying computer processing of natural language are: (a) understanding language; (b) understanding intelligence (language as the window into the mind); (c) natural language would be a very desirable way to communicate with computers, and would "democratise" computer use; (d) it is interesting.

Artificial Intelligence research has contributed to the area of *computational linguistics*, which seeks computer algorithms for parsing sentences to exhibit their underlying syntactic structure and hence to elicit their "meaning" in a sense appropriate to the task in hand; it also seeks algorithms for generating sentences to express a given "meaning". The desire to tackle practical computer applications involving language processing has led AI research to give more weight to questions of semantics than most formal linguistic research, where until recently most of the effort has been put into syntactic questions; an important question for AI has been how we use our common-sense knowledge of the world in disentangling what a sentence could mean.

What kind of applications motivate this research? It is now quite common to store large amounts of information in computer databases, about airline reservations, about orders and stocks in a factory, about car licences or about the location and availability of railway carriages. But it is hard to make simple enquiries about this data, e.g. "How many serviceable carriages are at Crewe?", "How many orders for 2 H.P. motor armatures did we have from China last year?" To make a flexible and easy to use enquiry system, natural language input would be of enormous value, and much effort is now being put into increasing the "naturalness" of formal enquiry languages. Similarly we would like to tell the computer what to do in our language, rather than its own, e.g. "Put the axle into the hole at the front of the car body" or "Delete the third occurrence of 'idiotic' and replace it by 'somewhat inappropriate'". In general the usefulness of computers to us is limited not so much by what they can do as by how well we can communicate with them.

There is a lot of work going on in AI studies of natural language, much of it on particular facets of the problems involved. Of the working systems that demonstrate some ability for understanding language by a computer the best known is Winograd's 1970 program, which internally models a collection of blocks, boxes and pyramids on a table top, displays it on a screen and is able to accept commands and answer questions, e.g. "Find a block that is taller than the one you are holding and put it into the box"

59

and "How many blocks are not in the box?". It is able to communicate about this very limited situation using quite a variety of syntactic forms. Another well-known program, by Woods, answers questions from a database of information about moon rocks.

What are the difficulties encountered in computer processing of natural language? They are certainly formidable:

(a) The sheer size and complexity of English (or Eskimo) syntax.
(b) The ambiguity of words and phrases in natural language, which must be resolved from context and background knowledge. (Even determining which person a pronoun like "he" refers to is a hard task. The need to consider all possibilities, and to follow trails that may later turn out false, complicates the programming.)
(c) The large amount of common-sense knowledge needed to understand even simple pieces of text, such as stories written for five-year-olds.
(d) The difficulty of finding suitable notions of "meaning" for parts of sentences, and of representing these meanings in a computer.
(e) The need to keep within practical bounds the potentially very large amount of computer time needed to process a sentence; this involves clever search and coding techniques, which make programs hard to write and to describe.

The AI approach to language has been directed to the more obvious practical aspects; it has left aside all the emotional and poetic content that is so important in human use of language.

These notes try to introduce you to computational linguistics by building up programs to perform simple tasks; generating sentences, parsing sentences, and answering questions about a very simplified version of Winograd's blocks model. Using this as a concrete basis for understanding we can then look at Winograd's much more elaborate system (still a gross simplification of human linguistic behaviour). This work is mainly concerned with the meanings of noun phrases, e.g. "the green pyramid that is on the box", so we conclude with a brief look at verbs and the important notion of "case", which relates a number of nouns to a verb. All this is a first nibble at a complex and exciting area of research.

References. For further reading the following are recommended:

E. Charniak and Y. Wilks, eds (1976) *Computational Semantics. Fundamental Studies in Computer Science No. 4*. North-Holland. A series of linked articles giving a good introduction to the area.

R.C. Schank and K.M. Colby, (1973) *Computer Models of Thought and Language*. San Francisco: Freeman. Contains tutorial papers by several leading researchers.

R.C. Schank, E. Charniak, Y. Wilks, T. Winograd and W.A. Woods (1977) Invited panel discussion, in *Proc. Fifth International Joint Conf. on*

Artificial Intelligence, pp.1007-13. Cambridge, Mass: MIT. A discussion highlighting current interests and uncertainties.

2.1.2 The Insult Program

Here is a program to generate insults such as "GET LOST YOU FILTHY BEAST". (See section 2.1.5 for the program in LISP.)

```
TO ELEMENT 'N 'L
  10 IF :N=1 THEN RESULT FIRST :L
  20 RESULT ELEMENT (:N-1) (BUTFIRST :L)
END                                        nth element of L

TO CHOOSEANY 'L
  10 NEW 'R
  20 MAKE 'R (RANDOM ((COUNT :L)-1))+1
  30 RESULT ELEMENT :R :L
END                                 chooses a random element of L

TO DOANY 'L
  10 APPLY CHOOSEANY :L          executes a random element of L,
END                                 a list of procedure names

TO OUT 'X
  10 TYPE SPACE AND TYPE :X
END                          prints its argument preceded by a space

TO SUGGEST1
10 OUT 'GET AND OUT 'LOST
END

TO SUGGEST2
  10 OUT 'GO AND OUT 'JUMP AND OUT 'IN AND OUT 'THE
     AND OUT 'LAKE
END

TO SUGGEST
  10 DOANY [SUGGEST1 SUGGEST2]
END

TO MISNAME1
  10 OUT 'ROTTEN AND OUT 'SWINE
END

TO MISNAME 2
  10 OUT 'FILTHY AND OUT 'BEAST
END

TO MISNAME
  10 DOANY [MISNAME1 MISNAME2]
END
```

```
TO  INSULT
  10  SUGGEST  AND  OUT  'YOU  AND  MISNAME
  20  PRINT  NL
END
```

2.1.3   The Insult Grammar

We can generate these insults by a *grammar*, which expresses succinctly
the rules of generation embodied in the above program.

insult ⟶ suggest 'you misname
suggest ⟶ 'get 'lost
suggest ⟶ 'go 'jump 'in 'the 'lake
misname ⟶ 'rotten 'swine
misname ⟶ 'filthy 'beast

A *context-free grammar* is a set of *production rules*, made from *non-
terminal symbols* (naming phrases) and *terminal symbols* (quoted words).
Each production rule consists of a non-terminal (on the left) and a list of
terminals and/or non-terminals (on the right). There is also a *starting
symbol* (here it is insult). You can think of the grammar in two ways: (a) as
an inductive definition:

'filthy 'beast is a misname
'rotten 'swine is a misname
'go 'jump in 'the 'lake is a suggest
'get 'lost is a suggest

A suggest followed by 'you followed by a misname is an insult.

or (b) as a recipe for generating sentences:

To generate an insult generate a suggest then 'you then a misname
To generate a suggest generate 'get then 'lost

or   To generate a suggest generate 'go then 'jump then 'in then 'the
then 'lake
To generate a misname, etc.

Exercise 2.1.1. Write a grammar to produce at least 100 insults in any
language you choose. (Try to manage with less than 100 production
rules.)

2.1.4   Number Grammar

Here is a grammar for the English numbers from "one" to "nine hundred
and ninety-nine".

ump ⟶ 'one
ump ⟶ 'two
     . . .
ump ⟶ 'nine
umpteen ⟶ 'ten
umpteen ⟶ 'eleven
     . . .
umpteen ⟶ 'nineteen
umpty ⟶ 'twenty

62

. . .
umpty⟶ 'ninety
upto99⟶ ump
upto99⟶ umpteen
upto99⟶ umpty
upto99⟶ umpty ump
umphun⟶ ump 'hundred
upto999⟶ upto99
upto999⟶ umphun
upto999⟶ umphun 'and upto99

(This grammar is essentially due to H.C. Longuet-Higgins.)

Exercises (* means a hard exercise, ** means a mini-project)

2.1.2. Continue by defining upto999999.

2.1.3. Do it in French or German or Gaelic or whatever.

2.1.4. Program the random generation for upto999 (you can pretend 3 to 8 don't exist to avoid tedium).

*2.1.5. Write a program to take a number expressed as a list of digits and print its name.

**2.1.6. Adapt 2.1.5 to write a teaching program that generates lists of digits at random, generates the English and French (or language X) name, *simultaneously* prints one, asks the user for the other, and tells him if he is right.

*2.1.7. We could represent the grammar by

```
TO GRAMMAR
10 [[UMP QUOTE ONE] [UMP QUOTE TWO] . . . [UMP
   QUOTE NINE] [UMPTEEN QUOTE TEN] . . . [UMPTY
   QUOTE TWENTY] . . . [UPTO99 UMP] [UPTO99
   UMPTEEN] [UPTO99 UMPTY UMP] . . .]]
END
```

Write a function to generate random number names from this representation of the grammar instead of the representation by individual functions we used before.

2.1.5 The Insult Program in LISP

```
(DEFUN ELEMENT (N L)
    (COND ((EQ N 1) (CAR L))
          (T (ELEMENT (1- N) (CDR L)))))

(DEFUN CHOOSEANY (L)
  (PROG (R)
    (SETQ R (1+ (RANDOM (LENGTH L))))
    (RETURN (ELEMENT R L))))

(DEFUN DOANY (L)
    (APPLY (CHOOSEANY L) NIL))
```

```
(DEFUN OUT (X)
   (TYO 40) (PRIN1 X))

(DEFUN SUGGEST1 ()
   (OUT 'GET) (OUT 'LOST))

(DEFUN SUGGEST2 ()
   (OUT 'GO) (OUT 'JUMP) (OUT 'IN) (OUT 'THE) (OUT 'LAKE))

(DEFUN SUGGEST ()
   (DOANY '(SUGGEST1 SUGGEST2)))

(DEFUN MISNAME1 ()
   (OUT 'ROTTEN) (OUT 'SWINE))

(DEFUN MISNAME2 ()
   (OUT 'FILTHY) (OUT 'BEAST))

(DEFUN MISNAME ()
   (DOANY '(MISNAME1 MISNAME2)))

(DEFUN INSULT ()
   (TERPRI) (SUGGEST) (OUT 'YOU) (MISNAME) (TERPRI))
```

2.2 GENERATING BLOCKS WORLD SENTENCES

2.2.1 The Blocks World

A world rather simpler and less disturbing than our own, although perhaps
a trifle dull, is the Blocks World.

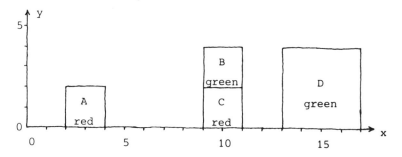

There are four square blocks A,B,C,D of fixed size (2 units for A,B,C and 4
units for D), of fixed colour (red or green) and of variable position (x,y)
denoting mid-point of base, e.g. A has x=3, y=0, and B has x=10, y=2, in
the above figure.

There are relations between any blocks a and b:

a is *to the left of*	b if $x_a + \frac{1}{2} size_a + \frac{1}{2} size_b \leq x_b$
a is *to the right of*	b if b is to the left of a
a is *on*	b if $y_a = y_b + size_b$ and a is not
	to the left of, or to the right of, b.

Exercise 2.2.1. Define *above* similarly. (But what exactly does *above* mean in English? Does it mean anything exactly?)

2.2.2 Sentences About Blocks World

Assertions There is a green block to the left of the big block.

The small green block is on a red block.

The block to the left of the small green block is

to the right of the big green block.

Questions Is a small block to the left of a green block?

Is a block to the right of a red block a green block?

The following grammar will generate these and similar sentences:

noun ⟶ 'block		
adj ⟶ 'big		
adj ⟶ 'small		
adj ⟶ 'red		
adj ⟶ 'green		
prep ⟶ 'on		
prep ⟶ 'to 'the 'left 'of		
prep ⟶ 'to 'the 'right 'of		e.g.
nounphr ⟶ noun		(block)
nounphr ⟶ adj nounphr		(big block)
nounphr ⟶ nounphr qualif		(block on a red block)
qualif ⟶ prep clnounphr		(on a red block)
clnounphr ⟶ 'a nounphr		(a red block)
clnounphr ⟶ 'the nounphr		(the block on a green block)
assertion ⟶ 'there 'is 'a nounphr		(there is a green block)
assertion ⟶ clnounphr 'is qualif		(a red block is on a red block)
question ⟶ 'is clnounphr qualif		(is a red block on a red block)
sentence ⟶ assertion		
sentence ⟶ question		

(clnounphr means closed noun phrase: no more adjectives can be prefixed)

Exercises

2.2.1. Use a penny to hand-simulate RANDOM and generate three sentences at random.

2.2.2. Try to find some stupid sentences generated by this grammar. (Not just lies, but stupid sentences.)

*2.2.3. Add rules to generate each of the following kinds of sentence: What is on the small red block?; The big block is green; A block between the small red block and the big block is green.

*2.2.4. Make up a grammar for recipes in cookery books (add a pound of sugar, mix in a spoonful of flour, bake slowly). If you try cooking your random recipes you will discover that syntax without semantics is nothing but a pain in the gut.

2.2.3   Structure of Sentences

A sentence like "the small green block is on a red block" has a syntactic structure. Here is one way of showing it

[[THE [[SMALL][[GREEN][BLOCK]]]] IS [[ON][A[[RED][BLOCK]]]]]

or as a tree

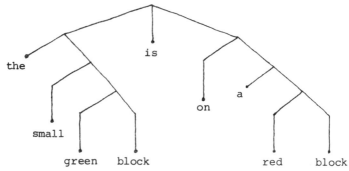

It does *not* have the structure

[[THE [SMALL]][[GREEN][BLOCK]IS ON] [A[RED]]]BLOCK]

because [BLOCK IS ON] and [A RED] are not grammatical entities (phrases). But for the former structure we have:

[BLOCK] - noun
[GREEN BLOCK] - nounphr
[SMALL GREEN BLOCK] - nounphr
[THE SMALL GREEN BLOCK] - clnounphr
[BLOCK] - noun
[RED BLOCK] - nounphr
[A RED BLOCK] - clnounphr
[ON] - prep
[ON A RED BLOCK] - qualif
[THE SMALL GREEN BLOCK IS ON A RED BLOCK] - assertion

We could easily make the generating program type out an indication of the structure by making each procedure like nounphr print out its own name before it starts, so that we get

QUALIF PREP on CLNOUNPHR a NOUNPHR ADJ red NOUNPHR
NOUN block

or pictorially as a tree

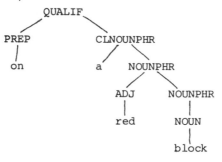

66

2.2.4   Ambiguity

The phrase "red block on a green block" could have the structure (omitting some brackets)

[RED[BLOCK[ON A GREEN BLOCK]]]

or   [[RED BLOCK] [ON A GREEN BLOCK]]

Intuitively these mean the same, so the syntactic ambiguity is harmless. But "green block to the left of the big block on a red block" could mean

[[GREEN BLOCK TO THE LEFT OF THE BIG BLOCK] ON A RED BLOCK]

which is B in the figure of section 2.2.1, or it could mean

[GREEN BLOCK[TO THE LEFT OF THE BIG BLOCK ON A RED BLOCK]]

and there is no big block on a red block. This is semantic ambiguity.

Exercise 2.2.5. Check that the grammar really will generate these two readings of "green block to the left of the big block on a red block", and draw their trees as above.

2.3   PARSING

2.3.1   Some Problems of Context-Free Grammars

Remember that a grammar describes a set of sentences, just as "the even numbers not divisible by 5" describes a set of numbers. Problems are:

1. (Generation) Given a grammar, list the set of sentences it describes.
2. (Parsing) Given a sentence and a grammar, test whether the sentence is one of those described by the grammar.
3. (Induction) Given a set of sentences, make up a grammar that describes them.
4. (Equivalence) Given two grammars, do they describe the same set of sentences.

What do you think is the order of difficulty of these?

The *parsing* problem is the one that interests us next. For example, does the grammar of the last lecture produce these sentences?

(a) There is a small block on a red block

(b) Is a red block on a red block on a red block?

(c) A green block is there on the red block

More important, what structure if any does it attribute to them? Is this structure unique?

2.3.2   An Example to Help Us Understand the Parsing Problem

Here is an easy grammar G, starting symbol P: (using lower case instead of ')

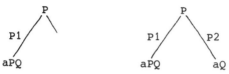

$$P \longrightarrow a\, P\, Q \qquad \text{(P1)}$$
$$P \longrightarrow a\, Q \qquad \text{(P2)}$$
$$Q \longrightarrow c\, Q \qquad \text{(Q1)}$$
$$Q \longrightarrow b \qquad \text{(Q2)}$$

Does cca come from it? How about ab or aacb? Try generating the sentences of G systematically. When you have generated even part of a sentence you can see whether it could be cca by comparing the terminal symbols (a,b,c) at the front.

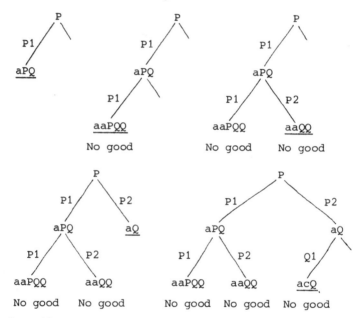

So cca does *not* come from the grammar G. How about ab?

Continue this systematically. Can you generate ab?

Exercise 2.3.1. Try to generate systematically sentences from the above grammar to get aacbb.

2.3.3 A Parsing Program for This Grammar

Our convention will be that each phrase has a parsing procedure, which is given a string to parse and returns the remainder of that string after removing the phrase it is looking for; but if it fails to find it then it returns FAIL. We will write a collection of procedures for the grammar just given. (See section 2.3.6 for the program in LISP.)

68

TAKEOFF just tries to remove a given word from a string of words. P tries P1 and, if that doesn't work, P2. Similarly Q tries Q1 and, if that doesn't work, Q2. P1 takes off 'A, if the result is OK it removes a P, and if still OK it removes a Q.

```
TO TAKEOFF 'WORD 'STRING
  IF EMPTYQ :STRING THEN RESULT 'FAIL
  IF NOT (:WORD=F :STRING) THEN RESULT 'FAIL
  RESULT BF :STRING
END
```

Examples: TAKEOFF 'A [A B C] = [B C],
            TAKEOFF 'D [A B C] = 'FAIL.

```
TO OK 'X
  NOT (:X='FAIL)
END
```

```
TO P 'STRING                                (remove a P from front or fail)
  NEW 'STRINGREM                                      (remainder string)
  MAKE 'STRINGREM P1 :STRING                            (remove a P1)
  IF OK :STRINGREM THEN RESULT :STRINGREM
  MAKE 'STRINGREM P2 :STRING                   (otherwise remove a P2)
  IF OK :STRINGREM THEN RESULT :STRINGREM
  RESULT 'FAIL                                 (P2 didn't work either)
END
```

```
TO Q 'STRING
  as P but using Q1 and Q2
END
```

Examples: Q[C B A A] ⟶ [A A], Q[A B] ⟶ 'FAIL,
            P[A B C A] ⟶ [C A]

```
TO P1 'STRING                                       (remove 'A P Q)
  MAKE 'STRING TAKEOFF 'A :STRING             (takeoff 'A if possible)
  IF NOT OK :STRING THEN RESULT 'FAIL      (fail if can't take off 'A)
  MAKE 'STRING P :STRING
  IF NOT OK :STRING THEN RESULT 'FAIL       (fail if can't take off P)
  MAKE 'STRING Q :STRING
  RESULT :STRING                           (result is remainder or FAIL)
END
```

```
TO P2 'STRING                                       (remove 'A Q)
  MAKE 'STRING TAKEOFF 'A :STRING
  IF NOT OK :STRING THEN RESULT 'FAIL
  MAKE 'STRING Q :STRING
  RESULT :STRING
END
```

69

```
TO Q1 'STRING
  . . .
END

TO Q2 'STRING
  . . .
END
```

Exercise 2.3.2. Write out some of the procedures needed to parse
numbers with the number grammar given previously (not for all the
productions, just enough to get the idea). Try your procedures on the
machine.

2.3.4 A More General Parsing Program

The program that we gave in section 2.3.3 has three disadvantages:
1. (practical) it is rather long, each production needing a substantial
   procedure
2. (theoretical) it will sometimes fail to find a parse when one exists.

To understand (2) consider the grammar, starting with R,

$$R \longrightarrow a \ Q \ d$$
$$Q \longrightarrow b$$
$$Q \longrightarrow b \ c$$

Trying this on [A B C] using a program like that of section 2.3.3 we get
function calls:

R[A B D]	$\longrightarrow$ [ ]
R1[A B D]	$\longrightarrow$ [ ]
Q[B D]	$\longrightarrow$ [D]
Q1[B D]	$\longrightarrow$ [D]

But on [A B C D] we get

R[A B C D]	$\longrightarrow$ FAIL
R1[A B C D]	$\longrightarrow$ FAIL
Q[B C D]	$\longrightarrow$ [C D]
Q1[B C D]	$\longrightarrow$ [C D]

whereas Q2[B C D] $\longrightarrow$ [D], which eventually makes P succeed.

3. (theoretical) it goes into an infinite recursion if given productions of
   the form $P \longrightarrow P. \ldots$ But this is not fatal, because it is always possible
   to rewrite a grammar to avoid such productions.

Disadvantage (2) suggests that we define a function P', which takes a
string as argument and produces a *set of strings* as result (the empty set
now corresponds to FAIL).

Disadvantage (1) suggests that we go further in search of brevity and
define a function P', which takes a *set of strings* as argument and
produces a set of strings as result. To be technical, suppose P is a symbol
in the grammar. Let P be a set of strings, all strings generable from P. Let
P's, where s is a string, be the set of all strings t such that s=pt for some
string p in P'. Let P''S, where S is a set of strings, be the set of all strings t

70

such that s=pt for some string s in S and some string p in P.

We will now write a program for the grammar of section 2.3.3 with a function P'' for each symbol P (we just call it PP, not P'', in LOGO). We have corresponding functions, from sets of strings to sets of strings, for each production. For terminal symbols we define a special function TAKEOFF, which takes a word and a set of strings to a set of strings.

For each production we simply do the functions corresponding to its components in sequence. For each non-terminal symbol we do the function for each of its productions and join up the result. We start the whole process on a set whose only element is the given string and expect as result a set whose only element is the empty string (i.e. nothing remains when a P is removed from the front.) We represent both strings and sets by lists (confusing, but that is all LOGO offers).

The non-terminal P generates a set of strings, [ab,acb,accb, aabb,aabcb, . . .]. There is a corresponding procedure PP which, given a set of strings, say [abxyz,accbuvw,bbcc] tries to take off each of the generated strings from each of these (getting xyz from abxyz, uvw from accbuvw, nothing from bbcc, [xyz,uvw] in all). Similarly Q generates [cb,ccb,cccb, . . .] and has an analogous procedure QQ.

To define these we need a basic procedure TAKEOFF to take a single word off each of a set of strings, given word a and set of lists [axyz,cc,abc] it gives [xyz,bc]. Do not worry how TAKEOFF is written, just understand what it does.

Here is the program, followed by some examples (we call the functions PP and QQ because P is already used for PRINT). (See section 2.3.7 for the program in LISP.)

```
TO TAKEOFF 'WORD 'STRINGS
  10 NEW 'STRING
  20 IF EMPTYQ :STRINGS THEN RESULT [ ]
  30 MAKE 'STRING F :STRINGS AND MAKE 'STRINGS BF
     :STRINGS
  40 IF EMPTYQ :STRING THEN RESULT TAKEOFF :WORD
     :STRINGS
  50 IF :WORD=F :STRING THEN RESULT FPUT (BF :STRING)
     (TAKEOFF :WORD :STRINGS)
  60 RESULT TAKEOFF :WORD :STRINGS
END

TO PP 'STRINGS
  10 IF EMPTYQ :STRINGS THEN RESULT [ ]
  20 RESULT JOIN P1 :STRINGS P2 :STRINGS
END
```

```
TO QQ 'STRINGS
  10 IF EMPTYQ :STRINGS THEN RESULT [ ]
  20 RESULT JOIN Q1 :STRINGS Q2 :STRINGS
END

TO P1'STRINGS
  10 RESULT QQ PP TAKEOFF 'A :STRINGS
END

TO P2 'STRINGS
  10 RESULT QQ TAKEOFF 'A :STRINGS
END

TO Q1 'STRINGS
  10 RESULT QQ TAKEOFF 'C :STRINGS
END

TO Q2 'STRINGS
  10 RESULT TAKEOFF 'B :STRINGS
END

TO PARSE 'STRING
  10 NEW 'STRINGS
  20 MAKE 'STRINGS PP  《 :STRING 》
  30 IF (COUNT :STRINGS)= 0 THEN RESULT 'NOGOOD
  40 IF (COUNT :STRINGS) >1 THEN RESULT FPUT 'AMBIGUOUS
     :STRINGS
  50 IF NOT EMPTYQ F :STRINGS THEN RESULT FPUT 'TOOLONG
     F :STRINGS
  60 RESULT 'GOOD
END
```

Example
```
TAKEOFF 'A [[A B C]] ⟶ [[B C]]
TAKEOFF 'A [[D C]] ⟶ [ ]
TAKEOFF 'A [[A B C] [A D E] [D C]] ⟶ [[B C] [D E]]
P2[[A B D] [A A B B E]] ⟶ [[D]]
P1[[A B D] [A A B B E]] ⟶ [[E]]
PP[[A B D] [A A B B E]] ⟶ [[D] [E]]
```

2.3.5 Limitations of Context-Free Grammars

The notion of context-free grammar is a very important one, particularly in computational linguistics. It has been very useful for describing programming languages but it has long been realised that it is inadequate for describing natural languages. That is to say it is practically (and even theoretically) impossible to write such a grammar to generate all the "grammatical" sentences of English but no "ungrammatical" ones. Not only would the number of non-terminal symbols (phrase names) get unreasonably large, but the whole exercise would give very arbitrary generation tree-structures to sentences, failing to show similarities between closely related sentences.

Chomsky's notion of *Transformational Grammar* has been widely explored in linguistics; the idea is to generate some basic sentences by a context-free grammar and then apply transformations to get variants such as passives and negations. Unfortunately this model is based on generating sentences and gives us no clue as to how to parse them. Since parsing is the main point of interest and difficulty in Artificial Intelligence work on language understanding, transformational grammars have been of little use.

Winograd makes use of Halliday's *Systemic Grammar*, which enables one to get over the multiplicity of arbitrary phrase names in context-free grammars by using a much smaller number of grammatical classes qualified by a suitable collection of features. We will also look at Fillmore's idea of *Case Grammar*, which is designed to show up the relationship between verbs and the noun phrases that play different roles with respect to them.

Nevertheless, many AI systems use relatively simple context-free grammars, even if not explicit ones, to impose a structure on the sentences but without excluding all ungrammatical ones. It is then possible to use "semantic routines" written in some programming language, together with suitable 'dictionary' data structures, to rule out impossible interpretations and so reduce ambiguity. This seems the best way to handle restrictions like agreement of gender or number, and verbs like "eat", which require an animate subject.

2.3.6 The Parsing Program in LISP

This is the program of section 2.3.3.

```
(DEFUN TAKEOFF (WORD  STRING)
    (COND (NULL STRING) 'FAIL)
           ((NOT (EQ WORD (CAR STRING))) 'FAIL)
           (T (CDR STRING))))

(DEFUN OK (X)
    (NOT (EQ X 'FAIL)))

(DEFUN P (STRING)
   (PROG (STRINGREM)
      (SETQ STRINGREM (P1 STRING))
      (COND ((OK STRINGREM) (RETURN STRINGREM)))
      (SETQ STRINGREM (P2 STRING))
      (COND ((OK STRINGREM) (RETURN STRINGREM)))
      (RETURN 'FAIL)))
```

```
(DEFUN Q (STRING)
  (PROG (STRINGREM)
    (SETQ STRINGREM (Q1 STRING))
    (COND ((OK STRINGREM) (RETURN STRINGREM)))
    (SETQ STRINGREM (Q2 STRING))
    (COND ((OK STRINGREM) (RETURN STRINGREM)))
    (RETURN 'FAIL)))

(DEFUN P1 (STRING)
  (PROG ()
    (SETQ STRING (TAKEOFF 'A STRING))
    (COND ((NOT (OK STRING)) (RETURN 'FAIL)))
    (SETQ STRING (P STRING))
    (COND ((NOT (OK STRING)) (RETURN 'FAIL)))
    (SETQ STRING (Q STRING))
    (RETURN STRING)))

(DEFUN P2 (STRING)
  (PROG ()
    (SETQ STRING (TAKEOFF 'A STRING))
    (COND ((NOT (OK STRING)) (RETURN 'FAIL)))
    (SETQ STRING (Q STRING))
    (RETURN STRING)))

(DEFUN Q1 (STRING)
  (PROG ()
    (SETQ STRING (TAKEOFF 'C STRING))
    (COND ((NOT (OK STRING)) (RETURN 'FAIL)))
    (SETQ STRING (Q STRING))
    (RETURN STRING)))

(DEFUN Q2 (STRING)
  (PROG ()
    (SETQ STRING (TAKEOFF 'B STRING))
    (COND ((NOT (OK STRING)) (RETURN 'FAIL)))
    (RETURN STRING)))
```

2.3.7   The General Parsing Program in LISP

This is the program of section 2.3.4.

```
(DEFUN TAKEOFF (WORD STRINGS)
  (PROG (STRING)
    (COND ((NULL STRINGS) (RETURN NIL)))
    (SETQ STRING (CAR STRINGS))
    (SETQ STRINGS (CDR STRINGS))
    (COND ((NULL STRING) (RETURN (TAKEOFF WORD STRINGS)))
          ((EQ WORD (CAR STRING))
```

```
                    (RETURN (CONS (CDR STRING) (TAKEOFF  WORD
                                                      STRINGS))))
            (T  (RETURN  (TAKEOFF  WORD  STRINGS))))))

(DEFUN  PP  (STRINGS)
    (COND ((NULL  STRINGS)  NIL)
            (T  (APPEND  (P1  STRINGS)  (P2  STRINGS)))))

(DEFUN  QQ  (STRINGS)
    (COND ((NULL  STRINGS)  NIL)
            (T  (APPEND  (Q1  STRINGS)  (Q2  STRINGS)))))

(DEFUN  P1  (STRINGS)
    (QQ  (PP  (TAKEOFF  'A  STRINGS))))

(DEFUN  P2  (STRINGS)
    (QQ  (TAKEOFF  'A  STRINGS)))

(DEFUN  Q1  (STRINGS)
    (QQ  (TAKEOFF  'C  STRINGS)))

(DEFUN  Q2  (STRINGS)
    (TAKEOFF  'B  STRINGS))

(DEFUN  PARSE(STRING)
   (PROG  (STRINGS)
     (SETQ  STRINGS  (PP  (LIST  STRING)))
     (COND ((EQ  (LENGTH  STRING)  0)  (RETURN  'NOGOOD))
             (( >(LENGTH  STRING)  1)
               (RETURN  (CONS  'AMBIGUOUS  STRINGS)))
             ((NOT  (NULL  (CAR  STRINGS)))
               (RETURN  (CONS  'TOOLONG  (CAR  STRINGS))))
             (T  (RETURN  'GOOD)))))
```

2.4   TRANSLATION

2.4.1   Introduction

We have written random generator programs for insults and for sentences
about blocks, also a parser for a b c sentences. The parser just said
whether a string of words belonged to the grammar; can we go further
and produce a "meaning" for a sentence? (What is a meaning? Good
question.) Let us try, as a very simple example, to get the actual number
from a number name. We will use ⟨ (. . .) ⟩ for 'the meaning of . . .', and we
will express the way in which the meaning of a string depends on the
meanings of its components by writing equations, one alongside each
production.

Number grammar with meanings

ump⟶ one	⟨(ump)⟩=1
ump⟶ two	⟨(ump)⟩=2
...	
umpteen⟶'ten	⟨(umpteen)⟩=10
...	
umpty⟶'twenty	⟨(umpty)⟩=20
...	
upto99⟶ ump	⟨(upto99)⟩=⟨(ump)⟩
upto99⟶ umpteen	⟨(upto99)⟩=⟨(umpteen)⟩
upto99⟶ umpty	⟨(upto99)⟩=⟨(umpty)⟩
upto99⟶ umpty ump	⟨(upto99)⟩=⟨(umpty)⟩+ (ump)⟩
umphun⟶ ump 'hundred	⟨(umphun)⟩=⟨(ump)⟩*100
upto999⟶ upto99	⟨(upto999)⟩=⟨(upto99)⟩
upto999⟶ umphun	⟨(upto999)⟩=⟨(umphun)⟩
upto999⟶ umphun 'and upto99	⟨(upto999)⟩=⟨(umphun)⟩+⟨(upto99)⟩

Example

[one] is ump	⟨([one])⟩=1
[twenty] is umpty	⟨([twenty])⟩=20
[twenty one] is upto99	⟨([twenty one])⟩ =
	⟨([twenty])⟩+⟨([one])⟩=20+1=21

Notice that we use the syntax symbols (ump, etc) as variable names in the equations standing for any string of that syntactic class. If a production involved more than one occurrence, e.g. P⟶ a Q b Q, we would have to use subscripts, e.g. ⟨(P)⟩ = ... ⟨(Q₁)⟩ ... ⟨(Q₂)⟩ ... .

This way of specifying meaning goes rather naturally with the notion of context-free grammar. Such grammars and our meaning equations are restrictive but, as you will see, we can extend their usefulness still using the same basic ideas. Our approach here has been influenced both by "syntax-directed compiling" and "denotational semantics" in Computer Science and by Montague's work on the formal semantics of Natural Language; the main idea is to find a suitable denotation for each phrase and to say succinctly for each phrase how the meaning of the phrase depends on the meaning of its constituent phrases.

Reference. R. Montague (1974) *Formal Philosophy* (ed. R.H. Thomason) Yale University Press. A fundamentally interesting but difficult-to-read set of papers on the logic of natural language.

2.4.2 A Translation Program

To program a translater instead of a parser, we need to have functions that handle not just remainder strings but also meanings. In general a string of words will produce a string of meanings, rather than just one meaning. We can think of the translation process as taking words off the front of the word string and putting meanings on the back of the meaning string. Thus an (intermediate) *state* of the translation consists of a *string of meanings* (its left) and a *string of words* (its right).

Consider the states produced in translating "two hundred and twenty seven", with the rules used to obtain them:

Rule	Left (meaning string)	Right (word string)
	[ ]	[two hundred and twenty seven]
ump/2	[2]	[hundred and twenty seven]
umphun/1	[200]	[and twenty seven]
	[200]	[twenty seven]
umpty/1	[200 20]	[seven]
ump/7	[200 20 7]	[ ]
upto99/4	[200 27]	[ ]
upto999/3	[227]	[ ]

We finish with a unit string of meanings on the left and an empty string of words on the right.

We want to use the same technique as our second parsing program, adapted by using states instead of just strings of words. So our translation functions will all take a *set of states* as argument and produce a *set of states* as result. They are:

MEANINGOF word ⟶ meaning

takes an individual word to its meaning (or NOMEANING if it has none).

MKSTATE meaning-string word-string ⟶ state

makes a state represented by a list of the two.

BEGINS word state ⟶ T

produces TRUE if the right of the state begins with the word, FALSE otherwise.

NEWSTATE word state1 ⟶ state2

only used if state1 begins with the word. Removes this word from the right and puts its meaning (if any) on the back of the left.

TAKEOFF word state-set1 ⟶ state-set2

for each state in state-set1 that begins with the word, remove the word from the right and get a new state with the meaning of the word on the back of the left.

Example. If MEANINGOF 'TWO = 2,
TAKEOFF 'TWO MKSTATE[1] [TWO THREE FOUR]⟶
[[1 2] [THREE FOUR]]

We need some way of associating some semantics with each production. Consider

upto99 ⟶ umpty ump   ⟨(upto99)⟩ = ⟨(umpty)⟩ + ⟨(ump)⟩

After we have used this production and called the UMPTY and UMP functions we should have a set of states each of whose left is [. . . x y], where x is the meaning of the umpty part and y is the meaning of the ump part. We need to add these two together to produce a state with x + y on the end instead. A general function DOSEMANTIC will do all this for any semantic operation, not just addition.

NARGS function-name $\longrightarrow$ N (number of arguments, 1 or 2)

DOSEMANTIC1 function-name state $\longrightarrow$ state-set

where function-name names an arbitrary semantic function. This is applied to the last element of the left of the state and the result replaces it (or if NARGS gives 2 to the last two elements and the result replaces them). A set consisting of just this state is produced, unless the result of applying the given function was FAIL when the empty set is produced (production was semantically inapplicable).

Example. DOSEMANTIC1 'SUM MKSTATE [1 2 3] [FOUR FIVE]
$\longrightarrow$ [[1 5] [FOUR FIVE]]

DOSEMANTIC function-name state-set1 $\longrightarrow$ state-set2

does DOSEMANTIC1 to each state of state-set1 and collects together all the results.

Here then are the general procedures for writing translater programs. (See section 2.4.4 for the program in LISP.)

```
TO MKSTATE 'LEFT 'RIGHT
  10 RESULT  《 :LEFT :RIGHT 》
END

TO BEGINS 'WORD 'STATE
  10 NEW 'RIGHT
  20 MAKE 'RIGHT F BF :STATE
  30 IF EMPTYQ :RIGHT THEN RESULT FALSE
  40 IF :WORD=F :RIGHT THEN RESULT TRUE
  50 RESULT FALSE
END

TO NEWSTATE 'WORD 'STATE
  10 NEW 'LEFT 'RIGHT 'MEANING
  20 MAKE 'LEFT F :STATE AND MAKE 'RIGHT F BF :STATE
  30 MAKE 'MEANING MEANINGOF :WORD
  40 IF :MEANING='NOMEANING THEN RESULT MKSTATE :LEFT
     (BF :RIGHT)
  50 RESULT MKSTATE (LASTPUT :MEANING :LEFT) (BF :RIGHT)
END

TO TAKEOFF 'WORD 'STATES
  10 NEW 'STATE
  20 IF EMPTYQ :STATES THEN RESULT [ ]
  30 M 'STATE F :STATES AND M 'STATES BF :STATES
```

78

```
40 IF BEGINS :WORD :STATE THEN RESULT FPUT
   (NEWSTATE :WORD :STATE) (TAKEOFF :WORD :STATES)
50 RESULT (TAKEOFF :WORD :STATES)
END

TO DOSEMANTIC1 'FN 'STATE
  10 NEW 'LEFT 'RIGHT 'FNRESULT
  20 MAKE 'LEFT F :STATE AND MAKE 'RIGHT F BF :STATE
  30 IF 1=NARGS :FN THEN M 'FNRESULT APPLY :FN (LAST
     :LEFT)
  35 IF 1=NARGS :FN THEN M 'LEFT BL :LEFT
  40 IF 2=NARGS :FN THEN M 'FNRESULT APPLY :FN (LAST BL
     :LEFT) (LAST :LEFT)
  45 IF 2=NARGS :FN THEN M 'LEFT BL BL :LEFT
  50 IF :FNRESULT='FAIL THEN RESULT [ ]
  60 RESULT  《MKSTATE (LASTPUT :FNRESULT :LEFT) :RIGHT》
END

TO DOSEMANTIC 'FN 'STATES
  10 IF EMPTYQ :STATES THEN RESULT [ ]
  20 RESULT JOIN (DOSEMANTIC1 :FN F :STATES)
     (DOSEMANTIC :FN BF :STATES)
END
```

2.4.3 Using the Translation Program on Number Names

To use the procedures defined above to translate a particular grammar
with particular meaning specification, we need to write some more
procedures corresponding to the rules of that grammar. Below are the
procedures for the number-name grammar up to 99. The final procedure
TEST1 tries UPTO99 on a given string of words, putting a full stop at the
end and ensuring that only final states that have devoured all the string up
to the stop are printed.

Exercises
2.4.1. Try to work out on paper in outline the computation produced by
TEST1 [TWENTY TWO]. What procedures are called with what
arguments? (Don't do all the details.)
2.4.2. Write the extra procedures needed to do UPTO99.

Number-name translation procedures. (See section 2.4.5 for the program
in LISP.)

```
TO MEANINGOF 'WORD
  10 IF :WORD='ONE THEN RESULT 1
  20 IF :WORD='TWO THEN RESULT 2
  30 IF :WORD='TWENTY THEN RESULT 20
  40 RESULT 'NOMEANING
END
```

79

```
TO NARGS 'FN
  10 IF :FN='SUM THEN RESULT 2
  20 IF :FN='TIMES100 THEN RESULT 1
  30 BREAK
END

TO UMP 'STATES
  10 JOIN UMP1 :STATES UMP2 :STATES
END

TO UMP1 'STATES                    TO UMP2 'STATES
  10 TAKEOFF 'ONE :STATES            10 TAKEOFF 'TWO :STATES
END                                END

TO UMPTEEN 'STATES                 TO UMPTEEN1 'STATES
  10 UMPTEEN1 :STATES               10 TAKEOFF 'TEN :STATES
END                                END

TO UMPTY 'STATES                   TO UMPTY1 'STATES
  10 UMPTY1 :STATES                 10 TAKEOFF 'TWENTY :STATES
END                                END

TO UPTO99 'STATES
  10 JOIN JOIN JOIN UPTO991 :STATES UPTO992
     :STATES UPTO993 :STATES UPTO994 :STATES
END

TO UPTO991 'STATES                 TO UPTO992 'STATES
  10 UMP :STATES                    10 UMPTEEN :STATES
END                                END

TO UPTO993 'STATES                 TO UPTO994 'STATES
  10 UMPTY :STATES                  10 DOSEMANTIC 'SUM UMP
END                                   UMPTY :STATES
                                   END

TO TEST1 'WORDSTRING
  10 P TAKEOFF 'STOP UPTO99   《 MKSTATE [ ]
     (LPUT 'STOP :WORDSTRING) 》
END
```

2.4.4   The Translation Program in LISP

This is the program of section 2.4.2.

```
(DEFUN MKSTATE (LEFT RIGHT)
  (LIST LEFT RIGHT))

(DEFUN BEGINS (WORD STATE)
  (PROG (RIGHT)
```

```
                (SETQ RIGHT (CADR STATE))
                (COND ((NULL RIGHT) (RETURN NIL))
                        ((EQ WORD (CAR RIGHT)) (RETURN T))
                        (T (RETURN NIL)))))

(DEFUN NEWSTATE (WORD STATE)
    (PROG (LEFT RIGHT MEANING)
        (SETQ LEFT (CAR STATE))
        (SETQ RIGHT (CADR STATE))
        (SETQ MEANING (MEANINGOF WORD))
        (COND ((EQ MEANING 'NOMEANING)
                (RETURN (MKSTATE LEFT (CDR RIGHT))))
                (T (RETURN (MKSTATE (APPEND LEFT (LIST
                                        MEANING)) (CDR RIGHT)))))))

(DEFUN TAKEOFF (WORD STATES)
    (PROG (STATE)
        (COND ((NULL STATES) (RETURN NIL)))
        (SETQ STATE (CAR STATES))
        (SETQ STATES (CDR STATES))
        (COND ((BEGINS WORD STATE)
                (RETURN (CONS (NEWSTATE WORD STATE)
                                (TAKEOFF WORD STATES))))
                (T (RETURN (TAKEOFF WORD STATES))))))

(DEFUN LAST (LST)
        (CAR (REVERSE LST)))

(DEFUN BUTLAST (LST)
        (REVERSE (CDR (REVERSE LST))))

(DEFUN DOSEMANTIC1 (FN STATE)
    (PROG (LEFT RIGHT FNRESULT)
        (SETQ LEFT (CAR STATE))
        (SETQ RIGHT (CADR STATE))
        (COND ((EQ (NARGS FN) 1)
                (SETQ FNRESULT (APPLY FN (LIST (LAST LEFT))))
                (SETQ LEFT (BUTLAST LEFT)))
                ((EQ (NARGS FN) 2)
                (SETQ FNRESULT (APPLY FN (LIST (LAST (BUTLAST
                                        LEFT))(LAST LEFT))))
                (SETQ LEFT (BUTLAST (BUTLAST LEFT)))))
        (COND ((EQ FNRESULT 'FAIL) (RETURN NIL))
                (T (RETURN (LIST(MKSTATE (APPEND LEFT (LIST
                                        FNRESULT)) RIGHT))))))))
```

```
(DEFUN DOSEMANTIC (FN STATES)
  (COND ((NULL STATES) NIL)
    (T (APPEND (DOSEMANTIC1 FN (CAR STATES))
               (DOSEMANTIC FN (CDR STATES))))))
```

2.4.5 The Number-Name Translation Program in LISP
This is the program of section 2.4.3.

```
(DEFUN MEANINGOF (WORD)
  (PROG()
    (COND ((EQ WORD 'ONE) (RETURN 1))
          ((EQ WORD 'TWO) (RETURN 2))
          ((EQ WORD 'TWENTY) (RETURN 20))
          (T (RETURN 'NOMEANING)))))

(DEFUN NARGS (FN)
  (COND ((EQ FN '+) 2)
        ((EQ FN 'TIMES100) 1)
        (T (BREAK NARGS T))))

(DEFUN UMP (STATES)
  (APPEND (UMP1 STATES) (UMP2 STATES)))

(DEFUN UMP1 (STATES)
  (TAKEOFF 'ONE STATES))

(DEFUN UMP2 (STATES)
  (TAKEOFF 'TWO STATES))

(DEFUN UMPTEEN (STATES)
  (UMPTEEN1 STATES))

(DEFUN UMPTEEN1 (STATES)
  (TAKEOFF 'TEN STATES))

(DEFUN UMPTY (STATES)
  (UMPTY1 STATES))

(DEFUN UMPTY1 (STATES)
  (TAKEOFF 'TWENTY STATES))

(DEFUN UPTO99 (STATES)
  (APPEND (UPTO991 STATES) (UPTO992 STATES)
          (UPTO993 STATES) (UPTO994 STATES)))

(DEFUN UPTO991 (STATES)
  (UMP STATES))

(DEFUN UPTO992 (STATES)
  (UMPTEEN STATES))
```

```
(DEFUN  UPTO993  (STATES)
    (UMPTY  STATES))

(DEFUN  UPTO994  (STATES)
    (DOSEMANTIC  '+  (UMP  (UMPTY  STATES))))

(DEFUN  TEST1  (WORDSTRING)
    (PRINT  (TAKEOFF  'STOP  (UPTO99  (LIST
        (MKSTATE  NIL  (APPEND  WORDSTRING  '(STOP)))))))))
```

2.5   CONVERSATIONS ABOUT BLOCKS

2.5.1   Simple Approach: Phrases Translate to Sets

Let us try to use our translation program on simple sentences about the
blocks world, the sentences generated by the grammar we gave earlier. It
is reasonable to take the phrases to have the following meaning:

noun	
simplenounphr	a set of
nounphr	blocks
clnounphr	
adj	a property of
qualif	blocks
prep	a relation between blocks
assertion	
question	no meaning, just a printing effect
sentence	

How should we represent these meanings in our program? The most
straightforward way is:

set of blocks	set of blocks
property of blocks	set of blocks with that property
relation between blocks	set of pairs of blocks in that relation

where as usual we use LOGO lists for sets, and we use words to name
blocks. For example:

block	[A B C D]
red	[A C]
small	[A B C]
small red block	[A]
left	[[A C] [B D] [C D] [A D]]
left of red block	[A]
big block left of red block	[ ]

We can manufacture these meanings with three main semantic functions:

    DOPROP :XS :YS

a list of all elements occurring in both the lists XS and YS (intersection)

    DOREL :XYS :YS

where XYS is a list of pairs. The result is the list of first elements of those
pairs whose second element is in YS.

83

UNIQUE :XS

if the list XS has exactly one element then result is XS, otherwise prints a grumble.

For example,

DOPROP [A B C] [B A D] = [A B],

DOREL [[A C] [B D] [C D]] [B D] = [B C].

Now we write down the meanings of phrases as before:

simpnounphr—▸noun	⟨(noun)⟩
simpnounphr—▸adj simpnounphr	doprop⟨(adj)⟩⟨(simpnounphr)⟩
nounphr—▸simpnounphr qualif	doprop⟨(qualif)⟩⟨(simpnounphr)⟩
nounphr—▸simpnounphr	⟨(simpnounphr)⟩
qualif—▸prep clnounphr	dorel⟨(prep)⟩⟨(clnounphr)⟩
clnounphr—▸'a nounphr	⟨(nounphr)⟩
clnounphr—▸'the nounphr	unique⟨(nounphr)⟩
assertion—▸'there 'is	if emptyq⟨(nounphr)⟩
'a nounphr	then p 'liar else p 'correct
assertion—▸'clnounphr	if emptyq doprop⟨(qualif)⟩
'is qualif	⟨(clnounphr)⟩ then p 'liar
	else p 'correct
question—▸'is clnounphr	if emptyq doprop⟨(qualif)⟩
qualif	⟨(clnounphr)⟩ then p 'yes
	else p 'no

Here then is the program, using TAKEOFF and DOSEMANTIC as above.

Naive blocks program. (See section 2.5.3 for program in LISP.)

```
TO MEANINGOF 'W
 10 IF :W='BLOCK THEN RESULT [A B C D]
 20 IF :W='BIG THEN RESULT [D]
 30 IF :W='SMALL THEN RESULT [A B C]
 40 IF :W='RED THEN RESULT [A C]
 50 IF :W='GREEN THEN RESULT [B D]
 60 IF :W='ON THEN RESULT [[B C]]
 70 IF :W='LEFT THEN RESULT [[A C] [B D] [C D]]
 80 IF :W='RIGHT THEN RESULT [[C A] [D B] [D C]]
 90 RESULT 'NOMEANING
END

TO MEMBERQ 'X 'XS
 10 IF EMPTYQ :XS THEN RESULT FALSE
 20 IF (F :XS)=:X THEN RESULT TRUE
 30 RESULT MEMBERQ :X BF :XS
END

TO DOREL 'XYS 'YS
 10 NEW [XY FIRSTSOFBF]
 20 IF EMPTYQ :XYS THEN RESULT [ ]
```

84

```
   30 M 'XY F :XYS
   40 M 'FIRSTOFBF DOREL BF :XYS :YS
   50 IF NOT MEMBERQ (F BF :XY) :YS THEN RESULT
      :FIRSTSOFBF
   60 IF MEMBERQ F :XY :FIRSTSOFBF THEN RESULT :FIRSTSOFBF
   70 RESULT FPUT F :XY :FIRSTSOFBF
END

TO DOPROP 'XS 'YS
   10 IF EMPTYQ :XS THEN RESULT [ ]
   20 IF MEMBERQ F :XS :YS THEN RESULT FPUT (F :XS)
      (DOPROP BF :XS :YS)
   30 RESULT DOPROP BF :XS :YS
END

TO DOPROPREV 'XS 'YS
   10 DOPROP :YS :XS
END

TO UNIQUE 'XS
   10 IF (COUNT :XS)= 1 THEN RESULT :XS
   20 IF (COUNT :XS)= 0 THEN RESULT 'FAIL
   30 P 'AMBIGUOUS AND QUIT
END

TO TESTEMPTY 'XS
   10 IF NOT EMPTYQ :XS THEN P 'CORRECT ELSE P 'LIAR
END

TO TESTNONEINBOTH 'XS 'YS
   10 IF EMPTYQ (DOPROP :YS :XS) THEN P 'LIAR ELSE P
      'CORRECT
END

TO ANSWEREMPTY 'XS 'YS
   10 IF EMPTYQ (DOPROP :YS :XS) THEN P 'YES ELSE P 'NO
END

TO NOUN 'STATES
   10 TAKEOFF 'BLOCK :STATES
END

TO ADJ 'STATES
   10 JOIN JOIN JOIN TAKEOFF 'BIG :STATES TAKEOFF 'SMALL
      :STATES TAKEOFF 'RED :STATES TAKEOFF 'GREEN :STATES
END

TO PREP 'STATES
   10 JOIN JOIN PREP1 :STATES PREP2 :STATES PREP3 :STATES
END
```

```
TO PREP1 'STATES
 10 TAKEOFF 'ON :STATES
END

TO PREP2 'STATES
 10 TAKEOFF 'OF TAKEOFF 'LEFT TAKEOFF 'THE TAKEOFF 'TO
    :STATES
END

TO PREP3 'STATES
 10 TAKEOFF 'OF TAKEOFF 'RIGHT TAKEOFF 'THE TAKEOFF 'TO
    :STATES
END

TO SIMPNOUNPHR 'STATES
 10 JOIN SIMPNOUNPHR1 :STATES SIMPNOUNPHR2 :STATES
END

TO SIMPNOUNPHR1 'STATES
 05 IF EMPTYQ :STATES THEN RESULT [ ]
 10 NOUN :STATES
END

TO SIMPNOUNPHR2 'STATES
 10 DOSEMANTIC 'DOPROP SIMPNOUNPHR ADJ :STATES
END

TO NOUNPHR 'STATES
 05 IF EMPTYQ :STATES THEN RESULT [ ]
 10 JOIN NOUNPHR1 :STATES NOUNPHR2 :STATES
END

TO NOUNPHR1 'STATES
 10 DOSEMANTIC 'DOPROPREV QUALIF SIMPNOUNPHR :STATES
END

TO NOUNPHR2 'STATES
 10 SIMPNOUNPHR :STATES
END

TO QUALIF 'STATES
 10 DOSEMANTIC 'DOREL CLNOUNPHR PREP :STATES
END

TO CLNOUNPHR 'STATES
 10 JOIN CLNOUNPHR1 :STATES CLNOUNPHR2 :STATES
END

TO CLNOUNPHR1 'STATES
 10 NOUNPHR TAKEOFF 'A :STATES
END
```

```
TO CLNOUNPHR2 'STATES
 10 DOSEMANTIC 'UNIQUE NOUNPHR TAKEOFF 'THE :STATES
END

TO ASSERTION 'STATES
 10 JOIN ASSERTION1 :STATES ASSERTION2 :STATES
END

TO ASSERTION1 'STATES
 10 DOSEMANTIC 'TESTEMPTY NOUNPHR TAKEOFF 'A TAKEOFF
    'IS TAKEOFF 'THERE :STATES
END

TO ASSERTION2 'STATES
 10 DOSEMANTIC 'TESTNONEINBOTH QUALIF TAKEOFF 'IS
    CLNOUNPHR :STATES
END

TO QUESTION 'STATES
 10 DOSEMANTIC 'ANSWEREMPTY QUALIF CLNOUNPHR
    TAKEOFF 'IS :STATES
END

TO SENTENCE 'STATES
 10 JOIN ASSERTION :STATES QUESTION :STATES
END
```

To use this translater we need a main function that makes a set containing just one state from a given list of words, applies a given phrase function to this set of states, then prints the meaning part of each resulting state (there should only be one unless the phrase is ambiguous):

```
TO DO 'PHRASE 'WS
 10 APPLY :PHRASE    《 《 [ ] :WS 》 》
 20 MAPLIST IT [PRINT F EACH]
END
```

For example, we should get:

```
        DO 'NOUNPHR [SMALL RED BLOCK]
        [A C]   (result)
        DO 'SENTENCE [THERE IS A BIG BLOCK ON A BLOCK]
        LIAR     (printed by assertion1)
```

2.5.2   A More Flexible Approach: Translation to Functions

The program in the last section is rather inflexible. Suppose we want to change the world by moving, or painting, some block. We have to adjust the meanings of all the words affected: 'ON, 'LEFT, 'RIGHT, 'RED, 'GREEN. So a conversation with commands like "put the red block on the big block" would be hard to implement. We can get over this by having a separate *world model* and computing the meanings of words like 'ON

87

when we encounter them, using this model. The model can be changed; it can also be displayed to give non-verbal output.

The world model can be just a list of pairs, each a block name and a block description as follows: colour, dimension, x-coordinate, y-coordinate. For the world we had before:-

```
[[A [RED 2 2 0]]
 [B [GREEN 2 5 2]]
 [C [RED 2 5 0]]
 [D [GREEN 4 11 0]]]
```

We can write basic functions COLOF, DIMOF, XOF, YOF, which take the name of a block and give its colour, dimension, x-coordinate and y-coordinate in the current world. Now we can program a meaning function for each word in a natural way. Let us use the name ØXYZ for the meaning function associated with the word 'XYZ.

Øblock   → list of blocks (i.e. their names)

Øred block   → truthvalue

Øon block block → truthvalue

and so on.

```
TO MAKEWORLD
  10 M 'WORLD [[A [RED 2 2 0]] [B [GREEN 2 5 2]]
                [C [RED 2 5 0]] [D [GREEN 4 11 0]]]
END
```

```
TO LOOKUP 'X 'XYS
  10 IF :XYS=[ ] THEN TYPE :X AND P 'NOTFOUND AND QUIT
  20 IF :X=F F :XYS THEN RESULT F BF F :XYS
  30 LOOKUP :X (BF :XYS)
END
```
(finds the y corresponding to x in the list of x-y-pairs xys)

```
TO COLOF 'B                    TO XOF 'B
  10 F LOOKUP :B :WORLD          10 F BF BF LOOKUP :B :WORLD
END                            END
```

```
TO DIMOF 'B                    TO YOF 'B
  10 F BF LOOKUP :B :WORLD       10 F BF BF BF LOOKUP :B :WORLD
END                            END
```

(Note COLOF :B, XOF :B, etc., now depend on the state of the world. We lazily made this a global variable instead of passing it to each function as a parameter.)

```
TO ØBLOCK
  10 MAPLIST :WORLD 'F
END
```

88

```
TO ØBIG 'B                          TO ØRED :B
  10 (DIMOF :B)>2                      10 (COLOF :B)='RED
END                                 END

TO ØSMALL 'B                        TO ØGREEN :B
  10 (DIMOF :B)<3                      10 (COLOF :B)='GREEN
END                                 END

TO ØON 'B1 'B2
  10 IF NOT((YOF :B1)=(YOF :B2)+(DIMOF :B2)) THEN RESULT
     FALSE
  20 IF EITHER(ØLEFT :B1 :B2) (ØRIGHT :B1 :B2) THEN RESULT
     FALSE
  30 RESULT TRUE
END

TO ØLEFT 'B1 'B2
  10 (XOF :B1)+(DIMOF :B1)<= (XOF :B2)
END

TO ØRIGHT 'B1 'B2
  10 LEFT :B2 :B1
END

TO MEANINGOF 'W
  10 IF :W='BLOCK THEN RESULT ØBLOCK
  20 IF :W='BIG THEN RESULT ØBIG
  ETC.
END
```

See section 2.5.4 for the program in LISP.

Now we have to rewrite DOPROP and DOREL to cope with a function name as first argument instead of a list. But wait, how do we handle qualif?

      qualif→prep clnounphr

Its meaning is a property of blocks, but we cannot easily produce a LOGO function to represent this property. We will just have to use a list as we did before, so DOPROP must accept lists as well as function names.

     DOPROP(function-name or set-of-blocks) set-of-blocks →

                                       set-of-blocks

     DOREL function-name set-of-blocks → set-of-blocks

```
TO DOPROP 'PROP 'YS
  10 IF EMPTYQ :YS THEN RESULT [ ]
  20 IF LISTQ :PROP THEN RESULT OLDDOPROP :PROP 'YS
  30 IF APPLY :PROP (F :YS)
     THEN RESULT FPUT (F :YS) (DOPROP :PROP (BF :YS))
```

```
  40 DOPROP :PROP (BF :YS)
END
```
(subset of YS which have the property;OLDDOPROP is DOPROP of last section)

```
TO DOREL 'REL 'YS
  10 FILTER ØBLOCK :REL :YS
END
```

```
TO FILTER 'XS 'REL 'YS
  10 IF EMPTYQ :XS THEN RESULT [ ]
  20 JOIN(FILTER1(F :XS) :REL :YS) (FILTER (BF :XS) :REL :YS)
END
```
(finds all X in XS which are related to some Y in YS)

```
TO FILTER1 'X 'REL 'YS
  10 IF EMPTYQ :YS THEN RESULT [ ]
  20 IF APPLY :REL :X (F :YS) THEN RESULT 《 :X 》
  30 FILTER1 :X :REL (BF :YS)
END
```
(《 :X 》 if X related to some Y in YS, else emptylist)

With redefinitions our program should work as before but more flexibly, since its behaviour depends on the current value of the variable WORLD.

2.5.3　The Naive Blocks Program in LISP

```
(DEFUN NARGS (FN)
    (COND ((EQ FN 'DOPROP) 2)
          ((EQ FN 'DOPROPREV) 2)
          ((EQ FN 'DOREL) 2)
          ((EQ FN 'UNIQUE) 1)
          ((EQ FN 'TESTEMPTY) 1)
          ((EQ FN 'TESTNONEINBOTH) 2)
          ((EQ FN ANSWEREMPTY) 2)
          (T (BREAK NARGS T))))

(DEFUN MEANINGOF (W)
    (COND ((EQ W 'BLOCK) '(A B C D))
          ((EQ W 'BIG) '(D))
          ((EQ W 'SMALL) '(A B C))
          ((EQ W 'RED) '(A C))
          ((EQ W 'GREEN) '(B D))
          ((EQ W 'ON) '((B C)))
          ((EQ W 'LEFT) '((A C) (B D) (C D)))
          ((EQ W 'RIGHT) '((C A) (D B) (D C)))
          (T 'NOMEANING)))
```

```
(DEFUN MEMBERQ (X XS)
    (COND ((NULL XS) NIL)
          ((EQ (CAR XS) X))
          (T (MEMBERQ X (CDR XS)))))

(DEFUN DOREL (XYS YS)
  (PROG (XY FIRSTOFBF)
      (COND ((NULL XYS) (RETURN NIL)))
      (SETQ XY (CAR XYS))
      (SETQ FIRSTOFBF (DOREL (CDR XYS) YS))
      (COND ((NOT (MEMBERQ (CADR XY) YS)) (RETURN
                                              FIRSTOFBF))
            ((MEMBERQ (CAR XY) FIRSTOFBF) (RETURN
                                              FIRSTOFBF))
            (T (RETURN (CONS (CAR XY) FIRSTOFBF))))))

(DEFUN DOPROP (XS YS)
  PROG ()
      (COND ((NULL XS) (RETURN NIL))
            ((MEMBERQ (CAR XS) YS) (RETURN (CONS (CAR XS)
                                       (DOPROP (CDR XS) YS))))
            (T (RETURN (DOPROP (CDR XS) YS)))))

(DEFUN DOPROPREV (XS YS)
    (DOPROP YS XS))

(DEFUN UNIQUE (XS)
  (PROG ()
      (COND ((EQ (LENGTH XS) 1) (RETURN XS))
            ((EQ (LENGTH XS) 0) (RETURN 'FAIL))
            (T (PRINT 'AMBIGUOUS) (QUIT)))))

(DEFUN TESTEMPTY (XS)
  (PROG ()
      (COND ((NOT NULL RIGHT)) (RETURN NIL)) (parse incomplete)
            ((NOT (NULL XS)) (PRINT 'CORRECT))
            (T (PRINT 'LIAR)))))

(DEFUN TESTNONEINBOTH (XS YS)
  (PROG ()
      (COND ((NOT (NULL RIGHT)) (RETURN NIL)) (parse incomplete)
            ((NULL (DOPROPREV XS YS)) (PRINT 'LIAR))
            (T (PRINT 'CORRECT)))))

(DEFUN ANSWEREMPTY (XS YS)
  (PROG ()
      (COND ((NOT (NULL RIGHT)) (RETURN NIL)) (parse incomplete)
            ((NULL (DOPROPREV XS YS)) (PRINT 'NO))
            (T (PRINT 'YES)))))
```

```
(DEFUN NOUN (STATES)
    TAKEOFF 'BLOCK STATES))

(DEFUN ADJ (STATES)
    (APPEND (TAKEOFF 'BIG STATES) (TAKEOFF 'SMALL STATES)
            (TAKEOFF 'RED STATES) (TAKEOFF 'GREEN STATES)))

(DEFUN PREP (STATES)
    (APPEND (PREP1 STATES) (PREP2 STATES) (PREP3 STATES)))

(DEFUN PREP1 (STATES)
    TAKEOFF 'ON STATES))

(DEFUN PREP2 (STATES)
    (TAKEOFF 'OF (TAKEOFF 'LEFT (TAKEOFF 'THE
                                (TAKEOFF 'TO STATES)))))

(DEFUN PREP3 (STATES)
    (TAKEOFF 'OF (TAKEOFF 'RIGHT (TAKEOFF 'THE
                                (TAKEOFF 'TO STATES)))))

(DEFUN SIMPNOUNPHR (STATES)
    (COND ((NULL STATES) NIL)
          (T (APPEND (SIMPNOUNPHR1 STATES)
                     (SIMPNOUNPHR2 STATES)))))

(DEFUN SIMPNOUNPHR1 (STATES)
    (COND ((NULL STATES) NIL)
          (T (NOUN STATES))))

(DEFUN SIMPNOUNPHR2 (STATES)
    (DOSEMANTIC 'DOPROP (SIMPNOUNPHR (ADJ STATES))))

(DEFUN NOUNPHR (STATES)
    (COND ((NULL STATES) NIL)
          (T (APPEND (NOUNPHR1 STATES) (NOUNPHR2
                                STATES)))))

(DEFUN NOUNPHR1 (STATES)
    (DOSEMANTIC 'DOPROPREV (QUALIF (SIMPNOUNPHR
                                STATES))))

(DEFUN NOUNPHR2 (STATES)
    (SIMPNOUNPHR STATES))

(DEFUN QUALIF (STATES)
    (DOSEMANTIC 'DOREL (CLNOUNPHR (PREP STATES))))

(DEFUN CLNOUNPHR (STATES)
    (APPEND (CLNOUNPHR1 STATES) (CLNOUNPHR2 STATES)))
```

```
(DEFUN CLNOUNPHR1 (STATES)
    (NOUNPHR (TAKEOFF 'A STATES)))

(DEFUN CLNOUNPHR2 (STATES)
    (DOSEMANTIC 'UNIQUE (NOUNPHR (TAKEOFF 'THE
                                              STATES))))

(DEFUN ASSERTION (STATES)
    (APPEND (ASSERTION1 STATES) (ASSERTION2 STATES)))

(DEFUN ASSERTION1 (STATES)
    (DOSEMANTIC 'TESTEMPTY (NOUNPHR (TAKEOFF 'A
                    (TAKEOFF 'IS (TAKEOFF 'THERE STATES))))))

(DEFUN ASSERTION2 (STATES)
    (DOSEMANTIC 'TESTNONEINBOTH
                (QUALIF (TAKEOFF 'IS (CLNOUNPHR STATES)))))

(DEFUN QUESTION (STATES)
    (DOSEMANTIC 'ANSWEREMPTY (QUALIF (CLNOUNPHR
                                (TAKEOFF 'IS STATES)))))

(DEFUN SENTENCE (STATES)
    (APPEND (ASSERTION STATES) (QUESTION STATES)))

(DEFUN DO (PHRASE WS)
   (PROG ()
     (MAPC '(LAMBDA (EACH)
            (COND ((CAAR EACH) (PRINT (CAAR EACH)))))
            (APPLY PHRASE (LIST (LIST NIL WS)))))))
```

2.5.4   The More Flexible Approach, in LISP

The World Model

```
(DEFUN LISTQ (L)
    (OR (EQ (TYPEP L) 'LIST) (EQ L NIL)))

(DEFUN MAKEWORLD NIL
    (SETQ WORLD '((A (RED 2. 2. 0.))
                  (B (GREEN 2. 5. 2.))
                  (C (RED 2. 5. 0.))
                  (D (GREEN 4. 9. 0.)))))

(DEFUN LOOKUP (X XYS)
   (PROG NIL
     (COND ((NULL XYS)
            (PRINT X)
            (PRIN1 'NOTFOUND)
            (QUIT))
```

```
          (COND ((EQ X (CAAR XYS)) (RETURN (CADAR XYS))))
          (RETURN (LOOKUP X (CDR XYS))))))

(DEFUN COLOF (B) (CAR (LOOKUP B WORLD)))

(DEFUN XOF (B) (CADDR (LOOKUP B WORLD)))

(DEFUN DIMOF (B) (CADR (LOOKUP B WORLD)))

(DEFUN YOF (B) (CADDDR (LOOKUP B WORLD)))

(DEFUN ØBLOCK NIL (MAPCAR 'CAR WORLD))

(DEFUN ØBIG (B) ( >(DIMOF B) 2.))

(DEFUN ØSMALL (B) (< (DIMOF B) 3.))

(DEFUN ØRED (B) (EQ (COLOF B) 'RED))

(DEFUN ØGREEN (B) (EQ (COLOF B) 'GREEN))

(DEFUN ØON (B1 B2)
       (COND ((NOT (EQ (YOF B1) (+ (YOF B2) (DIMOF B2)))) NIL)
             ((OR (ØLEFT B1 B2) (ØRIGHT B1 B2)) NIL)
             (T)))

(DEFUN ØLEFT (B1 B2) (NOT ( >(+ (XOF B1) (DIMOF B1)) (XOF
                                                       B2))))

(DEFUN ØRIGHT (B1 B2) (ØLEFT B2 B1))

(DEFUN MEANINGOF (W)
       (COND ((EQ W 'BLOCK) (ØBLOCK))
             ((EQ W 'BIG) 'ØBIG)
             ((EQ W 'SMALL) 'ØSMALL)
             ((EQ W 'RED) 'ØRED)
             ((EQ W 'GREEN) 'ØGREEN)
             ((EQ W 'ON) 'ØON)
             ((EQ W 'LEFT) 'ØLEFT)
             ((EQ W 'RIGHT) 'ØRIGHT)
             (T 'NOMEANING)))
```

DOPROP and DOREL

```
(DEFUN DOPROP (PROP YS)
  (PROG NIL
     (COND ((NULL YS) (RETURN NIL))
           ((LISTQ PROP) (RETURN (OLDDOPROP PROP YS)))
           ((APPLY PROP (LIST (CAR YS)))
           (RETURN (CONS (CAR YS) (DOPROP PROP (CDR YS)))))
           (T (RETURN (DOPROP PROP (CDR YS)))))))
```

```
(DEFUN DOREL (REL YS)
    (FILTER (0BLOCK) REL YS))

(DEFUN FILTER (XS REL YS)
    COND ((NULL XS) NIL)
          (T (APPEND (FILTER1 (CAR XS) REL YS)
                     (FILTER (CDR XS) REL YS)))))

(DEFUN FILTER1 (X REL YS)
    (COND (NULL YS) NIL)
          ((APPLY REL (LIST X (CAR YS))) (LIST X))
          (T (FILTER1 X REL (CDR YS)))))

(DEFUN OLDDOPROP (XS YS)
  (PROG NIL
    (COND ((NULL XS) (RETURN NIL))
          ((MEMBERQ (CAR XS) YS)
           (RETURN (CONS (CAR XS) (OLDDOPROP (CDR XS)
                                                   YS))))
          (T (RETURN (OLDDOPROP (CDR XS) YS)))))))
```

2.6   A LA RECHERCHE DU TEMPS PERDU

2.6.1   History and Time Contexts

So far all our sentences about blocks have referred to a single state of the
world, the present one. Let us try to extend our system to discuss the past,
giving the blocks world a history. This brings up the important idea of
interpreting a phrase in a context, in our case a time context. Other
contexts would be place ("come *here*") or speaker("*I* killed Cock Robin").

Let us simply take Monday, Tuesday, . . ., as the times, and define the
blocks history as a set of day-world pairs. If we use the notation X → Y to
abbreviate [X Y] for readability we have as a possible history:

```
[MONDAY    [A→[RED 2 2 0]    B→[GREEN 2 5 2]
           C→[RED 2 5 0]     D→[GREEN 4 11 0]]
 TUESDAY   [A→[RED 2 5 4]    B→[GREEN 2 5 2]
           C→[RED 2 5 0]     D→[GREEN 4 11 0]]
 WEDNESDAY→[etc.
```

(Nothing much happened between Monday and Tuesday except that the
red block to the left of a red block was put on the small green block.)

We also need to know what day it is today, say Thursday. So global
variables HISTORY and TODAY describe our model (they can be set up by
a procedure MAKEHISTORY corresponding to our previous
MAKEWORLD). If we want to know what the world was like on Monday
LOOKUP 'MONDAY :HISTORY will tell us, and LOOKUP 'TODAY
:HISTORY gives us the news.

What sort of sentences should we have? How about: "The block which was to the left of a red block on Monday is on a block", or "On Wednesday the block which was to the left of the block which was on a big block on Monday on Tuesday was to the right of the block which was on a red block on Thursday". Has the big block been on a small block? The point is that we can't evaluate "on a big block" to find which blocks it describes until we know which day we are talking about. So when we translate such a phrase we cannot pass on a list of blocks as the result, as we did previously.

So let us pass back a *description*, which can be evaluated for a given day when we have read enough to know what day it is. This description can be a list of lists of lists . . ., that is a tree structure, using markers OBJ (object), PROP (property), REL (relation), UNIQUE (to handle 'the). The tips of the tree can be the names of semantic functions ØBLOCK, ØRED, etc. The phrase [RED BLOCK ON THE BIG BLOCK] would give the tree

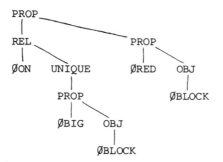

This would be represented by lists thus
```
    [PROP [REL ØON [UNIQUE [PROP ØBIG [OBJ ØBLOCK]]]]
          [PROP ØRED [OBJ ØBLOCK]]]
```
We could also allow such descriptions to have as components lists of blocks, which we have already evaluated. Such trees are easily constructed by functions MAKEOBJECT, etc; thus:
```
TO MKOBJ 'X            TO MKPROP 'PR 'X 》
   10 《 'OBJ :X 》          10 《 'PROP :PR :X 》
END                    END
```
and similarly for MKREL and MKUNIQUE.

Now we need a function to evaluate descriptions for a given day and produce a list of blocks. It can use our previous functions DOPROP, DOREL and UNIQUE, thus:

```
TO EVAL 'DESCRIP 'DAY
    NEW 'WORLD
    M 'WORLD LOOKUP :DAY :HISTORY
    IF WORDQ :DESCRIP THEN RESULT :DESCRIP        (e.g. ØBIG)
```

```
          IF 'OBJ=F :DESCRIP THEN RESULT APPLY SECOND :DESCRIP
          IF 'PROP=F :DESCRIP THEN RESULT DOPROP
                                (EVAL SECOND :DESCRIP :DAY)
                                (EVAL THIRD :DESCRIP :DAY)
          IF 'REL=F :DESCRIP THEN RESULT DOREL
                                (EVAL SECOND :DESCRIP :DAY)
                                (EVAL THIRD :DESCRIP :DAY)
          IF 'UNIQUE=F :DESCRIP THEN RESULT UNIQUE
                                (EVAL SECOND :DESCRIP :DAY)
          RESULT :DESCRIP       (i.e. set of blocks, already evaluated)
END
```

(*Note* SECOND is F BF, THIRD is F BF BF). See section 2.6.4 for the LISP translation.

Now DOPROP and DOREL, which make reference to :WORLD, will have the right world to work in, since it is set up as a local variable and made to be the world for the day supplied. EVAL just calls itself recursively to evaluate sub-trees (think of it as solving sub-problems of evaluation).

2.6.2   Semantics for Blocks with Tense

Here then is the semantic specification for blocks with reference to past time. The new productions are marked with an asterisk. Coding the specification as LOGO procedures is tedious but straightforward. Notice that a production that does not know what day it is makes a description; one that is given a day evaluates descriptions.

simpnounphr → noun	mkobj ⟨(noun)⟩
simpnounphr → adj simpnounphr	mkprop ⟨(adj)⟩ ⟨(simpnounphr)⟩
nounphr → simpnounphr qualif	mkprop ⟨(qualif)⟩ ⟨(simpnounphr)⟩
nounphr → simpnounphr	⟨(simpnounphr)⟩
*nounphr → simpnounphr tqualif	mkprop ⟨(tqualif)⟩ ⟨(simpnounphr)⟩
qualif → prep clnounphr	mkrel ⟨(prep)⟩ ⟨(clnounphr)⟩
*tqualif → 'which 'was qualif 'on 'day	eval ⟨(qualif)⟩ ⟨(day)⟩
clnounphr → 'a nounphr	⟨(nounphr)⟩
clnounphr → 'the nounphr	mkunique ⟨(nounphr)⟩
assertion → 'there 'is 'a nounphr	not emptyq(eval ⟨(nounphr)⟩ today)
*assertion → 'on day 'there 'was 'a nounphr	not emptyq(eval ⟨(nounphr)⟩ ⟨(day)⟩)
question → 'is clnounphr qualif	exercise
*question → 'has clnounphr 'been qualif	exercise
sentence → assertion	if ⟨(assertion)⟩ then p 'correct else p 'liar

sentence ⟶ question	if ⟨(question)⟩ then
	p 'yes else p 'no
*sentence ⟶ 'today 'is day	m 'today⟨(day)⟩

2.6.3   Exercises

2.6.1. Fill in the semantics of questions.

2.6.2. Hand-simulate in outline the action of the EVAL procedure on the description tree given above and day MONDAY, using the history given at the beginning.

2.6.3. Write LOGO procedures for the new productions, using those for the "more flexible program" of section 2.5.2 as prototypes.

2.6.4   The Block-Listing Function in LISP

```
(DEFUN MKOBJ (X)
    (LIST 'OBJ X))

(DEFUN MKPROP (PR X)
    (LIST 'PROP PR X))

(DEFUN EVAL* (DESCRIP DAY)
  (PROG ()
    (SETQ WORLD (LOOKUP DAY HISTORY))
    (COND ((ATOMP DESCRIP) (RETURN DESCRIP))
          ((EQ 'OBJ (CAR DESCRIP)) (RETURN (APPLY (CADR
                                               DESCRIP))))
          ((EQ 'PROP (CAR DESCRIP))
           (RETURN (DOPROP (EVAL* (CADR DESCRIP) DAY)
                           (EVAL* (CADDR DESCRIP) DAY))))
          ((EQ 'REL (CAR DESCRIP))
           (RETURN (DOREL (EVAL* (CADR DESCRIP) DAY)
                          (EVAL* (CADDR DESCRIP) DAY))))
          ((EQ 'UNIQUE (CAR DESCRIP))
           (RETURN (UNIQUE (EVAL* (CADR DESCRIP) DAY))))
          (T (RETURN DESCRIP)))))
```

2.7   WINOGRAD'S CONVERSATIONAL PROGRAM

2.7.1   Introduction

Winograd's program for conversing about a simple world of blocks and pyramids was a landmark in natural language processing by computers. It simulates a system of blocks, pyramids and boxes and displays the current state on a screen. The user can give it commands and ask it questions, not only about the current state of the world but about its own past actions and reasons for them. We will not describe the program here since there is a very clear description in Winograd's 1973 paper; we just give a portion of Winograd's sample dialogue and make a few comments relating to it and to our previous work with LOGO.

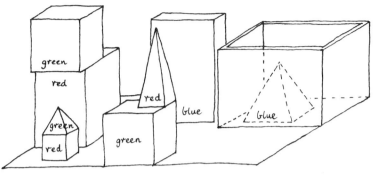

1. pick up a big red block
    OK
2. grasp the pyramid
    I DON'T UNDERSTAND WHICH PYRAMID YOU MEAN
3. find a block which is taller than the one you are holding
    and put it into the box.
    BY "IT", I ASSUME YOU MEAN THE BLOCK WHICH IS
    TALLER THAN THE ONE I AM HOLDING
    OK
4. what does the box contain?
    THE BLUE PYRAMID AND THE BLUE BLOCK
5. what is the pyramid supported by?
    THE BOX
6. how many blocks are not in the box?
    FOUR OF THEM
7. is at least one of them narrower than
    the one which I told you to pick up?
    YES, THE RED CUBE
8. is it supported?
    YES, BY THE TABLE
9. can the table pick up blocks?
    NO
10. can a pyramid be supported by a block?
    YES
11. can a pyramid support a pyramid?
    I DON'T KNOW
12. stack up two pyramids
    I CAN'T.
13. the blue pyramid is mine
    I UNDERSTAND
14. I own all blocks which are not red,
    but I don't own anything which supports a pyramid
    I UNDERSTAND

15. do I own the box?
    NO
16. do I own anything in the box?
    YES, TWO THINGS: THE BLUE BLOCK AND THE BLUE
    PYRAMID
17. will you please stack up both of the red blocks
    and either a green cube or a pyramid?
    OK
18. which cube is sitting on the table?
    THE LARGE GREEN ONE WHICH SUPPORTS THE RED
    PYRAMID
19. is there a large block behind a pyramid?
    YES, THREE OF THEM: A LARGE RED ONE, A LARGE GREEN
    CUBE AND THE BLUE ONE
20. put a small one onto the green cube which supports a pyramid
    OK
21. put the littlest pyramid on top of it
    OK
22. how many things are on top of green cubes?
    I'M NOT SURE WHAT YOU MEAN BY "ON TOP OF" IN THE
    PHRASE "ON TOP OF GREEN CUBES"
    DO YOU MEAN:
    1 — DIRECTLY ON THE SURFACE
    2 — ANYWHERE ON TOP OF?
23. had you touched any pyramid before you put the green one on the
    little cube?
    YES, THE GREEN ONE
24. when did you pick it up?
    WHILE I WAS STACKING UP THE RED CUBE, A LARGE RED
    BLOCK AND A LARGE GREEN CUBE
25. why?
    TO GET RID OF IT
26. why did you do that?
    TO CLEAR OFF THE RED CUBE
27. why did you clear off that cube?
    TO PUT IT ON A LARGE GREEN CUBE
28. why did you do that?
    TO STACK UP THE RED CUBE, A LARGE RED BLOCK
    AND A LARGE GREEN CUBE.
29. why did you do that?
    BECAUSE YOU ASKED ME TO

2.7.2 Semantics: Some Remarks

(a) Our LOGO program computes a set (list) of blocks when it is unsure
which one is meant, e.g. [GREEN BLOCK] gives list [B D]. Winograd in
his Planner system chooses one of the blocks and uses a "back-track"

facility in Planner to go back and repeat with the next block. We can't do this in LOGO, but computing the list seems about as good.

(b) Winograd actually creates some Planner program and then runs it. We just run existing program. His Planner program looks rather like sentences in logic. For example:

a red cube which supports a pyramid
(GOAL (IS ?X1 BLOCK))
(GOAL (COLOR-OF ?X1 RED))
(GOAL (EQUIDIMENSIONAL ?X1))
(GOAL (IS ?X2 PYRAMID))
(GOAL (SUPPORT ?X1 ?X2))

This is more sophisticated than our description trees in the final LOGO program.

(c) Even the dictionary of word meanings had the names of procedures in it. (Similarly in our LOGO program MEANINGOF 'ON is a procedure name 'ØON.)

(d) Notice the complexity of a word like "the". Sentence 2 "Grasp the pyramid" is ambiguous, but "Grasp the red pyramid" is OK since the model world only has one red pyramid. In sentence 5 "What is the pyramid supported by?" there·is no ambiguity, since a particular pyramid has just been mentioned; here the ambiguity is resolved by syntactic context, not by reference to the model. Our LOGO program could not do this unless we made procedures like NOUNPHR store the meaning and the corresponding input string or tree.

2.7.3 Syntax: Some Remarks

(a) Notice the complexity of the syntax Winograd's program can handle compared with ours. Ours, with only a few kinds of phrases, was still a bit hard to keep in one's head. If we simply invented 199 more kinds of phrases we would get in a muddle.

(b) To avoid a very big context-free grammar with lots of arbitrary names of phrase classes Winograd uses "systemic grammar", due to Halliday (he doesn't regard the choice as crucial, just helpful). There are just four basic kind of phrase:

CLAUSE	'Is it red?', 'it is on the table', 'on which he sat'
NOUN GROUP	'A big man', 'the man in a hurry', 'cars'
PREPOSITION GROUP	'On top of the table', 'with', 'in the iron mask'
VERB GROUP	'lives', 'will have been living', 'to be kissed'

But each of these is subdivided (into species and subspecies as a biologist would say). The subdivisions are characterised by features,
DETERMINED, MASCULINE, SINGULAR, ANIMATE, TRANSITIVE,

INTERROGATIVE, etc. So instead of a class

    MASCSINGCLNOUNPHRASE (!!!)

we might have NOUN GROUP with features MASCULINE, SINGULAR, CLOSED. This makes it easy to ensure that subject and verb agree in number without writing separate procedure rules for each case (in French they must also agree in gender). We can also ensure more easily that verbs like "loves" get ANIMATE subjects. Notice, too, that one would expect the semantics of "loves" to be different according to whether the object is animate or not. "John loves Mary" implies that John is in love, but "John loves ice cream", doesn't.

The subdivisions of CLAUSE are very complicated (see Winograd 1972 pp.48, 49). Even this does not exhaust the matter because we can also make distinctions based on transitivity/intransitivity.

(c) Winograd writes his parser in a special language, PROGRAMMAR, which is not all that different from LOGO but is specially designed for parsing. For example, we do not need to mention the string S all the time, and the grammar

    S ⟶ NP VP
    NP ⟶ DETERMINER NOUN
    VP ⟶ VERB/TRANSITIVE NP
    VP ⟶ VERB/INTRANSITIVE

corresponds to the PROGRAMMAR program

```
(PDEFINE SENTENCE
(((PARSE NP) NIL FAIL)
((PARSE VP) FAIL FAIL RETURN)))

(PDEFINE NP
(((PARSE DETERMINER) NIL FAIL)
((PARSE NOUN) RETURN FAIL)))

(PDEFINE VP
(((PARSE VERB) NIL FAIL)
((ISQ H TRANSITIVE) NIL INTRANS)
((PARSE NP) RETURN NIL)

INTRANS
((ISQ H INTRANSITIVE) RETURN FAIL)
```

In the second line above (PARSE NP) has two "directions", NIL and FAIL, after it. It uses the first if it succeeds, the second if it doesn't. (PARSE VP) has a third direction, RETURN, which is used if it succeeds and there is not more string left. NIL means go onto next instruction. FAIL means output a fail and restore string to the previous one (like CHECK). RETURN outputs a result, after attaching the new node to the parse tree (rather like TRY).

(d) It is not clear from Winograd's papers how well the program does when interrogated by a user other than the author, and to what extent the syntax is tailored to the particular dialogue in the examples. Writing the syntax in procedural form is a flexible approach but may make it harder to forsee all possible interactions of the various parsing procedures.

2.7.4 References

T. Winograd (1973) A procedural model of language understanding, in *Computer Models of Thought and Language* (eds Schank & Colby) San Francisco: Freeman.

T. Winograd (1972) *Understanding Natural Language*. Edinburgh University Press. (A full account if you want more detail.)

2.8 VERBS AND THEIR MEANINGS

2.8.1 Verbs

In our LOGO program dealing with a simplified blocks world we had nouns, adjectives and prepositions, but avoided verbs except the verb *to be*. Winograd allows a rather restricted set of verbs such as *put* and *support*, but their use is limited since there is only one "person" in the blocks world, namely the program (called SHRDLU). Sentences with more interesting verbs are:

John *sold* Fred a donkey.

Fred *bought* a donkey.

Mary *put* the pie in the oven and *switched* it on.

Mary *told* Tim to *eat* his pie.

Two points of importance for generating or understanding sentences with verbs are

1. How does the verb relate to the noun phrases? For example how does *sold* relate to *John, Fred, a donkey*.
2. Can verbs be analysed into more primitive ideas? For example, is there some primitive idea common to *bought* and *sold*?

The first question is the concern of "case grammar". The second involves the search for "semantic" or "conceptual" primitives.

We should study both of them if we wanted to write a program to answer questions about a simple story in order to demonstrate its understanding, e.g. the story might say "John sold Fred a donkey" and we might ask "What did Fred buy?"

2.8.2 Case Grammars

The grammatical notion of case goes back to the Greek grammarians. English has three cases, nominative, accusative and genitive (I, me, my; he, him, his; Bill, Bill, Bill's), but Latin has six, Finnish fifteen. These are distinguished by word endings. In all three languages the genitive case has very similar meaning.

103

For semantics we are interested not in "surface" case, distinguished by word endings, but in "deep" case, which analyses what kind of role the noun plays with respect to the verb. Thus in "John sold Fred a donkey" there are no case endings, but we may distinguish four deep cases:

Agent	(John)
Object	(donkey)
Source	(John)
Goal	(Fred)

Filmore (1968) gives the following cases:

Agent (A)	the instigator of the event

Counter-
  Agent (C)
	the force of resistance against which
	  the action is carried out

Object (O)	the entity that moves or changes or whose position or existence is in consideration
Result (R)	the entity that comes into existence as a result of the action
Instrument (I)	the stimulus or immediate physical cause of an event
Source (S)	the place from which something moves
Goal (G)	the place to which something moves
Experience (E)	the entity that receives or accepts or expe- riences or undergoes the effect of an action

Any one verb can accept only a subset of these cases, and from this subset not all need be supplied in any one sentence. Thus "open" can be used in four ways:

The door opened	(O)
John opened the door	(AO)
The wind opened the door	(IO)
John opened the door with a chisel	(AOI)

A translation program might have a "case frame" for each verb telling us:
(a) which cases the verb can take
(b) which of these are compulsory (e.g. object for *open*)
(c) how each case is to be detected, by word endings or preposition
(d) any semantic restrictions on the case (e.g. agent of *open* must be animate, object of *open* must be physical-object)

This information can be used to remove any ambiguity of sentences (especially d), and to impose a structure on the sentence which is more useful than the parse tree for drawing inferences or translating to another language. For example a traditional parse of "John calmly broke the window with a hammer" might be:

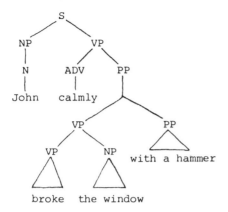

A case grammar might parse it thus:

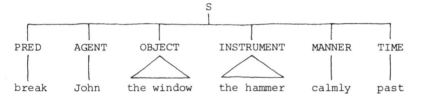

Here *break* is the predicate (verb), AGENT, OBJECT and INSTRUMENT are cases, and MANNER and TIME are verb modifiers. (The example is from Bruce 1975.) Most recent AI programs for natural language use some form of case analysis, but there is no agreed system of cases.

A more semantic way of looking at cases is to think of a narrative as describing "events". A verb is then a property of an event (a "falling" event, "selling" event, etc.) and the cases specify important relations between the event and individuals (agent relates individual John to event e). Events, unlike people, do not have proper names, and the information provided by the cases helps to specify them unambiguously.

2.8.3 Semantic Primitives

Pairs of verbs like *sell-buy*, *lend-borrow*, *come-go* clearly have some elements of meaning in common with each other. We might hope to analyse them into more primitive meaning constituents. For example, Schank uses about a dozen such constituents for notions such as transfer, propel and ingest.

As we have seen, such analysis could enable us to answer questions about a story even if a question refers to the same event by a word differing from the one used in the story. Furthermore, if we want to do inferences, e.g. to derive facts implied by, but not explicitly stated in, a story, it is far more economical to give rules for the small number of primitives than to give them for each word in the language. Of course semantic analysis into primitives can also be done to some extent for nouns (father = male

105

parent, or should it be parent = mother or father?) but we will talk here about verbs.

Let us take as an example an analysis of verbs proposed by Jackendoff (1975) following Gruber. He distinguishes GO, BE and STAY verbs

GO   The train travelled from Detroit to Cincinnati
        The hawk flew from its nest onto the ground
BE   Max is in Africa
        The cat lay on the couch
STAY   The bacteria stayed in his body
        Bill kept the book on his shelf

We might do a case analysis of the second sentence above as:

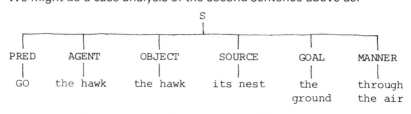

eliminating "flew" in favour of the primitive GO.

But there is another dimension of variation: Position, Possession, Identification. The verbs above were all positional, thus GO_{posit}, BE_{posit}, $STAY_{posit}$. Analogues for Possession are:

$GO_{possess}$ Harry gave the book to the library
$BE_{possess}$ Max owned an iguana
$STAY_{possess}$ The library kept the book

and for identification

GO_{ident} The ice became mushy
BE_{ident} The metal was red
$STAY_{ident}$ The redness persisted

Jackendoff further distinguishes two kinds of agent, "causal" as in "Linda lowered the rock" and "permissive" as in "Linda dropped the rock". These distinctions enable him to analyse important components of meaning in a considerable number of common verbs. He can then build up rather general inference rules applicable to these verbs, such as (using case notation):

If GO(object: X, source: Y, goal: Z) at time t
then for some times t', t'' with t' < t < t''
BE(object: X, location: Y) at t'
BE(object: X, location: Z) at t''

On the other hand it is unclear which are the best primitives, for example Schank makes other distinctions, principally between transferring a physical object (*put* a brick) and a mental object (tell him that . . .) (See his paper in Schank and Colby's 1973 book already referred to). Appropriateness of any system of primitives needs further demonstration by working programs, whilst case systems have already proved their value in this way.

All this analysis of verbs has led Schank and others to suggest that parsing should be done not by the traditional context-free syntax analysis or a variant thereof, but by finding the verbs and then looking around in the sentence for nouns to fill in the appropriate case slots. In programs working on a limited domain of discourse, such as electronic circuits, it seems possible to make good use of known case frames of verbs which may take very specific kinds of noun in each case position (e.g. connect-to-).

2.8.4   Exercises

2.9.1. Attempt a case analysis of the following sentences:
Fred peeled the apple with his knife
The heavens opened
John went to the restaurant and ordered a steak from the waiter
Don't eat peas with your spoon
He learnt Artificial Intelligence from a tape recorder in his bath
He left it in the park
2.9.2. Suggest a way in which case parses might be represented in LOGO.
2.9.3. Try to analyse the verbs in the above sentences in terms of semantically more primitive concepts.

2.8.5   References

Bruce (1975) Case systems for natural language. *AI J. 6*, 4. An excellent review.

Jackendoff (1975) A system of semantic primitives, in *Theoretical Issues in Natural Languages Processing* (eds Schank & Nash-Webber).

Schank (1973) in *Computer Models of Thought and Language* (eds Schank & Colby).San Francisco: Freeman.

2.9   ACKNOWLEDGEMENTS

Rod Burstall, who wrote the notes on natural language, would like to thank Stephen Isard for very helpful criticism, and Joseph Goguen for useful advice. He would also like to thank three generations of students for their tolerance to a lecturer on natural language processing whose professional competence (if any) is mainly in the theory of computation. Thanks also to Mark Adler for translating LOGO programs into LISP.

3. QUESTION ANSWERING AND INFERENCE

This section is about computer reasoning. The rules of formal logic can be programmed on a computer together with some heuristic search strategies to enable the machine to prove mathematical theorems. After many years of hard research programs exist that can prove standard theorems at about undergraduate mathematics level. But inferring conclusions from premises is useful outside the domain of mathematics, and somewhat simpler methods of computer reasoning have been applied both in natural language systems, like Winograd's, and in systems that answer questions from databases of information. A rather limited set of inference procedures are available in LOGO, and we shall explore their use here, starting with a consideration of the limitations of our previous approach to question answering.

3.1 THE INFERENCE SYSTEM

3.1.1 Introduction

We wrote a LOGO program to accept sentences about the blocks world and to make some primitive responses to them. But the model to which the sentences referred was put in as a collection of lists described in LOGO. It was not the result of our conversation. This might be a fair representation of a system that answers questions about a scene it sees through a TV camera or even about some specific body of data like airline timetables. But often we derive our knowledge from sentences: "Read this passage and answer the questions below", as the school books say. So we need to represent an *incomplete model* in a way that is *easy to add to or change*. The list representation was specific (it knew just where everything was), not too easy to change and needed special LOGO code for concepts like ON. An alternative to *lists + procedures* is *facts + inference rules*.

3.1.2 Memory

The program must store some information about the blocks world, for instance "The block is red". We adopt the same method as we used in the geometric analogy problems and the making of structural descriptions, and for the same reasons: i.e. we use symbolic descriptions. We could choose, say, [RED BLOCK] or [COLOUR BLOCK RED]. The latter will be most versatile, for instance if we wanted to answer the question "What is the colour of the block?".

Typically we will want to store a large collection of such facts inside the computer. As a first approximation we can imagine a list of them, e.g.
[[COLOUR BLOCK RED] [BELONGS BLOCK ME] [BIG BLOCK]
[ON BLOCK1 BLOCK] . . .]
Such a collection of facts is usually called a *database*.

Retrieval. How would the program use this database to answer the question "Is the block coloured red?". First it would have to analyse the sentence and build up the description [COLOUR BLOCK RED]. Then it would call:

AMONGQ [COLOUR BLOCK RED] :DATABASE

and print YES or NO as the result of this call was TRUE or FALSE. (Should it be NO or DO NOT KNOW?)

The problem of building up descriptions from the English input has been the subject of our natural language lectures.

3.1.3   Organising the Database

Unfortunately the number of facts that have to be stored in most non-trivial domains, is very large. Searching down a long list, as AMONGQ does, take a long time. It is rather as if one was searching for a book in the library by looking at every book. Our solution to this problem is similar to the library's: we index the database. Various indexing systems are used to organise databases. We have made a system available in LOGO (available through BORROWFILE or LIBRARY as 'ECMI01 'INFERENCE). You can add a fact to the database with the command ASSERT, e.g.

ASSERT [COLOUR BLOCK RED]
ASSERT [BIG BLOCK]

To decide whether a fact is present we have provided the test function ISQ, i.e.

ISQ [COLOUR BLOCK RED]

corresponds to

AMONGQ [COLOUR BLOCK RED] :DATABASE

3.1.4   Blocks World

Let us fill the database with some facts about a little world consisting of two blocks, both red, one big and one light (in weight). We must choose proper names for the blocks, say block1 and block2. The procedure SETUPWORLD will set this up for us:

```
TO SETUPWORLD
 10 CLEARDATABASE
 20 ASSERT [COLOUR BLOCK1 RED]
 30 ASSERT [COLOUR BLOCK2 RED]
 40 ASSERT [BIG BLOCK1]
 50 ASSERT [LIGHT BLOCK2]
END
```

3.1.5   Semantic Networks

These sequences of assertions are a little difficult to read, so, just as in the structural description problem, we can represent them as a network (these networks are variously called semantic networks, relational nets or graphs in the literature).

109

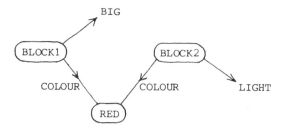

3.1.6 "Wh" Questions

Suppose we ask the question "What colour is block1?". What do we want the program to do? The program should look for a fact of the form: [COLOUR BLOCK ??] in the database, where ?? is any argument whatever, and returns as its result whatever ?? turns out to be (in this case RED).

We have already met something in LOGO that plays a similar role to ??, namely a LOGO variable, e.g. 'COL. We will use the same notation here and write [COLOUR BLOCK 'COL]. Originally COL will be unassigned, but during the course of answering the question it will be assigned a *value,* in this case RED. So we need a procedure, say FINDANY, which takes [COL] and [COLOUR BLOCK1 'COL] as arguments and returns RED as result, e.g.

    1: <u>PRINT FINDANY [COL] [COLOUR BLOCK1 'COL]</u>
    RED

This procedure will have to compare [COLOUR BLOCK1 'COL] against facts in the database, looking for one that *matches*, e.g. [COLOUR BLOCK1 RED]. Matching [COLOUR BLOCK1 'COL] against a fact consists of checking that the first and second items of the fact are COLOUR and BLOCK respectively and then assigning the third item to 'COL (i.e. MAKE 'COL 'RED). FINDANY will then return a list containing just :COL as its result. Similarly "What is coloured red?" could be translated into:

    FINDANY ['OBJ] [COLOUR 'OBJ RED]

Not just "Wh" questions (Which . . .?, What . . .?, Who . . .?, How . . .?, etc.) need to use variables. We might ask "Is anything red?". This naturally translates into:

    ISQ [COLOUR 'OBJ RED]

which should return TRUE if any fact in the database matches [COLOUR 'OBJ RED] (assigning the appropriate item to 'OBJ in the process).

3.1.7 Conjunctions

Suppose we ask "Is there something light and red?" or "What is light and red?". We clearly want these to succeed if both [LIGHT 'OBJ] and [COLOUR 'OBJ RED] match with facts in the database *and 'OBJ is assigned the same item in both matches.*

110

We will want both ISQ and FINDANY to take a list of descriptions as input. They will take the first description, [LIGHT 'OBJ], and compare it with facts from the database until they find one that matches (e.g. [LIGHT BLOCK2], when OBJ will be assigned the value BLOCK2). It will not do to continue the process by looking for something to match with [COLOUR 'OBJ RED], because OBJ may be assigned some other value than BLOCK2. Rather the database must now be searched for something to match with [COLOUR BLOCK2 RED], i.e. having found a value for OBJ, we replace all remaining occurrences of X by this value. We signify this to the procedures ISQ and FINDANY by putting a quote in front of any OBJ that is to be assigned a value, and a colon in front of any OBJ that is to be replaced by its value, i.e. we write

ISQ [[LIGHT 'OBJ] [COLOUR :OBJ RED]]
FINDANY [OBJ] [[LIGHT 'OBJ] [COLOUR :OBJ RED]]

To sum up:

'OBJECT means OBJECT is a variable that is to be assigned a value in the match, called an unbound variable.

:OBJECT means OBJECT is a variable that is to be replaced by the value of 'OBJECT, called a bound variable.

OBJECT means OBJECT is a *constant* that stands for itself, like RED, BLOCK2 or COLOUR.

3.1.8   Failure

If ISQ and FINDANY are working properly they should fail to find an object that is both big and light, i.e.

ISQ [[BIG 'OBJECT] [LIGHT :OBJECT]]

should return FALSE. (FINDANY returns [ ].) If we had written:

ISQ [[BIG 'OBJECT] [LIGHT 'OBJECT]]

then ISQ would have returned TRUE by assigning first BLOCK1 to OBJECT then BLOCK2 to OBJECT.

What we do with this output of FALSE when we get it depends on our conventions about the database. If we assume that the database has complete knowledge of the domain and that any fact not stored is false, then we will print NO. On the other hand, if we admit the possibility that there may be things it does not know, then we may either print I DO NOT KNOW or try to show that no big things are light so that we can print NO. Either of these conventions can be useful in different circumstances. We should always be clear which we intend.

3.1.9   Search

Suppose we had asked "Is anything red and light?", i.e.

ISQ [[COLOUR 'OBJ RED] [LIGHT :X]]

There is a good chance that the initial comparison of [COLOUR 'OBJ RED] with facts in the database would have assigned BLOCK1 to 'OBJ. Since [LIGHT BLOCK1] is not in the database, ISQ would have returned

FALSE unless it was able to back-up, undo its assignment of BLOCK1 to 'OBJ and assign BLOCK2 instead. Thus ISQ and FINDANY must be prepared to search for assignments to the variables that simultaneously satisfy all the descriptions. With a lot of conjunctions and a lot of variables in the input, ISQ and FINDANY may have to do a lot of searching before they succeed (or fail). We can represent these searches by a search tree, e.g.

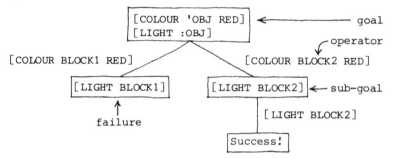

The nodes of the tree are goals or descriptions to be matched. The arcs or operators are facts from the database.

3.1.10 FINDALL

There may be several alternative assignments that lead to success. Both ISQ and FINDANY are satisfied with the first successful assignment they find, but there are occasions when we are interested in all the successful assignments. For instance, suppose we ask "Which things are red?". We would expect the answer "BLOCK1 and BLOCK2". A procedure FINDALL is provided in LOGO. Its syntax is similar to FINDANY, except that it returns a list of all successful assignments, e.g.

    FINDALL [THING] [COLOUR 'THING RED]

returns [[BLOCK1] [BLOCK2]] (N.B. not [BLOCK1 BLOCK2], for a reason that will soon be clear.)

3.1.11 Many Variables

Some questions may involve using several variables. For instance suppose we ask "What colour is the big object?". We would probably translate this into

    FINDANY [COL] [[BIG 'OBJ] [COLOUR :OBJ 'COL]]

which would return [RED]. In the process BLOCK1 would be assigned to OBJ and RED to COL. Only the value of COL is returned as the result of FINDANY, because [COL] was given as its first input. If we wanted the value of OBJ as well, for instance in answer to the question "What is the big object and what colour is it?", we would write

    FINDANY [OBJ COL] [[BIG 'OBJ] [COLOUR :OBJ 'COL]]

The result would be [BLOCK1 RED]. This explains why we have been using lists for the first input and the output of FINDANY and FINDALL.

FINDALL can also find the values of several variables. Consider the question "What are all the objects and their colours?". This translates into

    FINDALL [OBJ COL] [[COLOUR 'OBJ 'COL]]

The result of which is

    [[BLOCK1 RED] [BLOCK2 RED]]

which explains why the result of FINDALL is a list of lists.

3.1.12 Exercises

3.1.1. Write FINDANY in terms of ISQ (i.e. assume ISQ is provided, but FINDANY is not.)

3.1.2.

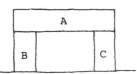

Represent the above picture as a procedure that makes a series of assertions in a database, e.g.

    TO ARCH1
      10 CLEARDATABASE
      20 ASSERT [ONEPARTIS GROUP A]   etc.

3.1.3. Translate the following questions into procedure calls that could access the database set up by ARCH1.

    Is A lying?
    What is lying?
    What is to the left of C?
    What is to the right of B?
    What things are supporting A?
    What is the arch constructed from?
    What are the supports of the arch?
    How many things are supporting A?

3.2   FORWARD AND BACKWARD DEDUCTION

3.2.1   Deduction

So far the knowledge in our database has been simple facts or assertions. Not all knowledge is of this type. Some knowledge is in the form of laws like "All big things are heavy" (people often use very rough generalisations). With this law, and the fact that block1 is big, we should be able to answer the question "Is block1 heavy?" in the affirmative. Perhaps the simplest way to ensure this would be to have a procedure which monitored all new additions to the database. Whenever a fact of the form [BIG 'X] was asserted this procedure would deduce [HEAVY :X] and add this to the database. We can add such a procedure to our world model using the procedure ASSERT. Let us edit the procedure SETUPWORLD

113

and add line
    15 ASSERT [IMPLIES [BIG 'X] [HEAVY :X]]
You should read this law "The fact that X is big implies the fact that X is heavy". The first description, [BIG 'X], is called the *antecedent* and the second, [HEAVY :X], is called the *consequent*. The procedure works by matching the antecedent against all incoming assertions. If a match succeeds the procedure asserts the consequent, replacing any variables with their assigned values. Such a procedure is sometimes called an "antecedent theorem", an "if asserted method", or a "demon", and the kind of deduction it does is variously called "forwards deduction", "forwards chaining", "bottom-up reasoning" or "hypotheses-driven deduction".

We should be sure to add such "demons" before asserting any facts, because they will only deduce consequences of facts asserted after they themselves have been asserted. Thus when line 40, which is
    40 ASSERT [BIG BLOCK1]
is executed, our demon will set to work and ASSERT [HEAVY BLOCK1]. (If line 40 were line 13, our demon would do nothing.) Now if we ask
    ISQ [HEAVY BLOCK1]
we will get the result TRUE.

3.2.2   Problems with Forwards Deduction
Unfortunately it is not always convenient to draw all possible conclusions from the things we assert. Typically an already large database will become cluttered with facts we may never need to know. Imagine, for instance, what would happen to our database if every time we asserted [HUMAN X], we deduced [HAS X HEART], [HAS X HEAD], [HAS X HAIR], [HAS X LUNG], etc. Any new assertion would lead to an explosion of deductions, and the database would become so full that we would find it increasingly hard to retrieve facts.

The situation is worse because some demons lead to a call of themselves. Consider "Every human has a human mother". If we asserted [HUMAN JANE1] we would deduce and assert [MOTHER JANE2 MUM1] and [HUMAN MUM1] where MUM1 was a new constant. This would lead to a new deduction [HUMAN MUM2] and so ad infinitum. Clearly some laws need to be kept for use only when needed.

3.2.3   Functions
In the previous example we cheated a bit. Each application of the law "Every human has a human mother", introduces a new constant, (e.g. MUM1, MUM2, . . .,etc.). But we have not yet discussed a mechanism for introducing new constants. We now correct this omission.

A first approximation might be to include a new constant in the statement of the laws, e.g.

[IMPLIES [HUMAN 'X] [HUMAN MUM]]
[IMPLIES [HUMAN 'X] [MOTHER :X MUM]]
This would work for the first application of the law to, say, [HUMAN
JANE] producing [HUMAN MUM] and [MOTHER JANE MUM], but the
second application (to [HUMAN MUM]) would produce [HUMAN MUM]
and [MOTHER MUM MUM], which would be silly. Clearly the new
constant should *depend on* the particular value of X at the time the law is
called. To deal with this problem we represent the new constant by
something like an explicit LOGO procedure call using the function name
MUMOF and taking :X as argument. So MUM1 will be represented by [
MUMOF JANE] and MUM2 by [MUMOF [MUMOF JANE]]. The law
"Every human has a human mother" can now be represented as
    [IMPLIES [HUMAN 'X] [HUMAN [MUMOF :X]]]
together with
    [IMPLIES [HUMAN 'X] [MOTHER [MUMOF :X]]]

Exercise 3.2.1. Represent the law "Every human has a head".

3.2.4   Backwards Deduction
What we need is a law that will only be invoked when it is needed to
answer some question, e.g. when we ask ISQ [HEAVY BLOCK1] it
changes the question to ISQ [BIG BLOCK1], which returns TRUE. But [
HEAVY BLOCK1] is *never* asserted. In LOGO we store such a law by
typing
    ASSERT [TOINFER [HEAVY 'X] [BIG :X]]
Read this law "To infer that X is heavy, deduce that X is big". ISQ [
HEAVY BLOCK1] first checks to see if [HEAVY BLOCK1] is in the
database. If not, it then checks in a database of laws to see if any are
relevant. This means matching the consequent of the law against the
current goal (e.g. [HEAVY 'X] against [HEAVY BLOCK1]). Then the
current goal is replaced by the antecedent of the law (with any assigned
variables replaced by their values), e.g. ISQ [HEAVY BLOCK1] is replaced
by ISQ [BIG BLOCK1].

Such laws are variously called "consequent theorems" or "if needed
methods", and the kind of deductions they do are called "backwards
deduction", "backwards chaining", "top-down reasoning" or "goal-
directed deduction".

We will want to allow the antecedent of our TOINFER laws to consist of
several descriptions, e.g.
    [TOINFER [METAL 'X] [HEAVY :X] [COLOUR :X GREY]]
This will cause no problems, since ISQ, etc., can handle conjunctions of
goals.

3.2.5   Search Again
Just as it was possible to make the wrong assignments to variables and
have to back-up, it is possible to apply the wrong law and have to back-up.

Suppose we edit SETUPWORLD to have two TOINFER laws, corresponding to "All metal things are heavy", and "All big things are heavy", i.e.

```
TO SETUPWORLD
  10 CLEARDATABASE
  13 ASSERT [TOINFER [HEAVY 'THING] [BIG :THING]]
  15 ASSERT [TOINFER [HEAVY 'THING] [METAL :THING]]
  20 ASSERT [COLOUR BLOCK1 RED]
  30 ASSERT [COLOUR BLOCK2 RED]
  40 ASSERT [BIG BLOCK1]
  50 ASSERT [LIGHT BLOCK2]
END
```

If we ask ISQ [HEAVY BLOCK1] in our current INFERENCE system the first law, "all metal things are heavy", will be used first and it will call ISQ [METAL BLOCK1]. This will fail, so if the original goal is not to fail, ISQ must be prepared to back up and try the second law.

We can represent the search by a tree:

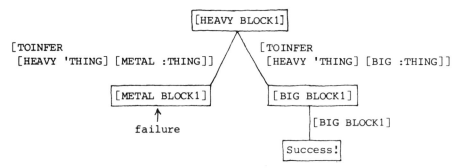

The arcs can now represent laws or facts from the database.

Even these TOINFER laws do not prevent explosions. For instance, suppose we added the law:

> [TOINFER [ON 'X 'X] [ON :X 'Y] [ON :Y :Z]]

corresponding to: if one block is on top of another and a third is on top of that, then the top block is on top of the bottom block. Suppose we now ask ISQ [ON BLOCK1 BLOCK2]. Since this is not in the database the law will be invoked and

> ISQ [[ON BLOCK1 'Y] [ON :Y BLOCK2]]

will be called. This will call

> ISQ [[ON BLOCK1 'Y1] [ON :Y1 'Y] [ON :Y BLOCK2]]

and so, ad infinitum.

3.2.6   Predicate Calculus

Those of you familiar with predicate calculus will find all this rather familiar. In fact this is a procedural version of a subset of predicate calculus. For that reason you will sometimes see programs like this referred to as "inference systems" or "theorem provers".

3.2.7 Logical Arguments

We can get the program to perform most of the logical deductions that you find in the literature. For instance, consider:

All Humans are Fallible
Turing is human
Socrates is human
Socrates is Greek

Who is a fallible Greek?

translate this into

ASSERT [TOINFER [FALLIBLE 'X] [HUMAN :X]]
ASSERT [HUMAN TURING]
ASSERT [HUMAN SOCRATES]
ASSERT [GREEK SOCRATES]
FINDANY [X] [[FALLIBLE 'X] [GREEK :X]]

to get [SOCRATES].

3.2.8 Exercises

3.2.2. Try the above translation with:

All men are mortal
Socrates is a man

Is Socrates mortal?

Ontology. We have met a very limited class of entities in this simple descriptive language, i.e. just:

Physical objects like block1, block2
Properties like red
Relations between them like colour, big
Assertions like [COLOUR BLOCK1 RED]
Laws like [IMPLIES [BIG 'X] [HEAVY :X]]

To conduct reasonable conversation we will have to represent: places; times; events; actions; substances, etc.

3.2.3. (a) Using the LOGO inference system translate each of the following sentences into a procedure call corresponding to its meaning:

The Pope is good
John Wayne is good
John Wayne is courageous
Anyone who is good and courageous is a hero

Who is a hero?

(b) Suppose the translations of the sentences above the line were used to set up a database, and the translation of the sentence below the line were

used to interrogate that database. Draw the search tree of that
interrogation.

3.2.4. If X is a parent of Y and Z is a sister of X then Z is an aunt of Y.
If X is a parent of Y and X is an aunt of Z then Y is a cousin of Z.
>   A mother or a father is a parent
>   Mary is the mother of John
>   Fred is the father of Jane
>   Mary is the sister of Fred
>   Daisy is the wife of Fred
>   ─────────────────────────────

>   Who is the cousin of Jane?
Draw the search tree of the above.

3.2.5. What additional laws do you need to answer "Who is the aunt of
John?"

3.2.6.

Using the LOGO INFERENCE system:
(a) Give a partial symbolic description of the above drawing of a face
sufficient to answer "yes" to the following questions, by direct database
lookup:
>   Is the mouth in the lower portion of the face?
>   Is the left eye in the upper portion of the face?
>   Is the nose in the centre of the face?
(b) In addition represent the laws that:
>   Anything in the centre of the face is also in the middle
>   portion.
>   Anything in the middle portion of something is always above
>   anything in the lower portion.
>   Anything in the upper portion of something is always above
>   anything in the middle portion.
(c) Represent the question:
>   Is the nose above the mouth?
Draw the complete search tree of its interrogation of the database.
(d) In addition represent the law:
>   To infer that x is above y
>   show that x is above z and z is above y.
and the question:
>   Is the mouth above the nose?
Draw some of the search tree of this interrogation. What problem arises?

118

How might it be overcome? Does your solution involve changing the LOGO INFERENCE system?

3.2.9 Recommended Reading

B. Raphael, (1964) A computer program which "understands", in *AFIPS Conference Proceedings* Vol.26, part 1, pp.577-99.

G.J. Sussman, T. Winograd & E. Charniak (1972) *Micro-Planner Reference Manual*. MIT AI Memo 203A. (Read lightly, not attempting to learn Microplanner.)

3.3 SUMMARY OF THE LOGO INFERENCE PACKAGE

3.3.1 Access

The INFERENCE system consists of a number of procedures available as a file in NEWLOGO. It provides facilities for making a database, retrieving from it and doing forward and backward inference.

3.3.2 Patterns

A pattern is a list of pattern elements or patterns. A pattern element is either
(a) A constant, i.e. a word or number
(b) A quoted variable, i.e. a quote followed by a variable name
(c) A colon variable, i.e. a colon followed by a variable name.
Examples of patterns:

    [LIKES JOE FOOD]
    [LIKES JOE 'XX]
    [NEAR 'XX :CURRENT]
    [LIKES JOE [DAUGHTEROF :XX]]
    [[LIKES JOE 'XX] [AVAILABLE :XX]]

A pattern is *simple* if its first is a pattern element, otherwise it is *compound*. Compound patterns are understood as conjunctions. (All but the last pattern above are simple.)

3.3.3 Procedures

Notation: Pat = pattern, T = truthvalue, L = list, Ll = list of lists, Vl = list of variables.

CLEARDATABASE	Clears the database.
ASSERT simple-pat	Adds pattern to database, any colon variables take their current values.

      Example: ASSERT [COLOUR RED :OBJ]

ISQ Pat → T	Tests whether pattern matches one in database. A quoted variable is assigned a value by the matching if possible. Colon variables take their current values whether assigned by MAKE or by matching.

New values are available after ISQ is finished. For a compound pattern each component is matched in succession, depth first.

Example: ISQ [[BIG 'XX] [BAD :XX]]

FINDANY VI Pat → L

The pattern is matched against the database; result is the list of subsequent values of the variables named in VI.

Example: FINDANY [XX] [BIG 'XX]

FINDALL VI Pat → LI

Like FINDANY, but finds all possible ways of matching the pattern with the database; result is the list of all possible lists of subsequent values of the variables named in VI.

3.3.4 Rules

ASSERT can also be used with a rule as argument. Rules use antecedents and consequents, which are simple patterns. There are two kinds of rules:

[IMPLIES antecedent consequent]
subsequently, when any pattern which matches the antecedent is asserted the consequent is also asserted (with the then current values of the variables, including assignments to variable while matching the antecedent).
Example: ASSERT [IMPLIES [STUDENT 'X] [INDUSTRIOUS :X]]

[TOINFER consequent antecedent1 antecedent2 . . .]
whenever the system tries to match some pattern of the same form as the consequent it can instead try to match the pattern(s) defined by the antecedent(s) (all of them conjunctively).
Example: ASSERT [TOINFER [MAN 'X] [MALE :X] [HUMAN :X]]

Restrictions.
1. No colon variables in the consequent of a TOINFER rule.
2. Variables occurring in the rules must not clash with any variables that appear in non-rule patterns. Adopt a convention like X,Y,Z only for rule-variables.

3.3.5 Negation

In a compound pattern any component after the first may be negated by [NOT [. . .]], e.g.
ISQ [[RED 'X] [NOT [SMALL :X]]].

4. VISUAL PERCEPTION

To expose some of the themes that arise when programming a computer to "see", we first consider how we ourselves might perceive simple drawings. Just as with problem solving, perceptual processes involve the formation and use of descriptions.

4.1 FORMING STRUCTURAL DESCRIPTIONS

4.1.1 Introduction

Task. How could we get a sensible description of the following figure?

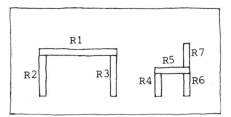

We would prefer "a chair near a table" to "5 vertical rectangles and 2 horizontal rectangles". Let us look again at the *process of achieving a symbolic description* of a picture we went through in the analogy lectures.

(a) We need to achieve uniformity of predicates. If several descriptions are possible, e.g. "a triangle inside a square", or "a square surrounding a triangle", we arbitrarily choose a predicate, say, "inside" and then stick to it, to enable rigorous comparison between descriptions.

(b) To avoid ambiguity, we express the elements involved in the relationship in a fixed order. [inside triangle square] must be distinguished systematically from [inside square triangle].

(c) We ignore superfluous words such as "with", "a", "it".

(d) In cases where we have two objects of the same shape, we distinguish them in the obvious way: triangle1, triangle2.

(e) We list the objects in the figure, explicitly, and our descriptions take the form:

⟨set of objects in figure⟩ ⟨set of relationships in figure⟩

4.1.2 Relations

Now consider our task figure. For convenience we abbreviate "rectangle" to "R", and the set of objects in the figure is [R1 R2 R3 R4 R5 R6 R7]. We could describe the spatial relationship between R1 and R2 using "above", "below", "under" or "on". "On" includes the idea of touching and suits our purposes best. Thus:

[on R1 R2] [on R1 R3] [on R5 R4] [on R5 R6] [on R7 R5]
We capture the different orientations thus:
[standing R2] [standing R3] [standing R4] [standing R6]
[standing R7] [lying R1] [lying R5]
Rather a lot of expressions are accumulating and we have not yet
expressed half the things we need to say about the picture. We need ways
of making it easier to see what is going on. Notice the threefold mention of
R1 — three facts about R1 have been asserted. We have a way of
grouping references to the same object by creating a node to represent the
object and using directed arrows to represent the relationships it has with
other objects.

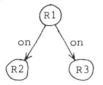

The third fact about R1 [lying R1] tells us about a property of R1 rather
than how it is related to other objects. We treat properties as one-place
relationships, in that the description of the property is attached to an
arrow from the node:

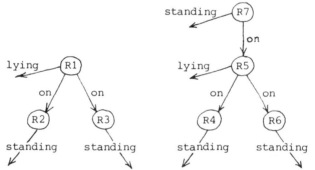

There are two interesting consequences of this representation:
  1. The objects form two clusters by virtue of their relations:
     group 1 is [R1 R2 R3], and group 2 is [R4 R5 R6 R7].
  2. We can readily see *patterns of relations*: "a lying object on two
     standing objects" is a pattern that occurs in each cluster, and
     suggests a derived predicate: "is supported by"
How does the first point, the grouping of objects, help us in our task? Let
us proceed with the business of adding relations to our network, e.g. R2 is
to the left of R3; R6 is to the right of R4. We choose, arbitrarily, "leftof" as
the canonical predicate and insert.

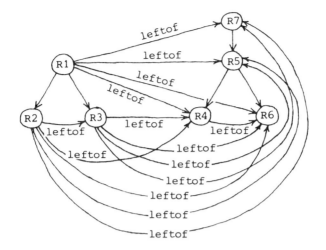

It is much more convenient to group the relations:

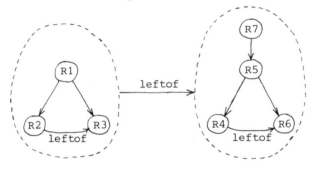

[leftof group1 group2] [leftof R2 R3] [leftof R4 R6]

But we need a way to refer to the dotted circles, and what do we mean by these circles anyway? We make explicit the relationship "one-part-is":

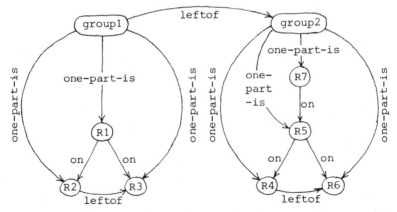

Our representation now reflects the grouping process explicitly and so enables our "seeing more easily".

4.1.3 More About Relations

1. Consider again the problem of choosing predicates: [inside triangle rectangle] has no intrinsic superiority over [outside rectangle triangle]. We could introduce explicitly the fact that the two are equivalent by using two arrows each time the relationship occurred in the network:

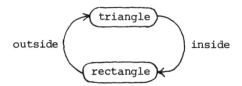

Alternatively, and more economically, we can provide this information once and for all in the form of an *inverse rule:*

> if obj1 inside obj2 then obj2 outside obj1. More generally, if one relation REL1 is the inverse of another relation REL2 then if [REL1 OBJ1 OBJ2] then [REL2 OBJ2 OBJ1].

Some relations, like "next to" or "near", are symmetrical and can be represented by a two-way arrow

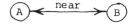

which would be equivalent to asserting both [near A B] & [near B A].

2. How about the relationship between R7 and R6 in the task picture? We have [on R7 R5] and [on R5 R6], and "on" is a particular kind of relation that is transitive. We could have a *transitive rule* of the form:

> If obj1 on obj2, and obj 2 on obj3, then obj1 on obj3.

Again, more generally, if a relation REL1 is transitive then

> if [REL1 OBJ1 OBJ2] and [REL1 OBJ2 OBJ3] then [REL1 OBJ1 OBJ3].

However, we cannot pursue this indefinitely for some relations, otherwise we could prove, say, that everything is near everything else. "Being near to" seems to include the idea of "distance away from" relative to some activity, i.e. near enough to be affected by.

3. In network terms, we have traversed two directed arrows in order to get [on R7 R6]; in both cases, the directed arrow had the label "on". In the same way, two successive arrows labelled "father-of" could give us "grandfather-of". We need not restrict ourselves to successive arrows having the same label. Thus "aunt-of" could be "mother-of" followed by "sister-of".

4. Problems arise in assigning predicates:
(a) Recall "is-supported-by" in the task figure, derived from grouping "one lying rectangle on two standing rectangles".

But what about this figure?

(b) Consider "leftof" and "above" in the following:

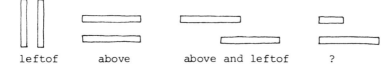

leftof   above   above and leftof   ?

(c) The cube is rightof the arch in the picture, but, in the real world scene that this represents, the cube is leftof the archway.

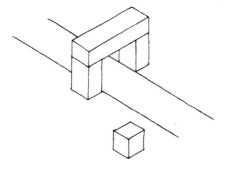

This is a matter of frame of reference in terms of which the relations are defined. The cube is to the left of the archway as seen from *the point of view* of someone in the right-hand part of our picture.

4.1.4 Point of View

Consider the task figure again. All the relations used in the description make an assumption about the figure, namely that we are looking at a *side view* of some scene and that, for example, points in the top part of the picture correspond to higher points in the scene than do those in the lower part of the picture.

Now let us assume that the picture represents an aerial view of some scene. What happens to our description?

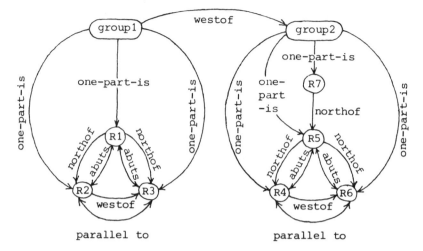

parallel to   parallel to

Notice that we have some symmetric relations, some transitive relations, and some inverse relations, and the same general rules already developed for these will hold.

A crucially important set of remarks. How difficult was it for you to see the picture as an aerial view? The familiar arrangement of parts triggers concepts we already have, i.e. it evokes the labels "table" and "chair" for group1 and group2 respectively. We can say it imposes the viewpoint. We see the three rectangles R1, R2 and R3 as a table. Parts take their names from the wholes they are seen to belong to, e.g. R1 becomes "table-top". No such ready interpretation emerges for an aerial view.

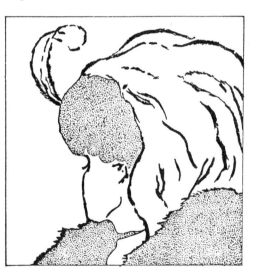

Rubin's figure   Boring's figure

126

We find that a global decision, such as viewpoint assignment, can determine which predicates will be included in the description.

Sometimes there are two equally strong possible interpretations. The so-called ambiguous figures that abound in the psychological literature have just this property, e.g. the Rubin figure, which can be seen sometimes as a vase and sometimes as two faces; or Boring's figure, which can be seen as a young girl or an old woman (see Gregory 1970).

We try out our method of forming structural descriptions on some standard displays used by Gestalt psychologists.

4.1.5   Grouping

Example (a). Consider this display of five vertical lines:

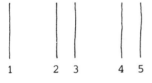

Our description might look like this:

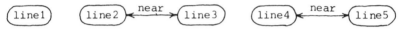

We could put in "parallel-to". But since each line is parallel to every other line, such a tag would only load up our description without providing any evidence for grouping. Similarly, properties like "vertical" and "straight" would occur attached to every node and would not affect our bias to form groups on the basis of a shared relation "near" as follows:

> group 1: line2 and line3 (abbreviate L2 & L3)
> group 2: L4 and L5
> group 3: L1

Example (b). Now we add four lines to our display to get:

The new feature is that certain lines are connected.

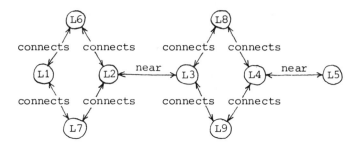

Again three groups fall out quite naturally on the basis of closed rings of links, thus:

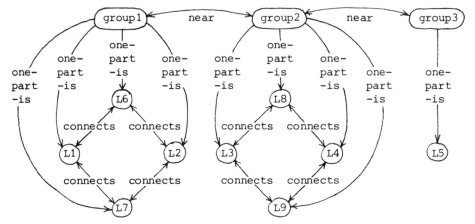

Notice how lines 2 and 3 have changed allegiance, and now *belong to* different groups. The nodes in groups 1 and 2 formed closed rings. To keep the skeleton of our description clear, we will not follow through the details of adding features, like "parallel-to" and "at-right-angles-to", necessary to provide the basis for *identifying* groups 1 and 2 as rectangles. Instead we look at example (c):

$$
\begin{bmatrix} 6 \\ 1 \\ 7 \end{bmatrix}
\begin{bmatrix} 8 \\ 2 \\ 9 \end{bmatrix}
\begin{bmatrix} 10 \\ 3 \\ 11 \end{bmatrix}
\begin{bmatrix} 12 \\ 4 \\ 13 \end{bmatrix}
\begin{matrix} \\ 5 \\ \end{matrix}
$$

This yields the following:

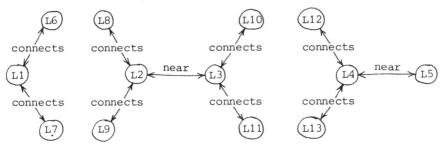

At first blush, we might seem to be back to the situation of example (a) with the same three groups. However by noticing the collinearity of the hanging lines 6 and 8, 7 and 9, 10 and 12, 11 and 13, we form a *conceptual closure* of the shape thus:

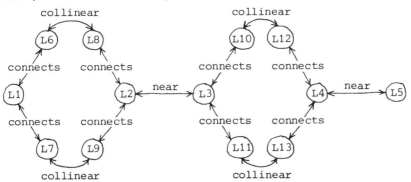

Now we are in situation (b). Indeed, if we had a description of the rectangles in (b) stored away, we could imagine that finding the "hook" [(L6-L1-L7) could invoke the stored description or model of a rectangle, i.e. trigger the expectation of a rectangle, and lead to an active search for the rest of the rectangle. More of this later.

Notice, however, that there is a bug in our recipe. Since we have granted our system the ability to notice collinearity in situation (c), we should have noticed the collinear lines in situation (b). When we allow this, we find that, because this relation involves only some nodes, it seriously affects our grouping. The description of situation (b) should have been:

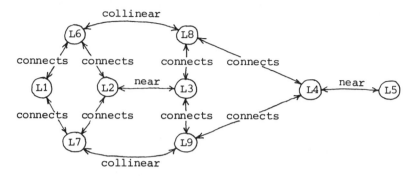

Now we can no longer claim that two groups fall out naturally. There is more than one way of extracting groups from this network. We need to have a way of ordering our grouping criteria. For example, if there are two possible closed rings to which any one node can belong, then choose the ring formed by relations of the same sort, or as nearly the same sort as possible. So, in our example, 6-1-7-2 are linked by a ring of "connects" and are preferred as a group to 6-2-3-8, which are linked by a diverse collection of relations.

Now we have to decide what to do about "collinear". One of the reasons for grouping is to form entities that at a higher level can themselves behave as primitive elements in a relation, e.g. group1 near group2. However, we would still want to retain the ability to relate part of one group to either the whole of another group, or to part of another group.

Consider again the task figure of section 4.1.1. We observe that the *bottom* lines of the two rectangles forming the "chair" are collinear, and that the same goes for the *bottom* lines of the rectangles forming the "table". Furthermore all these lines are collinear, i.e. part of part of the "chair" group is collinear with part of part of the "table" group, and we can, and probably do, use this as evidence of a support plane, the "floor".

Example (d). What do you see in this display?

At this point, I start seeing the letter E in several places. Can we get this description with the rules we have been using so far? Try this example yourselves. (Suggestion: There is a much deeper bug in our method, which was hinted at earlier by the remark that hooks of the form ⌐ might invoke the stored description or model of a rectangle.)

There is more to structuring a picture than is given directly in the picture.

4.1.6   The Relation "Belonging-to"

We now look at the following ambiguous figure, where P1 to P8 are sectors or pie slices, either *ribbed* (P1) or *striped* (P2), L1 to L8 are the shared lines separating P1-8, and R1 and R2 are examples of arcs.

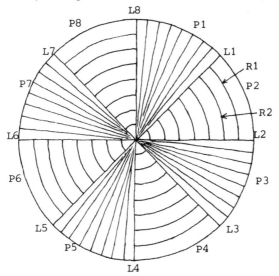

This can be seen either as a cross of four ribbed pie slices on a background disc of concentric circles, a target; or as a cross of striped pie slices on a background disc of radiating spikes. In the former case, the arcs are seen as the visible parts of complete circles; in the latter they are seen as true arcs.

We form a description, which reflects the facts that: (a) the areas cluster into two groups by virtue of their surface markings; and (b) in each group the members are identical to one another. We describe a typical group, and note the members.

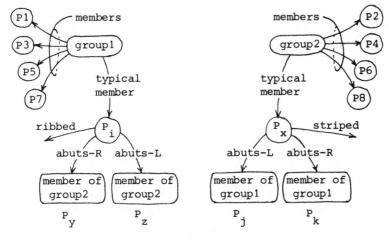

But what are we to do with lines 1-8? Consider L1 and the areas directly separated by it, i.e. P1 or P2. We could see L1 as belonging either to P1, or to P2, or to both. Let us follow through the consequences of each choice.

1. Suppose we choose to assign L1 as the boundary of P1. This leads us to expect L8 to form the other boundary of P1, which then achieves the status of a closed figure.

Rule: Try to group lines into closed figures.

Thus, P2 and P8 become background. If P1 is to remain a typical member of our group1, then we are led to postulate boundaries for all the other members of the group in the same way; the group now consists of four pie slices joined at the centre. Group2 consists of four bits of background, and we are likely to see them as one area patchily occluded by the cross of closed figures, by noticing that the arcs in these areas form matching sets of T-junctions with the figure boundaries:

Again we form *conceptual closures*, as we did in the earlier rectangle display, and see the arcs as passing under the figure to complete the circles. Our description now looks like this:

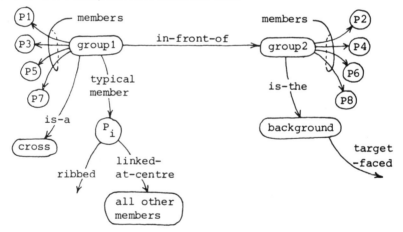

2. Suppose we choose to assign L1 to P2. Applying our closure rule, we get L2 belonging to P2 as well, to form a closed figure. The consequence of this spreads through the display, this time turning all group2 areas into closed figures joined at the centre to form a cross. Now we hallucinate radial spikes behind the figure. The description follows the previous pattern.

132

3. If we try to assign L1 to both P1 and P2, we run into difficulties. What is involved is conceptually splitting each line, and inhibiting the T-junction effect, in order to see a flat surface of alternately ribbed and striped figures. We just don't seem to do this very readily.

More examples of how context influences the structural descriptions being constructed are given in the figures at the end of this section.

In Summary. We have explored, in a tentative way, some of the methods we as human observers use to group lines into shapes into coherent structures. Grouping imposes an organisation on the figure, structures it into a meaningful whole.

Points to Notice.
1. Small local changes in the display can produce large global effects, e.g. by influencing the choice of grouping rule. We saw how lines changed their allegiance, i.e. what they are seen as *belonging to*, by virtue of changes elsewhere in the picture.

2. Grouping elements into larger units is part of an "effort after meaning", in which stored experience plays an important role.

3. We can systematically debug the rules we think we are using by spelling them out and then trying them out on a new display. It is very likely that you can find more bugs in the above account. That is good. It is a virtue of the methodology we are using that we can gradually refine our recipes by exposing them to new cases. The best way to find bugs that elude the kind of hand-testing we have been doing is to program up the rules and run the program on a set of examples. An issue that arises when we write such a program is the need to specify the stock of possible kinds of links that can appear in the descriptions.

4.   Choosing good examples is an important part of the story.

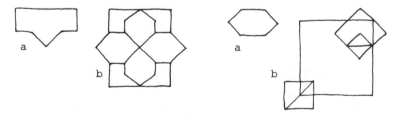

Try to find shape a in figure b in each case
(after Gottschaldt 1926).

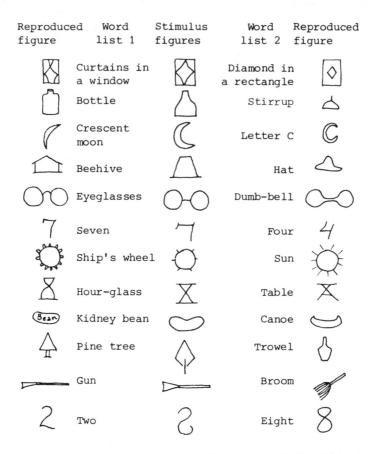

Reproduced figure	Word list 1	Stimulus figures	Word list 2	Reproduced figure
	Curtains in a window		Diamond in a rectangle	
	Bottle		Stirrup	
	Crescent moon		Letter C	
	Beehive		Hat	
	Eyeglasses		Dumb-bell	
	Seven		Four	
	Ship's wheel		Sun	
	Hour-glass		Table	
	Kidney bean		Canoe	
	Pine tree		Trowel	
	Gun		Broom	
	Two		Eight	

Ambiguous figures (after Carmichael et al.). Subjects were shown the series of stimulus figures in the central column, each of which could represent two things. As each figure was shown, names from list 1 were read out to one group; alternative names for each figure from list 2 were read out to another group. The two groups were then asked to draw what they had seen as accurately as possible.

4.1.7 References

F.C. Bartlett (1932) *Remembering*. Cambridge: University Press. This is a lovely book. It is the source of the notion of "effort after meaning" mentioned above. It provides a rich source of evidence for what will emerge as a central theme of these lectures, viz. the constructive nature of perceptual processes.

L. Carmichael *et al.* in *J. Exp. Psychol. 15*, 80.

K. Gottschaldt (1926) in *Experiments in Visual Perception* (ed. M.D. Vernon). Penguin Books.

R.L. Gregory (1970). *The Intelligent Eye.* New York: McGraw-Hill. (Especially the sections on ambiguous figures and illusions.)

Read about the "Gestalt laws of organisation" in the psychology text-book of your choice (e.g. J.E. Hochberg (1964) *Perception*, pp. 85-8, in the Foundations of Modern Psychology series, Prentice-Hall, N.J.) and compare them with the ideas presented here.

M. Wertheimer (1961) *Productive Thinking.* Tavistock Publications. An inspired treatise on the role of perceptual organisation in problem solving.

4.2 USING STRUCTURAL DESCRIPTIONS

4.2.1 Two-Dimension Drawings of Planar Solids

The three faces of a cube meet at a trihedral vertex. In a 2D drawing of a cube, the three edges forming such a vertex are represented by the junction of lines, forming either:

(a) a FORK junction: J7

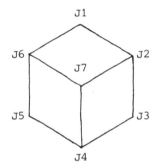

(b) an ARROW junction: J2 J4 J6

(one of three angles at junction$>180°$), or

(c) an ELL junction: J1 J3 J5

The number of visible faces at each vertex decides what the junction will look like:

    3 visible faces→a FORK junction in the picture

    2 visible faces→an ARROW junction in the picture

    1 visible face→an ELL junction in the picture

Going the other way, given a 2D representation of a collection of planar solids, we can decide which regions belong to which solids using rules, e.g.

(a) The FORK rule links all three regions surrounding a junction

(b) The ARROW rule links two of the regions contributing to the junction

For example: To segment an arch into its component parts, plant links wherever an arrow or a fork occurs.

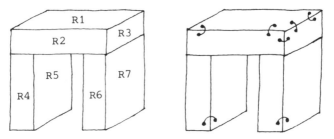

The regions can be grouped on the basis of these links into three groups

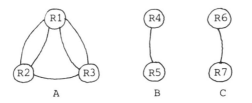

A   B   C

A segmentation process using rules like these forms the basis of a computer program written by Adolpho Guzman at MIT in 1968. This will be discussed in detail later.

4.2.2   Learning Structural Descriptions

We explore the problem of learning, using and extending the ideas of building and manipulating descriptions that we have developed so far. We will follow through a process of description refinement in response to a judiciously selected *training sequence*. This is a simple-minded version of a well-known program written by Pat Winston at MIT, and figure 4.1 a-d shows the sequence of exhibits he used to "teach" the concept of an ARCH.

Preliminary Account. The world consists of children's building blocks, brick-shaped or wedge-shaped, out of which the arches (and other simple structures) are built.

The idea is to set up an *Initial Description* of the first, good example of the concept, and then to gradually debug this description in the light of subsequent exhibits. The point of the exercise is to show the value of exhibiting something that is nearly an example but just fails to be so because of the presence or absence of only a few features: the *near miss*.

The process rests on comparing descriptions, a technique we used in the analogy problems. We build a description, for example, of the near miss, and compare it to the one we already have of a good example. The difference between the two tells us precisely why this new thing didn't

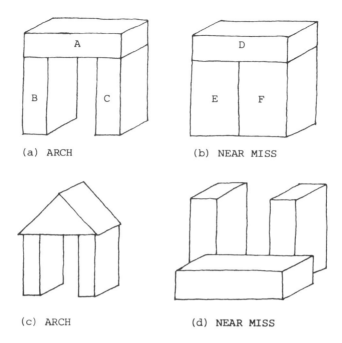

(a) ARCH   (b) NEAR MISS

(c) ARCH   (d) NEAR MISS

Figure 4.1. The concept of an arch.

make it: it highlights which of the features in our first (model) description are just not allowed to be missing. We enrich our description by adding this information about *mandatory* features of the concept.

Information comes too from new good examples: if this new thing is still a goodie and yet isn't the same as our standard good example with which we have compared it, then we need to loosen up our description to cover this new case.

Initial Descriptions. Consider figure 4.1a. We see that the arch consists of three bricks, one lying on and supported by the other two standing ones. This step is achieved in Winston's program by (a) using the segmentation program of Guzman mentioned above, and (b) using algorithms for determining relations like LEFTOF, ABOVE, SUPPORT, IN-FRONTOF. Our initial description would look like this:

137

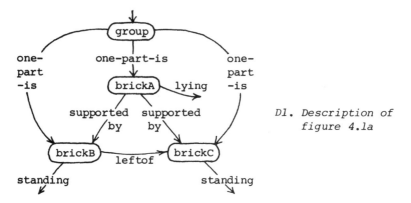

D1. *Description of figure 4.1a*

Note that the node labelled "group" is the distinguished entry node into the description. We set this description up as our mark 1 model of the concept of an arch.

Next we build up a description of figure 4.1b.

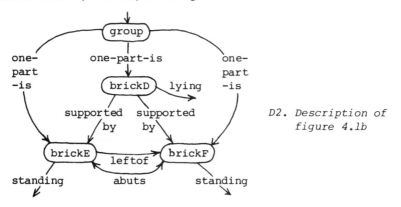

D2. *Description of figure 4.1b*

Comparing Descriptions. In each case we have a group of three bricks; we can match up the lying bricks (A, D) as each is supported by two other standing bricks. In each case, one of these standing bricks (B, E) is to the leftof of the other (C, F). But there is an extra "abuts" arrow connecting bricks E and F, and we conclude that this is the unwanted feature in D2 that makes it a non-example.

Let us spell out in greater detail how we might perform this comparison. The process involves matching the nodes in the two networks and deciding which nodes to pair up. We note that any node or arrow may be present in one description and not in the other.

(a) We start at the entry nodes. In each case we find a node with three arrows leaving it. Furthermore the arrows have the same labels. We decide to pair up these nodes as a *matched pair*.

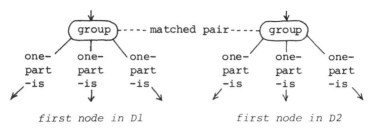

first node in D1   first node in D2

(b) We then follow any one of the arrows out of the D1 member of the linked pair, locate the node it connects to (the daughter node) and examine this node. For example, suppose we choose the arrow going to brick A. This node has three arcs leaving it and none coming in (apart from the one we arrived on). We compare this with each of the nodes one arrow along in D2 to find the one that is most similar. Brick E has three entering and two exit arrows while brick F has four coming in and one leaving. Brick D is the obvious winner because it has the same number of arrows as our criteria node, and moreover these have labels that match up exactly with those of the criteria nodes, so we link these nodes as follows:

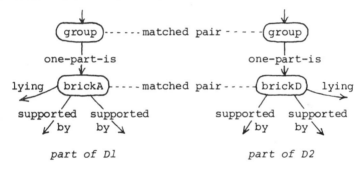

part of D1   part of D2

(c) Now we repeat step (b) for each of the other daughter nodes of "group" in D1, attempting in each case to find a node in D2 that best matches it.

For brick B, the comparison looks like this:

	incoming arrows	outgoing arrows
Brick B	supported by	standing; leftof
Brick E	supported by; abuts	standing; leftof
Brick F	supported by; leftof; abuts	standing

What do we need to do to brick E so that it will exactly match brick B?— remove the relations "abuts". What do we need to do to brick F so that it will exactly match brick B? — remove the relation "abuts" and invert the relation "leftof". The first change involves fewer steps than does the second, and we choose brick E as the pair to link to brick B, under the transformation [remove "abuts"]. The same transformation converts brick F into an exact match of brick C, and now our comparison is complete.

139

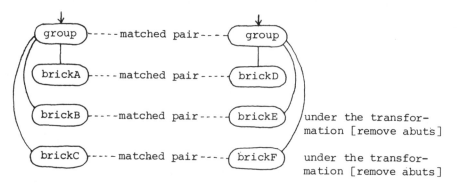

under the transfor-
mation [remove abuts]

under the transfor-
mation [remove abuts]

Now we have located the bug in figure 4.1b, and can describe it in terms of the transformation we had to make in order to get a match. Another way of saying this, is that [remove "abuts"] describes the mismatch. The way to ensure that we get a match in the first place is not to allow an "abuts" relation. We capture the information gained from analysing this bug by recording on our model a "must-not-have" note.

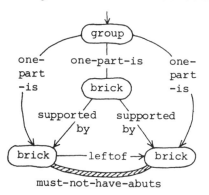

We have marked the "must-not-have" note using a crosshatched link. This is to emphasise its meta-comment nature, and to distinguish it from arrows that will participate directly in the matching.

Exercise 4.2.1. Repeat the process on figures 4.1c and d, omitting the detail in steps a-c above. Form descriptions of the figures, compare the new description with the model, find the mismatch by inspection, and update the model appropriately.

4.2.3   References

P.H. Winston (1970) Learning structural descriptions from examples. PhD thesis, AI technical report 231, MIT. See also chapter 5 in *The Psychology of Computer Vision* (ed. P.H. Winston), McGraw-Hill 1972. This gives more details of the processes discussed in this section, using a whole range of training sequences.

4.3 MACHINE PERCEPTION

4.3.1 Introduction
We are interested in studying machine vision for several reasons:
1. To increase understanding of human perception.
2. To increase understanding of intelligence: perception is a rich area in which to study knowledge-based reasoning.
3. Many connections with other branches of AI, e.g. perceptual strategies in game playing.
4. Application possibilities, e.g. the designing of industrial robots.

Kinds of Tasks.
1. Robot perception of real world scenes of simple objects
   (a) recognition of objects as a task in itself, e.g. the first set of Edinburgh robot programs recognised spectacles, cups.
   (b) as part of performing actions on such objects, e.g. assembly tasks, as in current Edinburgh robot project; pushing boxes around, as at Stanford Research Institute; copying structures from a collection of spare parts, as at MIT.
2. Understanding line drawings
   (a) line drawings as input using digitiser, e.g. Peanuts cartoons.
   (b) low level symbolic description of line drawings as input: typically drawings representing scenes from blocks world.

General Remarks. Much of the work has involved a simplified world of objects with flat surfaces. We know the world does not consist of only such objects; however, this simplification has been a very productive one, leading to the development of a series of programs, each built as a result of the experience gained from, and attempting to repair the limitations of, the previous ones and all contributing to an AI theory of perception.

It is convenient to start with a consideration of line drawings representing scenes of planar objects. We will come back to the problem of real world input later.

4.3.2 Interpretation of Line Drawings
We take up the story begun in section 4.2.1, where we introduced some of the ideas incorporated in Adolpho Guzman's program, SEE (Guzman (1968).

Points to Recall.
(a) The task under consideration is the *Segmentation* task. When we as observers look at a line drawing, say figure 4.2a, we see one cube lying on another. We allocate the regions to one or other of the cubes present. How do we do this? What information would we need to provide a program in order that it could perform this task?
(b) We follow Guzman's program and tackle the problem in two steps: (i) collect *local evidence* for linking regions, and (ii) *weigh this evidence* and

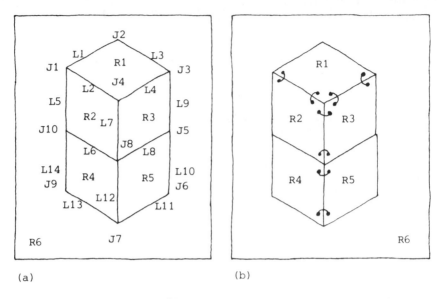

(a)

(b)

Figure 4.2. Linklist: [[R1 R2] [R2 R3] [R3 R1] [R1 R2]
[R4 R5] [R4 R5] [R3 R2] [R3 R1]]

accumulate groups of regions.

(c) What kind of local evidence can we use? We exploit the fact that some places in the picture contain more information than others, i.e. the points at which several lines meet: the *vertices* or picture *junctions*. As usual, we need some vocabulary for describing these picture fragments in order to be able to talk about and use them. To the set of junctions already mentioned — the FORK, the ARROW and the ELL — we add two more, the TEE junction and the PSI junction, and we also show the links that they all generate.

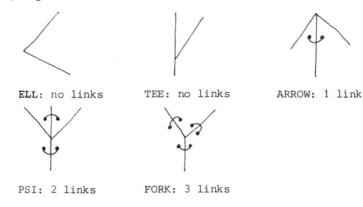

ELL: no links   TEE: no links   ARROW: 1 link

PSI: 2 links   FORK: 3 links

142

Linkage Generation.

(a) We have already considered the FORK rule, which links all three regions comprising the junction, and the ARROW rule, which links the pair of regions that flank the shaft of the arrow.

(b) An ELL junction contributes no links.

(c) The links generated by a PSI junction reflect its origin; that is to say, it is really an ARROW sitting on a FORK.

(d) A TEE provides powerful evidence for not linking the regions on opposite sides of its crossbar, e.g. in figure 4.3, the circled TEE junction is evidence that R1 and R4 belong to different objects.

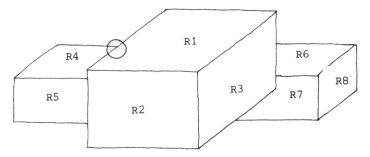

Figure 4.3

Programming Suggestions. Suppose we input the picture description as a list of junctions where each junction is specified by its name, the list of lines that form it, and the list of regions that meet at this point, given as the region name alternating with the size of the angle it contributes to the junction. For figure 4.2a, such a junctionlist would take the form:

        [[J1 [L1 L2 L5] [R1 60 R2 60 R6 240]]
         [J2 [L1 L3] . . .

         . . .
         [J10 [L5 L6 L14] [R2 120 R4 60 R6 180]]].

To *classify* a junction, we need to know: (a) how many lines meet at that junction, and (b) whether any of its regions contribute more than two of the quadrants around that junction.

We can now write a procedure for each junction type that embodies its behaviour, i.e. that knows how to recognise an instance of itself, and how to generate its characteristic links. Consider an ARROW procedure taking as input a junction specification in the form indicated above.

        TO ARROW 'JUNCTION
        Step 1 answers the question: Is this an arrow?

(a) find the number of lines that it comprises. If this is not equal to 3 then result false and stop.

(b) find a region that contributes a greater-than-180 angle to the junction. If none, then result false and stop.

143

Step 2 is reached only if :JUNCTION is a bona-fide ARROW.

(c) find the pair of regions around the shaft of the arrow.

(d) add this pair to a global linklist.

Exercise 4.3.1.

(a) Write a set of such procedures, one for each junction type.

(b) Using these, write a program to generate the linklist for figure 4.2a.

Grouping Regions using the Linklist. The linklist captures all the pieces of local evidence we have accumulated. We now need rules for weighing this evidence, such as a simple *one-link rule*:

Group all regions that are linked to one another by at least one link. Given a linklist such as that shown in figure 4.2b, and a global slot for accumulating all groups of connected regions, initially empty, which we call GROUPLIST, we can write a procedure for grouping regions containing the following steps:

```
TO  GROUP  'LINKLIST
Step 1  if :LINKLIST empty then stop
Step 2  choose a pair from :LINKLIST and set this up
          as a group
Step 3  find all pairs containing at least one element in
          common with this group and form into PAIRLIST
Step 4  form the union of all such pairs and
          add to :GROUPLIST
Step 5  call GROUP recursively with input
          LINKLIST-without-PAIRLIST
END
```

Applying this procedure to figure 4.2b, we would produce the GROUPLIST

[[R1 R2 R3] [R4 R5]]

What about R6?

Refining and Adding to our Rules.

1. *ADDING a matching TEE rule.* We need such a rule to segment figure 4.3.

This rule applies when we have a pair of TEE junctions whose shafts are collinear. We link regions on corresponding sides of the shafts. We have already met this rule in the pie-slice example of section 4.1.6; it enables us to hallucinate arcs passing behind the pie-slice to complete the circles. In figure 4.3, the effect of this rule is to enable us to "imagine" the part of the low flat object which lies behind and is *occluded by* the object lying in front of it.

144

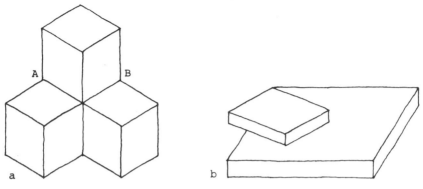

Figure 4.4

2. *Two-link rule*. When we try our simple one-link rule on figure 4.4a and b we come up with a single group in each case. Whilst this might do for 4a, it seems unsatisfactory for 4b, which ought to be seen as two separate bodies. One way out for this figure would be to require at least *two links* between regions before admitting them into the same group.

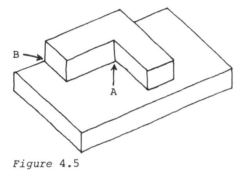

Figure 4.5

3. *Inhibiting Link-Formation*. While the two-link rule would produce a more reasonable solution for figure 4.4b, it would not help in figure 4.5. It is true that this could represent a single body with the top brick glued on to the bottom one; however, it would be nice if our program could separate these two. We can achieve this by introducing the idea of *inhibiting link formation in certain contexts*, i.e allowing the context of a junction to influence the information it yields. Thus, if the arm of a fork ends in the barb of an arrow, do not place the link across that arm: the dotted link is inhibited.

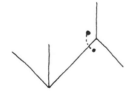

This gives the desired effect in figure 4.5.

145

Another inhibitory situation arises when one of the regions contributing to a junction is known to be background. In this case we do not place links between this and other regions. For example, at B in figure 4.5, we would only place one link; at A and B in figure 4.4a, we would also only place one link. Further examples require the addition of more inhibiting rules.

Summary of Guzman's Program in its Final Form. ✕

"In the first pass, the program gathers evidence through the vertex-inspired links that are not inhibited by adjacent vertices. In the second pass, these links cause binding together wherever two regions or sets of previously bound regions are connected by two or more links. It is a somewhat complex but reasonably talented program which usually returns the most likely partition of a scene [such as figure 4.6] into bodies."

This summary is taken from Winston (1972).

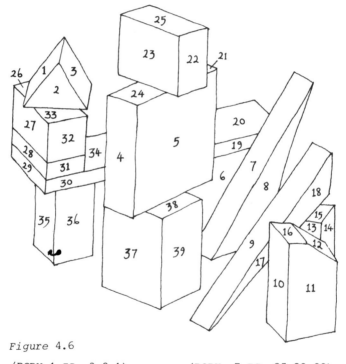

Figure 4.6

(BODY 1 IS :3:2:1)   (BODY 7 IS :25:23:22)
(BODY 2 IS :32:33:27:26)   (BODY 8 IS :14:13:15)
(BODY 3 IS :28:31)   (BODY 9 IS :10:16:11:12)
→(BODY 4 IS :19:20:34:30:29) (BODY 10 IS :18:9:17)
→(BODY 5 IS :36:35)   (BODY 11 IS :7:8)
(BODY 6 IS :24:5:21:4)   (BODY 12 IS :38:37:39)

4.3.3 Problems

The program comes to grief on figures 4.7 and 4.8. Try these. In 4.7, we notice that the program cannot *see* holes. In 4.8, it cheerfully accepts the impossible *Devil's pitchfork* as one body. An analysis of these deficiencies provides the basis for the next group of scene analysis programs.

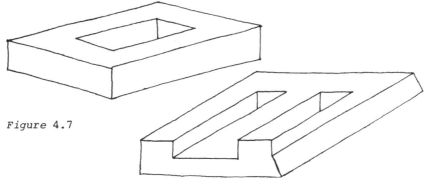

Figure 4.7

Figure 4.8

4.3.4 References

A. Guzman (1968) Decomposition of a visual scene into three-dimensional bodies, in *AFIPS proceedings of the Fall Joint Computer Conference 33*, 291-304. This gives a good account of the system, including the many link-inhibiting rules that his program needed to segment drawings of complex blocks-world scenes.

R.J. Popplestone (1977) A language for specifying robot assembly, in *Proc. Applied Robotics 77*, pp. 183-95. Karlovy Vary. This describes the Edinburgh robot work.

P.H. Winston (1972) The MIT robot, in *Machine Intelligence 7* (eds B. Meltzer & D. Michie) pp.431-63. Edinburgh: University Press.

4.4 INTERPRETATION, SEMANTICS AND MODELS

4.4.1 Introduction

Consider again the configuration in figure 4.5, which led us to postulate our first inhibitory rule. The source of the link that caused the trouble was the FORK at A, and the difference between this fork and the forks in the previous figures is that it occurs at a concavity in the object, whereas previous forks were at convex corners. Another way of saying this is, *whether or not a link-generating rule works depends on the 3D situation represented by the 2D drawing*, i.e. we need to attend to the 3D feature to which the 2D fragment corresponds. When we see figure 4.2a as one cube on another, we are using the following mapping rules from the picture domain into the scene domain: *lines* in the picture correspond to *edges* of solid objects; *regions* in the picture correspond to *surfaces*

147

meeting at these edges; and *junctions* in the picture correspond to *corners*, where two or more edges meet, i.e. where several surfaces meet.

4.4.2 The CLOWES-HUFFMAN line-labelling technique

As pointed out in section 4.2.1, when we look at a corner of a convex object end on, so that all three surfaces that meet at that corner are visible, we depict that corner as a fork in our line drawing. Our fork rule, which links all three regions, does so correctly. If we rotate the object (or walk round it) until just beyond the point where one of the surfaces disappears from view, a drawing from this point of view will show our same corner as an arrow. Again the two surfaces that remain visible are just the ones that the arrow rule links. But we would like to be able to handle concave objects as well.

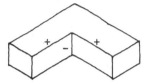

If we look at the concave edge of an L-shaped solid (labelled   -) we see that the corner at which it meets two convex edges (labelled +) is depicted as an ARROW. If we rotate this solid (anti-clockwise, say) until the (left-hand) surface disappears, that corner is now represented by an ELL.

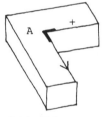

One arm of this ELL corresponds to the convex edge at which the remaining two visible surfaces meet. But now one of these surfaces disappears under the other arm of the ELL; this latter line depicts the edge of the occluding surface A. We call such an edge an *occluding* edge, and label it with an arrow. The labelling convention requires the occluding surface to be on the right when facing the direction of the arrow.

So our occluding surface is partly hiding one of the original three surfaces we could see, and totally hiding another. Notice that all three surfaces we have been talking about belong to the same body. In scenes containing several polyhedra, a so-called occluding edge can partially or completely hide surfaces of bodies other than the one it belongs to. The external edges of all bodies occlude the background.

Possible Interpretations of a Line.

1. The line represents an edge, both of whose contributing surfaces, A and B, are visible:

148

(a) convex, labelled +

A _____ + _____

B

(b) concave, labelled –

A _____ – _____

B

2. Only *one* of the contributing surfaces is visible; the arrowhead labels an edge that belongs to the (occluding) surface on the right (as you move in the direction of the arrow):

(c) occluding: in-pointing arrow

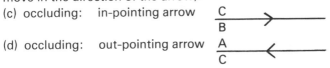

(d) occluding: out-pointing arrow

(C is further away and passes under A or B)

Pictorial Inference. Now label figure 4.8. You will notice that different ends of lines A, B and C have different labels on them. We have contravened a basic rule of polyhedral scene interpretation, that *a given line (in the picture domain) must have the same meaning (in the scene domain) all along its length.* Using this single *coherence* rule the line-labelling method (published independently by Clowes 1971 and Huffman 1971) correctly detects impossible objects like this devil's pitchfork.

4.4.3   The Effects of Adding all this Information

Since there are 4 possible interpretations of a single line, there are 4^2 possibilities for an ELL and 4^3 possibilities for each ARROW and each FORK. If we were to embark upon the task of automatically producing all possible labellings of a given picture, say, a simple cube, by systematically considering the possible labellings of each junction, the space of possibilities we would be searching over would be very large. We appear to have created a combinatorial explosion. The striking fact is that very few of these are physically possible. These can be visualised using the following reasoning:

The three planes that meet at a corner divide the space around that corner into eight octants. Some of these octants are filled with solid material and some are empty.

    1 octant filled implies all convex edges contributing to corner
    3 octants filled implies 2 convex and 1 concave edge
    5 octants filled implies 2 concave and 1 convex edge
    7 octants filled implies 3 concave edges

Any corner can be viewed from each unoccupied octant around it and *all views from a given octant give the same configuration.* Figure 4.9 shows the possible views for each corner type, and summarises the legal labellings that have a meaning in the real world. We have added semantic information to our system, but instead of searching over the whole space of theoretical possiblities, we need to search only over this restricted range of possible corner models.

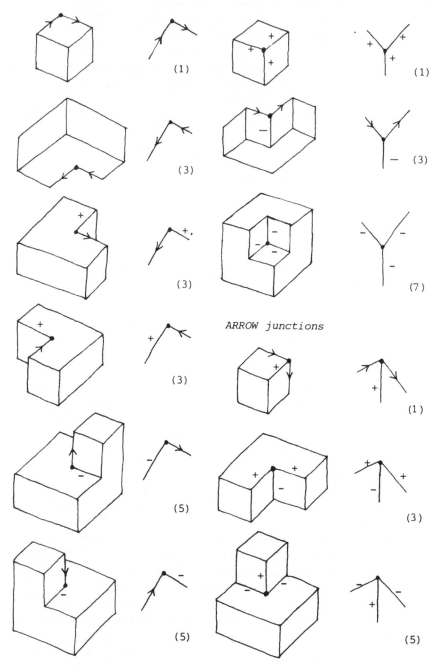

Figure 4.9. Legal labellings of various junctions. Numbers in brackets are the numbers of octants filled.

Exercise 4.4.1. Use the table of possible line-labellings to generate all possible labellings of a cube. (Notice that since the last choice has to mesh with the first, you will produce a graph, best represented on line drawings of a cube.)

4.4.4   Another Look at Guzman's Program

Now we can look back at the link-generating rules. We remarked (and in this, we use the analysis of Mackworth 1974) that Guzman's program works as well as it does because of the implicit assumption about convex bodies. Consider the legal labellings table again and eliminate all those possibilities that involve concave edges — there is now a unique labelling for each junction.

In the case of FORKS and ARROWS, if we disallow all lines labelled concave, we are left with the unique labellings

If we look at figure 4.9, showing how the various ELL labellings arise, we see that all but the first imply a hidden concave edge.

The importance of the Huffman-Clowes contribution in distinguishing the picture domain from the scene domain cannot be over-emphasised.

4.4.5   Progressive Constraint Satisfaction — The Waltz Effect

A dramatic reduction of the search space can be achieved by a *pairwise elimination of possibilities.* This involves the same rule we have already used, i.e. that a single line must have the same label along its entire length. By comparing adjacent pairs of junctions at the start of the search and satisfying their mutal constraints, we can filter out many of the possibilities from further consideration. For example, consider two adjacent junctions, one ELL and one ARROW:

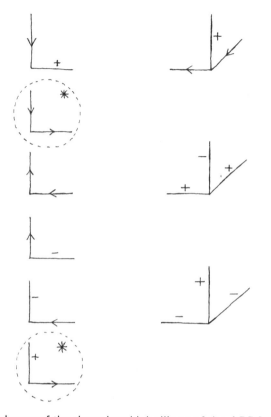

Whichever of the three legal labellings of the ARROW we choose, we will never have a match with the two starred possibilities of the ELL junction. So under these particular circumstances, these latter two need *never* be considered again. By repeating this process of pairwise constraint satisfaction on each adjacent pair and by allowing the consequences of each elimination to percolate through the whole figure, a remarkable reduction in the search space is achieved. To use an analogy, the more specified your piece of jigsaw puzzle is, i.e. noting its colour and surface markings as well as its contour, the fewer places it is likely to fit. (See Waltz 1972.)

Exercise 4.4.2. Try the effect of pairwise elimination on the cube example used previously.

4.4.6 Coplanarity
There is yet a further bug in our method, which shows up when we use it on the following figure.

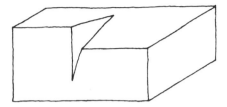

This is satisfactorily labelled, i.e. accepted as a legal figure, because the method cannot distinguish between different degrees of convexity or concavity and makes no requirement about *surface* coherence. More recent programs have been generated by this bug but these are beyond our present scope (see Mackworth 1974, Marr 1977). Locating and analysing surfaces and identifying the solids to which they belong leads us into the next section.

4.4.7 References

M.B. Clowes (1971) On seeing things. *Artificial Intelligence 2 (1)*, 79-112.

D.A. Huffman (1971) Impossible objects as nonsense sentences, in *Machine Intelligence 6* (eds B. Meltzer & D. Michie) pp.295-323, Edinburgh: University Press.

A.K. Mackworth (1973) Interpreting pictures of polyhedral scenes. *Artificial Intelligence 4*, 121-38.

D. Marr (1977) *Representing Visual Information*. MIT memo AIM 415.

D. Waltz (1972) Generating semantic descriptions from drawings of scenes with shadows, in *The Psychology of Computer Vision* (ed. P.H. Winston) McGraw-Hill.

P.H. Winston (1972) The MIT robot, in *Machine Intelligence 7* (eds B. Meltzer & D. Michie), Edinburgh: University Press.

Clowes gives an account of a computer program that does pictorial inference using the line-labelling technique, and Huffman presents a theoretical analysis that includes a preliminary discussion of curved objects. Waltz carries these ideas forward, showing how extending the range of information used helps the problem-solving process to converge. This is an important principle, which generalises to many domains. Mackworth's program POLY embodies general coherence rules that *surfaces* and edges must satisfy, using a dual-space representation that is plane-oriented.

4.5 OBJECT IDENTIFICATION
AND THE USE OF STORED PROTOTYPES

4.5.1 Introduction

We have a real world scene of 3D objects, and we wish to specify a perceiving system that can say what these objects are. This is the *identification* task. We restrict the objects to planar solids and provide a set of *prototypes* so that objects are *seen as* some transformation of these models. Such a system embodies the notion of the continual perception of familiar shapes under a wide variety of transformations — each model represents an invariant percept.

We base our discussion on a program implemented by Roberts in 1963; it predates the programs already described and does not use junctions or line-labelling.

To motivate the discussion, we illustrate the kind of answer we expect our system to produce. In the first example, the 2 x 1 cuboid is *seen as a cube* expanded along the Y-axis.

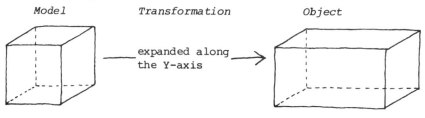

In the second example, the *composite* object, an L-beam, is *seen as* a combination of transformations of two instances of the *cube* prototype.

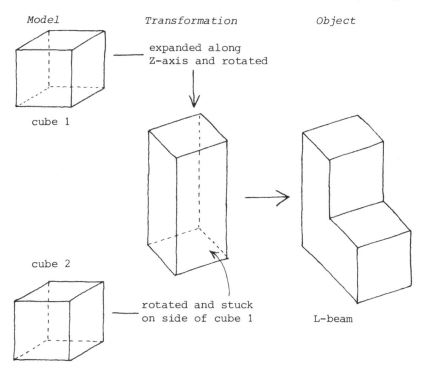

4.5.2   Method

In order to find the relation R between the model and the object, we take an indirect route via a TV camera picture of the unknown object. We set up the more tractable task of finding a *picture description* with which to compare our stored *model description* and so derive the relation H. Then we can use $R = H \times P^{-1}$ (the inverse transformation) to solve our problem.

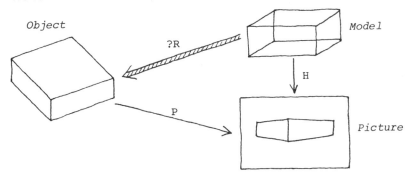

Picture Description. Taking a picture of the object corresponds to projecting 3D points in the object through a focal point on to a 2D picture plane. For a given camera and picture size, this transformation is known.

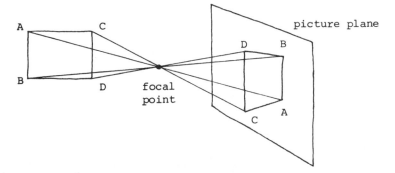

The first part of Roberts' program consists of converting digital intensity values of the picture input into a line drawing and finding closed picture regions. For present purposes, we assume that this (very considerable) task has been completed. The resultant *picture description* consists of:
(a) a set of lines represented by their endpoint coordinates, and
(b) a set of regions bounded by these lines.

Model Description. We use three prototypes, as shown below. A *model description* consists of:
(a) a set of point coordinates representing the corners of the model, and
(b) a list of the polygons surrounding each point.

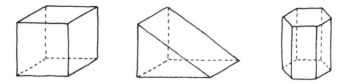

Given the three models shown, the set of *approved polygons* is restricted to convex polygons of sides 3, 4 or 6.

Each point on a CUBE model has 3 quadrilaterals around it.
Each point on a WEDGE model has 2 quadrilaterals and 1 triangle around it.
Each point on an HEXAGONAL PRISM model has 2 quadrilaterals and 1 hexagon around it.

Model-Picture Matching, i.e. finding the transformation H. Under ideal conditions, we need only know what the regions around a picture point are in order to assign it to the correct model. In practice, the matching process is complicated by two factors: (a) the presence of composite objects, e.g. the L-beam in section 4.5.1; and (b) occlusion of one object by another, as in figure 4.10.

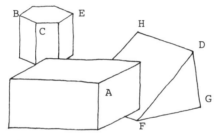

Figure 4.10

This means that regions in the picture may not belong to the set of approved polygons. Our task is to find the *largest picture fragment* that will home in on the right model most rapidly, where "right" means "contains a matching model fragment". Roberts provides an ordered sequence of four tests, allowing successively greater departure from the ideal, i.e. from a picture of a non-composite, non-occluded object. We illustrate this by considering a picture of a simple cube, and the collection of objects depicted in figure 4.10.

Test 1. Find a picture point that is completely surrounded by approved polygons. A is such a point:

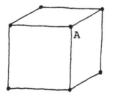

7 picture
points
required

(See also point A in figure 4.10.)

156

Test 2. Find a line that has an approved polygon on either side of it, e.g. line AB:

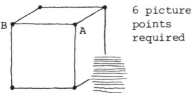

6 picture
points
required

(See also line BC in figure 4.10.)

Test 3. Try for an approved polygon with a line coming from one of its vertices, e.g. A B C D, with line B E:

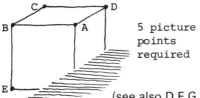

5 picture
points
required

(see also D F G, with line D H, in figure 4.10.)

Test 4. Find a point which three lines emerge, e.g. point D:

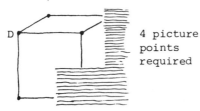

4 picture
points
required

(see also point E in figure 4.10.)

Selecting a Model. The next step is to use the best picture fragment (this will be the largest fragment that passes the above tests) as the basis for model selection. Roberts uses a predetermined order of models (cube — wedge — hexagonal prism) over which the program searches for a model fragment to correspond to the picture fragment. That is to say, it looks for a model point surrounded by the same polygon structure as the selected picture point and constructs a list of matching (i.e. topologically equivalent) model-picture points pairs.

If the object were identical in shape, size and orientation to the standard prototype, there would be an exact match (taking into account the loss of the third dimension) between the picture points projected by that object and the model points with which they have been paired. A *mismatch* reflects a transformed model. To get an intuitive feel for what this could mean, consider the upper surface of a cube as it is tilted backwards away from the vertical. Two of the angles, starting off as 90°, would become increasingly more acute, and the other two more obtuse. The degree of acuteness (obtuseness) reflects the degree of tilt. Roberts' program uses standard matrix manipulation to calculate the combination of

157

transformations (rotation/translation/perspective/expansion-along-an-axis) to account for the mismatch.

Finally, the selected model-plus-transformation is used to generate the rest of the picture, i.e. to *predict* all the remaining picture points not so far involved in the matching. These predicted points are compared with the actual picture points. Three possibilities arise:
(a) A fit means we have found the correct model and the trans-formation H.
(b) If some of the model-generated points fall outside the external boundary of the picture, this means we have the wrong model and we try another.
(c) If all the generated points fall inside the boundary but do not account for all the picture lines, this indicates that we are dealing with a picture of a composite object. We need to *decompose* the object into sub-parts that can be seen as transformed models.

Decomposition. Consider the L-beam on the left of the figure below. Finding a "good" picture fragment involves trying the four tests outlined above successively. There is no picture point surrounded by three approved polygons (test 1). Applying test 2 yields three possible candidates. Line 1, flanked by regions A and B, would find a matching fragment in the cube model, but when the rest of the picture is generated by this model, some points fall outside the picture boundary.

Line 2, flanked by polygons B and C, is more promising; the points predicted by the cube model that it matches would fall within the external boundary of the picture. Roberts decomposes the picture using the following steps:
1. All model lines and points are added to the picture if not already there (dotted lines)
2. If a model point falls on a picture line, insert the point (X)
3. Each visible model point in the picture that does not connect to any *non*-model line is marked "used" (⊙)
4. Delete all used points and their attached lines and polygons

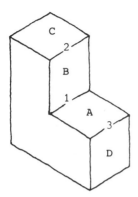

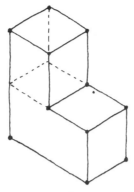

step 1

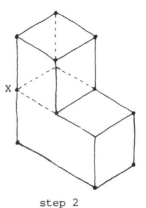

step 2

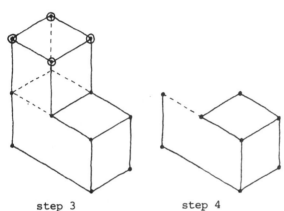

step 3   step 4

The remaining picture (step 4) is matched to the cube model under the transformation "expansion-in-Y-axis". Starting with line 3, flanked by A and D, corresponds to the example shown in section 4.5.1.

4.5.3 Notes

1. We observe that Roberts' first test, find a point surrounded by three approved polygons, corresponds to Guzman's FORK heuristic; and his second test, find a line flanked by accepted polygons, is just our old friend the ARROW rule.

2. Roberts' system incorporates a two-way addressing process whereby stimulus cues ("good" picture fragments) address or invoke internal models, which in turn suggest (predict) where the rest of the picture will be.

3. Combining the ideas of Roberts with those of Guzman, Clowes and Huffman, we see the possibility of a hierarchy of semantic models.

Points 2 and 3 will be taken up again later.

159

4.5.4 References

L.G. Roberts (1965) Machine perception of 3D objects, in *Optical and Electro-optical Information Processes* (eds Tippett *et al.*) pp. 159-97, MIT press.

4.6   LINE-FINDING

4.6.1   Introduction

Many AI systems developed to analyse real-world scenes have involved producing a line drawing as a definitive stage in the processing of the scene. Figure 4.11 shows typical stages in the process of transforming a TV camera picture into a description of the scene. We give a simple-minded version of the second stage of this process — the detection of discontinuities in the intensity array, using a local gradient operator and thresholding — and then discuss difficulties that arise and proposals for overcoming these problems.

```
INPUT                                      OUTPUT

Stage 1                      to produce
take TV camera picture      ─────────────> brightness array

Stage 2                      to produce
apply local gradient        ─────────────> edge point description:
operator and thresholding                  site of significant
at every point in image                    intensity gradients

Stage 3                      to produce
fit line segments           ─────────────> line drawing description:
to edge points and                         lines - endpoint
identify closed regions                             coordinates
                                           regions - boundary lines
                                                      and junctions
                                           junctions - coordinates
                                                       of points (2D)

Stage 4
compare line drawing     ╲
with stored prototypes:   ╲
surfaces - units normal
           to face
edges - length in
        real numbers
corners - 3D coordinates
                           to produce
AND                       ─────────────>  IDENTIFIED SOLIDS
                                          LOCATED IN 3-SPACE
use information about the
camera position and the
supporting plane of      ╱
the scene               ╱
```

Figure 4.11. Showing stages in scene analysis (after Falk 1972).

4.6.2 The Detection of Discontinuities

The Gradient Operator. A TV picture of a 3D scene records the light intensity or brightness level (a product of illumination and reflectance of the surface). The brightness intensity at each small area of the resultant picture is converted via an analogue-to-digital convertor into an integer to produce an array of numbers: the *digitised image*. A small portion of such an array (under near ideal conditions) might look like this:

columns	A	B	C	D	E	F	G
rows 11	1	1	2	4	5	5	6
12	1	1	1	5	5	6	5
13	1	1	1	5	6	5	5

We are interested in finding *picture edges* of interest, i.e. "significant" local changes in picture brightness. So we examine what is happening in the immediate neighbourhood of each point by passing a 3 x 3 grid across the whole array, and computing the gradient at each point as follows:

Point *D12* is flanked by
column E, which sums to 16 } column difference = 12
and column C, which sums to 4
and by row 13, which sums to 12 } row difference = 1
and by row 11, which sums to 11

Clearly there is a lot happening in the row direction and not very much in the column direction. In contrast, point B12 yields a column difference of 1 and a row difference of 1. We can compute the *gradient* as

(a) the *amount* of difference = (column difference^2 + row difference^2)$^{\frac{1}{2}}$
(b) the *direction of difference* (as its tangent)
= column difference / row difference

Note that the edge should be perpendicular to the gradient. Repeating the process for each picture point, we get an array of gradients. Since we are not interested in small differences, we eliminate these by applying a *threshold*, leaving only the edge points of interest.

Fitting Line Segments. Under ideal conditions, the edge points found in stage 2 should line up nicely. Unfortunately, difficulties arise with actual pictures of real world scenes due to mutual illumination, scattering effects at edges, smudges, shadows, object deformities such as surface chips, surface markings and a whole battery of instrument defects. Background noise is high; variations within a picture region can be larger than the step across to the next region. This gives rise to spurious points above the threshold, and if we increase the threshold we risk losing significant points. In general it is difficult to find a good compromise! Consequently a line finder that tries to piece together edge points by tracking at 90° to the gradient direction at each point, i.e. by "following its nose" in the direction of a putative edge, can be misled by wrong local data into going off in the wrong direction: and it can be hampered by *missing* edge points.

4.6.3
To overcome the difficulties mentioned above several approaches have been used, which include ideas of the following sort:

1. Brightness contrast across edges falls into 3 categories:

step   roof   peak

So Binford and Horn use a set of different *gradient operators* to facilitate detection of particular edge types.

2. Marr uses specific intensity profiles suggested by the neurophysiological finding of Hubel and Wiesel that simple cells of the visual cortex respond to EDGES and BARS in the scene. He passes EDGE masks and BAR masks

of varying widths and at a variety of orientations over the array. In addition he generates an *explicit* description of the range of information extracted. The result is a rich symbolic description of
(a) intensity changes, their position, spatial extent, contrast and type of change.
(b) 2D geometric relations, e.g. parallel relationships between nearby edges.

3. O'Gorman and Clowes look at edge points *globally* to find sets of collinear points.

4. Shirai finds external boundary lines first, since these are more easily found, and uses typical configurations in the contour to guide the search:

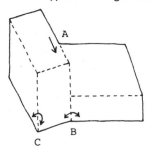

Concavities are good places to start. They could conceal a T-junction, e.g. at A, so look for one by looking along the extension of one arm of the concavity; find the third line at a junction, e.g. B, C, by doing a circular

162

scan; in either case try to find a line parallel to a contour line.

5. Falk doesn't try too hard for a complete line drawing at the preprocessing stage, and leaves it to high level programs to *complete* the picture by adding lines. He provides three procedures to do this job:

(a) JOIN, which can complete the face F by joining the two hanging collinear lines L1 and L2.

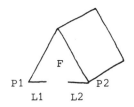

(b) ADDCORNER, which extends dangling lines L1 and L2 to complete the corner and so complete the face F.

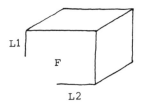

(c) ADDLINE, which looks for evidence that a complete line has been missed and adds a line between P1 and P2 to split F into two.

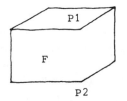

Note. The improvements in line-finding listed above involve using *global* properties, using progressively more *context*, using *partial results* to suggest the possible position and orientation of lines still to be found: e.g. collinearity of edge points (3 above); collinear lines already found (5a); parallelism (2, 3); known junction types (4, 5b and c). A knowledge of what is being looked for is deployed to provide goal-directed search.

4.6.4   Alternatives to Line-Finding

Instead of looking for discontinuities in the intensity array to find lines in the picture, we can look for *regions* of similar intensity, e.g. the programs used in the Edinburgh robot project to recognise spectacles, cups, etc., mentioned in section 4.3.1, used region finding.

163

We can use range-finders to locate surfaces of objects in the scene, e.g. (a) the *line-striping* technique in the current Edinburgh robot project, or (b) a laser beam, as used at Stanford and by vision workers in Japan.

4.6.5 Comments

The assumption that producing a line drawing is a necessary stage in the analysis of a scene is open to question. It would seem more profitable to regard line drawings as an expression of (i.e. as generatable from) an internal description that is itself a 3D description. This is not to say that the reverse process can't occur; it obviously can. When in fact a line drawing as such is input, e.g. as a diagram, or a PEANUTS cartoon, it can be readily seen as representing a 3D scene, as indeed can a drawing composed of dots. In a technical drawing, e.g. a circuit diagram, the conventions in terms of which the elements of the drawing map into concepts in the domain (e.g. —⋁⋁⋀— means resistor) must be explicitly acquired before the observer can make sense of the drawing. Strip cartoon devotees gradually acquire a great mass of conventions. For example, in a PEANUTS cartoon, "distance" means "distance from action", and there are three positions of importance in the picture: middle ground, where the centre of the action takes place; background, for observer status; and (blown-up) foreground, for emphasis. See Minsky and Papert (AI Memo 252) for a discussion of how children reveal their internal representations in their drawings.

4.6.6 References

T.O. Binford & B.K.P. Horn, *The Binford-Horn Line-Finder*, MIT AI memo AIM 285.

G. Falk (1972) Interpretation of line data as a three-dimensional scene. *Artificial Intelligence 3(2)*, 101-44. A complete scene-analysis system, which is an interesting combination and elaboration of earlier ideas, e.g. junction types, search space of 3D models, together with the completion heuristics mentioned above, and verification of hypothesised line drawings.

D. Marr (1976) Early processing of visual information. *Phil. Trans. Roy. Soc. London B, 275*, 483-519.

M. Minsky & S. Papert (1971) *Project MAC Progress Report VIII*, pp.129-224. MIT.

R.J. Popplestone *et al.* (1975) Forming models of plane-and-cylinder faceted bodies from light stripes. *Proc. 1975 IJCAI*, Tbilisi.

Y. Shirai (1973) A context-sensitive line-finder for recognition of polyhedra. *Artificial Intelligence 4(2)*, 95-119.

4.7 CONTRIBUTION TO A THEORY OF VISUAL PERCEPTION

We now draw together themes from previous sections.

4.7.1 The Formation and Use of Symbolic Descriptions

In our consideration of grouping processes, we built up the notion of a hierarchical description and suggested a role for an *intermediate* description (section 4.1.5): "if we had a description of a rectangle stored away, we could imagine that finding the "hook" could invoke this description".

We postulated (section 4.1.4) that it was easier to see the picture under consideration as a side view (of a chair and table) rather than as an aerial view, by noting that "the familiar arrangement of parts triggers concepts that we already have", and that "parts take their names from the wholes they are seen to belong to".

We saw (section 4.1.6) how lines can change their allegiance, i.e. what they are *seen as* belonging to, by virtue of changes elsewhere in the picture. Small local changes in the display produced large global effects. Grouping elements into larger units was part of an "effort after meaning" in which stored experience plays an important role.

In sections 4.3, 4.4 and 4.5, we considered programs (Guzman, Clowes-Huffman, Roberts) for analysing line drawings. These programs deploy a vocabulary of descriptions to refer to significant parts of the picture, e.g. arrow, forks, junctions, and a repertoire of procedures (rules) for manipulating these descriptions. Guzman showed how junctions provided pieces of evidence for linking the regions of which they were part into whole bodies (section 4.3.2) and how the effect of any one bit of local evidence could be modified by the context in which the junctions occurred, e.g. how the presence of a particular neighbouring junction could inhibit link formation (section 4.3.2).

Both the Clowes-Huffman line-labelling approach and Roberts' program introduce the notion of models. In the former, each of Guzman's picture parts has a set of possible models, e.g. there are four possible *edge* models for each line in the picture (section 4.4.2). Edges meeting at a point constitute *corner* models, and the number of physically possible corner models for each junction type was seen to be surprisingly small (figure 4.9). Since, in a complete line drawing, each line connects two junctions, applying a coherence rule that a single line must have the same edge model along its entire length captures the fact that the assignment of a meaning to each junction must take place within the context of its immediate neighbours. Interpretation of a picture is then equivalent to searching over the set of possible corner models for each junction in the picture and applying this rule.

165

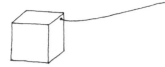

This acute angle is SEEN AS a right angle. Our cube schema has "right-angled" as part of its description. Recognition involves projecting a right angle onto the acute angle.

Our schemata include the rule: Things further away appear smaller; to get the correct size, enlarge correspondingly.

Converging lines mean "receding into the distance". So we project a larger man onto the stimulus of the same size.

H. Rorschach

PLATE IV. Inkblot

"We may regard pictures as lying in a kind of continuum. At one end there will be drawings, realistic paintings and photographs that are representational. ... At the other, the fantasy end, will be inkblots or pictures in the fire or in clouds...

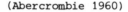

"For most people plate V will be at the fantasy end, meaning as little or as much as an inkblot. ... People appropriately trained in interpretation of radiographs will recognise it as a radiograph of part of a human head..."

(Abercrombie 1960)

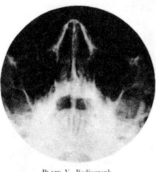

PLATE V. Radiograph

Figure 4.12

In this line-labelling scheme, concave objects are handled in the same way as convex objects. Roberts' system adopts an alternative possible mechanism, in which concave objects are seen as decomposable into a small set of prototype convex models. Finding the right model involves the topological matching of the polygon structure around picture points with the polygon structure around model points. It is point-dominated, and no intermediate models, e.g. edges or surfaces, are used. Again the search for a solution takes the form of a search over possible models. A more powerful, suggestive way of describing the seeing process is as a two-way addressing system whereby stimulus cues ("good" picture fragments) address (or invoke) internal models (or schemata) and these models, once invoked, suggest (or predict) what and where the rest of the picture might be.

We need both the stimulus patterns and bottom-up analysis of the Behaviourists, and the candidate models (or wholes) and top-down hypothesis-generation of the Gestaltists. By adopting this middle-ground position, we can account for such features of the human perceptual system as, for example, its *constructive* gap-filling nature, for models allow us to hallucinate the missing bits; and the role of mental set in perception in determining which models are to be considered. In figure 4.12 we show a selection of examples to illustrate this two-way process.

4.7.2 Knowledge-Driven Analysis

Notice (section 4.5.2) that when we had collected our model-picture point pairs, we did not expect an exact match. Instead we expected to be able to account for the *mismatch* by one of a given number of transformations, i.e. to interpret or make sense of the mismatch between the incoming perceptual pattern and the stored concept. A crucial element of stored conceptual structures must consist of knowledge of how to handle such mismatches.

In our discussion of the low-level process of line-finding, we showed (section 4.6.3) how a knowledge of what is being looked for can be deployed to provide a goal-directed search. The analysis is conducted in terms of assumptions (hypotheses, prejudices) about what is significant (relevant) and what is noise to be ignored. Notice (section 4.6.2) that surface markings are listed among the difficulties to be overcome. An alternative possibility would be to *exploit* their presence, which is exactly what the perception psychologist Gibson does in his demonstration of how surface texture can provide depth information: as the surface recedes, the markings get closer together. Shadows were regarded as a nuisance by the early vision programs, until Waltz showed how to use the evidence they provide to cut down the number of possible interpretations of a picture, as shown in the MIT film *Eye of the Robot*. Shadows tell us what the scene looks like from the viewpoint of the light source.

Developing vision systems capable of representing different varieties of knowledge, and allowing these to interact in different ways (in a heterarchical fashion), depending on on-going partial results, is the challenge currently being tackled by workers in AI vision projects e.g. the Fortran coding sheet project at Essex University; the "spotty pictures" project and the "puppet" project, both at Sussex University. This work is very much influenced by the seminal paper by Marvin Minsky (1975).

4.7.3 Action Perception

The view of the perceptual process as a constructive, interpretative activity in which we see the current situation in terms of what we know, is captivated by Clowes' slogan: "We can not SEE. We can only SEE-AS". Work in this department on action perception has involved an extension of these ideas to a richer domain, which includes moving objects. This can produce a dramatic increase in the range of concepts that enter into the interpretative process. Thus moving objects become participants in event-sequences or actions, in terms of which they acquire roles such as agent or patient. We become concerned with what caused the perceived movement and with the attribution of motives to the participants. The Belgian psychologist Michotte used simple 2D "meaningless" shapes such as squares, circles and triangles moving in relation to one another over a screen; subjects viewing such displays receive impressions of one object chasing another, pushing one another, fleeing from another, and so on. Except for isolated instances, these effects were independent of the particular shape used. These observations form an ideal basis for our task of modelling the *perception of moving objects* on a computer.

In the classical LAUNCHING experiment, the subject fixates a stationary red square (B) in the centre of a white screen, while from a point 40 mm left of centre a black square (A) travels towards B and stops when it reaches it; B then moves off to the right. Observers see object A bump into object B and give it a push. What we require in order to produce an "explanation" of, or to give an account of, the impressions reported by Michotte's subjects is, in the first instance, the development of a *vocabulary of symbols* appropriate to various levels of interpretation of the kinetic displays, for example:

low-level descriptions of position: bar (position P1 (time t1))
                                      bar (position P2 (time t2))
low-level description of change of position: A moves
intermediate description
        in relation to another object: A approaches B rapidly
        in relation to a previous movement: A moves to-and-fro
high-level description of causal sequence: A bumps into B and
                                      pushes it forward

Depending on the *reference point* chosen, the description of the movement of an object, e.g. A moves, can become:

    A approaches B
or A movesacross screen
or A withdrawsfrom B

An important issue is how to *represent moving objects* in the computer in such a way as to facilitate the generation of descriptions of their movements. We input the process continuum as successive time slices, or conceptual snapshots, depicted as a frame sequence rather like a strip cartoon. It is as though the observer takes successive samplings of the movement processes and forms descriptions of each, so that the *difference-descriptions* between successive frames express the changes that have occurred during a particular time interval. (Cf. use of difference-descriptions by Evans in his analogy program, and by Winston in his learning structural descriptions program.)

The experiments are input to the program in the form of low-level symbolic descriptions of a sequence of snapshots of moving objects. The program is required to build up a description of what is happening in the form of event-sequences to check relevant constraints, and so decide which of the act types it knows about corresponds to the input sequence.

There will in general be more than one way of pairing picture regions in successive frames, and we need a way of choosing which of the possible pairings corresponds to an *enduring object in motion*.

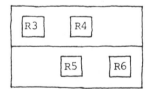

Which region should we combine with R5? R3 or R4, to which it is nearer? If we choose R4 we are left with pair R3-R6, but (R3-R5; R4-R6) is better in that it gives a combined pairing which involves the least overall change in position.

In Weir (1978) we detail the steps involved in forming descriptions from the experimental data, e.g. we show how the factors influencing the choice of a reference point radically affect the *intermediate descriptions* generated. Since these latter form the components of *action schemata*, this in turn influences which particular action schema will be evoked. Figure 4.13 gives a representation of some of the features of a pushing or launching schema. Any component could evoke this schema. Typically, an instance of [x collideswith y] would be responsible for an active search for the "withdrawal" of the patient y.

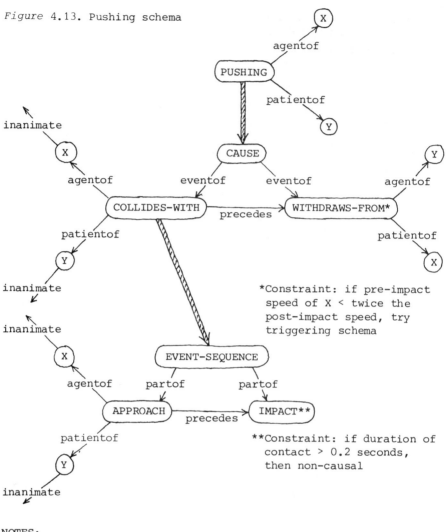

Figure 4.13. Pushing schema

*Constraint: if pre-impact speed of X < twice the post-impact speed, try triggering schema

**Constraint: if duration of contact > 0.2 seconds, then non-causal

NOTES:

(a)   is to be read as: the node A can be viewed as node B and all the nodes that hang from it

(b)   is to be read as: B (is the) C (of) A

(c)   is to be read as: A has the property B

(d) The variables X and Y have been used to avoid complicating the diagram by identity links between participants of events.

170

4.7.4 Summary

This brief description of the Michotte work has been included to indicate the potential of the two-way addressing system espoused in this account of perception. Exploring possible mechanisms to support the attribution of animacy and causality involved in these experiments suggests ways of thinking about the much more complex, elaborate processing underlying interpersonal perception.

4.7.5 References

M. L. J. Abercrombie (1960) *The Anatomy of Judgement.* Hutchinson.

R. Bornat & J.M. Brady (1976) Using knowledge in the computer interpretation of FORTRAN coding sheets. *Int. J. Man Machine Studies*.

T.G. Evans (1964) A heuristic program to solve geometric analogy problems. Spring *J.S.C.C.*

A. Michotte (1963) *The Perception of Causality* (trans. T. & E. Miles, original French edn 1946). Methuen.

M. Minsky (1975) A framework for representing knowledge, in *The Psychology of Computer Vision* (ed. P.H. Winston). McGraw-Hill.

F. O'Gorman & M.B. Clowes (1973) in *Proc. IJCAI 3* (ed. N. Nilsson). Stanford.

A. Sloman & S. Hardy (1976) Giving a computer gestalt experiences, in *Proc. AISB*, Edinburgh.

S. Weir (1978) The perception of motion: Michotte revisited. To appear in *Perception*.

5.   LEARNING

5.1   SAMUEL'S CHECKERS-PLAYER AND HILL-CLIMBING

5.1.1   Introduction

For the moment, we will restrict ourselves to issues directly related to one of the problems we discussed earlier, that of playing draughts. In this section we are not going to discuss basic questions like "what do we mean by learning?" or "How do we get a computer to learn?". We will spend some time on that in the next section, but for the present, without going into it more deeply, we will just say that the program we are going to discuss is a learning program because it improves its standard of play with experience.

5.1.2   Aspects of the Program

Recall: a game-playing program works by minimaxing back up a *game tree*, using an *evaluation function* on the terminal nodes which consists of a *weighted-sum-of-features score*. Typical features are: piece ratio, centre control, threat of fork, denial of occupancy, etc.:

$$S = w_1{}^*s_1 + w_2{}^*s_2 + \ldots \ldots + w_n{}^*s_n$$

We want to look at this evaluation function in a rather different way than we have done so far. Notice firstly that there are two different ways that the nodes in the search tree have values assigned to them:

(a) Nodes at the limits of the search get a value
     by calculating the evaluation function.
(b) Other nodes get their values
     by minimaxing the values from (a).

So the evaluation score is a result of static, featural analysis, and the backed-up value is a result of dynamic, exploratory analysis.

Notice secondly that the only reason we need an evaluation function at all is because we cannot afford to search the whole tree. If we *could* search the whole thing, we would be able to assign nodes their *true* value of $+1$ (win), 0 (draw), or -1 (lose). But in fact we have to terminate the search somewhere, and at these points we have to make do with an *approximation* to the true value. In other words, the evaluation score is a second-rate substitute for a full exploratory search. It is intended to tell us approximately what we *would* find, if we *were* able to carry out the full search.

5.1.3   Generalisation learning

The question now is this: in the "weighted sum of features score", where do the weights come from? What should they be? And the proposed answer is that the program should *learn* the appropriate weights by experience — it should continually be adjusting its weights to improve its standard of play. (It also chooses an appropriate set of features — more on this below.) The idea is for the program to play for a while, and see how well it is doing. It must then somehow *increase* the weights of the features that are helping to make the right decisions, and *decrease* the others.

How often should it do this? If it does it only once per game, the rate of learning is far too slow, and one is extracting far too little information from all the activity involved in playing. For example, even if the program lost a game, it may have been because of just one mistake: most of its decisions may still have been right. Or conversely, if the program won, does it mean that *all* its decisions were equally responsible for the success? (What we are discussing here is an aspect of what is known as the *credit assignment* problem.)

So we do the updating after each move. This is sufficiently frequent, but there is a difficulty. On what basis can the program decide "how well it is doing"? The simple description given above supposes that there is a trainer standing by to tell the program "Yes, that was a good move" or "No, you did the wrong thing". In the absence of such a trainer, how can the program itself, which is already making the best decisions it can, also know how good these decisions are?

The solution comes from the two points mentioned above, in section 5.1.2. There are two ways of finding the value of a board position: (a) by static evaluation function, (b) by dynamic search. Since it looks further ahead, score (b) is less dependent on the details of the evaluation function, and so it can be used as a criterion for the correctness of score (a).

To say the same thing a different way: remember that (a) is regarded as a *prediction* of (b), so that it can serve as a substitute for it. The better the evaluation function, the better that prediction. If the evaluation function were perfect, the two scores would be in agreement throughout the game. So all we have to do to see how good the evaluation function is, is to see how closely it corresponds to the backed-up score, i.e. for boards encountered during actual play, we compute

$$\Delta = \text{(backed-up score of board resulting from chosen move)}$$
$$- \text{(evaluation score for current board)}$$

If Δ is positive, then the evaluation score made an under-estimate, so the positive terms in the polynomial should have more weight, and the negative terms less weight. If Δ is negative, the score was an over-estimate or even led to the wrong choice of move, so the weights should be altered conversely.

In fact, the program keeps a cumulative average record of the "correlation" between the sign of each term and the sign of Δ, and this is used to adjust the weights after each move. The correlation of a given feature tells us how good a predictor it is, so the better it is, the more weight it is given.

173

Term Selection. The evaluation polynomial involves only 16 out of a possible 38 features. The program keeps track of which term has the lowest "correlation", and if any term is lowest too often it is replaced by a new term, which initially has zero weight. With experience this program becomes highly competent, a "better-than-average" player with good middle- and end-game play, though the openings remain weak and unconventional.

5.1.4 Hill climbing

Occasionally, during learning, the program is temporarily unable to improve its play any further. It is then necessary to give it a big "kick", by setting to zero the weight of the leading term in the polynomial. Why does this happen?

Samuel is essentially using the technique of *hill climbing* to optimise the program's performance. This technique is appropriate when for some reason you are unable to *analyse* the task in such a way as to deduce the best weights (e.g. in draughts, nobody knows how to do this). Instead you start from where the program is and make a long series of small improvements. Compare this with trying to reach the top of a hill on a foggy night, without a map. The general idea is to "keep going upwards". One can
(a) find the line of steepest slope and take a step along it; or
(b) try steps in different directions, and choose the best;
      etc.

This method suffers from various problems. The one that concerns us here is the problem of *secondary peaks* (or local maxima). You may have reached a peak, but is it the highest one? One solution is to try making random leaps. To do better, you have to know more about the structure of the problem. (Another difficulty is that of encountering a "mesa", a large area where there is no change whichever way you move, and therefore no clue to the correct direction.)

Hill climbing is a technique widely used and studied even outside of AI.

5.1.5 References

A.L. Samuel (1959) Some studies in machine learning using the game of checkers. *IBM Journal of Research and Development 3*, 211-29. Reprinted in *Computers and Thought* (eds E.A. Feigenbaum & J. Feldman) pp.71-105.

A.L. Samuel (1967) Some studies in machine learning using the game of checkers. II — Recent progress. *IBM Journal of Research and Development 11*, 601-17.

In his 1959 paper, in addition to the "generalised learning" discussed here, Samuel describes a form of "rote learning" in which selected board positions encountered during play are remembered, and used to increase the effective depth of search, thereby improving the program's play. See pp.79-83 in *Computers and Thought*.

5.2 STRUCTURAL LEARNING AND GENERAL COMMENTS

5.2.1 Digression: "Concept Identification" Experiments

We take a quick look at a chapter of experimental psychology in order to provide ourselves with certain terminology and ideas. In a "concept identification" experiment, the subject is presented with a set of objects varying in some systematic way, e.g. cards with shapes varying in outline, number, size, colour, etc. A "concept" is a subset of the objects specified by a simple rule. Different kinds of rules define different kinds of concepts:

    conjunctive, e.g. red and square

    disjunctive, e.g. red or square

    equivalence, e.g. both red and square, or neither.

For a given concept, certain attributes are *relevant*; e.g. for "red and square", colour and shape are relevant attributes, the rest are irrelevant. The subject is shown examples one at a time, and told whether or not they are instances of the concept the experimenter has in mind. The subject's task is to guess the rule.

A strategy commonly used for learning conjunctive concepts is "conservative focussing". Here the subject remembers the first positive

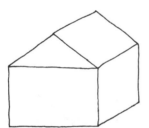

HOUSE

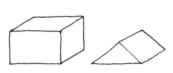

NEAR MISS

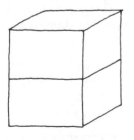

NEAR MISS

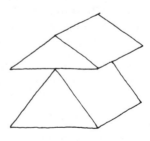

NEAR MISS

Figure 5.1. HOUSE

175

instance, and then gradually strips away its irrelevant attributes. We can see that if a new example differs from the first in several attributes but is still a positive instance, then those attributes must all be irrelevant. Whereas if the new example differs in just one attribute and is a non-instance (a "near-miss"), then that attribute must be relevant. This should all sound vaguely familiar.

The field was opened up by a book by Bruner, Goodnow and Austin in 1956. Since then more than 1200 similar experiments have been published.

5.2.2 Winston's Program Revisited

(a) Consider the process of building a model from a sequence of positive instances and "near-misses", e.g. HOUSE (see figure 5.1). The formation of the MUST-BE and MUST-NOT-BE links is the detection of the relevant attributes.

(b) When having to relax a requirement, Winston's program makes an *appropriate generalisation* by finding the first superordinate entity that includes both cases. For example, when learning ARCH (see section 4.2) it finds that both a BRICK and a WEDGE are acceptable as cross-members, so generalises them to PRISM, e.g.

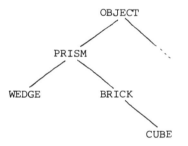

If something holds for both CUBE and WEDGE, the appropriate generalisation is to PRISM.

(c) Previously learned concepts can be used in new ones, e.g. ARCH as a component of ARCADE (see figure 5.2). Such a concept is necessarily hierarchical: ARCADE could not be learned *without* first learning ARCH — it would become hopelessly complicated.

(d) These iterative structures like ARCADE and COLUMN are handled in the same way as simple structures. The networks have a TYPICAL-MEMBER link, and a NUMBER-OF-MEMBERS that can be "appropriately generalised" to be an INTEGER (implicitly, > 2). See figure 5.3.

Discussion. Note the central importance of near misses for the learning. Successful learning is dependent on being given a good training sequence. Viewing learning as the building of an internal description gives us a

176

Figure 5.2. ARCADE

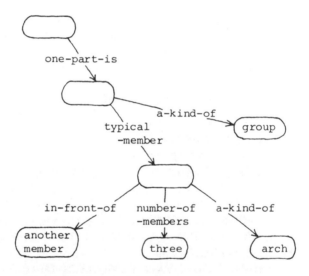

Figure 5.3. ARCADE

rational basis for discussing "good teaching". But does this go beyond what Bruner, Goodnow & Austin (1956) did? Compare this view with Bruner's own work on education (1960, 1966).

The *limitation* comes from the fact that the technique is essentially "conservative focussing", so it is restricted to learning conjunctive concepts. For example, could it learn the concept "two bricks in the same orientation" (either both lying or both standing)? What about the concept "cat"? Or "abuts"? Or "near to"?

5.2.3 Discrimination Nets

Consider the ANIMAL program you played with at the beginning of term:

THINK OF AN ANIMAL

IS IT A MOUSE? : no

OH DEAR, I DID NOT GET THAT ONE

WHAT ANIMAL WERE YOU THINKING OF? : pterodactyl

PLEASE ASK A QUESTION TO DISTINGUISH A
   MOUSE FROM A PTERODACTYL : is it prehistoric

WHAT WOULD THE ANSWER BE IN THE CASE OF A
   PTERODACTYL? : yes

THANK YOU, I WILL REMEMBER THAT

THINK OF AN ANIMAL

IS IT PREHISTORIC? : no

IS IT A MOUSE? : no

OH DEAR, I DID NOT GET THAT ONE

WHAT ANIMAL WERE YOU THINKING OF? : whale

PLEASE ASK A QUESTION TO DISTINGUISH A MOUSE FROM
   A WHALE : is it enormous

WHAT WOULD THE ANSWER BE IN THE CASE OF A WHALE?
   : yes

THANK YOU, I WILL REMEMBER THAT

THINK OF AN ANIMAL

IS IT PREHISTORIC? : yes

IS IT A PTERODACTYL : no

OH DEAR, I DID NOT GET THAT ONE

WHAT ANIMAL WERE YOU THINKING OF? : dinosaur

PLEASE ASK A QUESTION TO DISTINGUISH A PTERODACTYL
   FROM A DINOSAUR : is it spelled funny

WHAT WOULD THE ANSWER BE IN THE CASE OF A
   DINOSAUR? : no

THANK YOU, I WILL REMEMBER THAT

THINK OF AN ANIMAL

IS IT PREHISTORIC? : no

IS IT ENORMOUS? : yes

IS IT A WHALE? : yes

I GUESSED IT!!!

How does the program recognise an animal by testing for suitable features in a sensible way? By making use of a (binary) *discrimination tree*: a tree in which the *terminal* nodes are names of animals, and each *non-terminal* node has (a) a test; (b) a pointer to its YES-node; and (c) a pointer to its NO-node. For example, in the sequence above, when the program has learned the first discrimination it builds the structure:

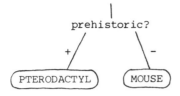

After adding the second discrimination, this becomes:

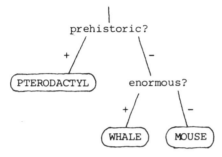

And so on.

Exercise 5.2.1. Draw a suitable discrimination tree to distinguish the objects CUBE, CYLINDER, PYRAMID, CONE, WEDGE, PRISM, BRICK. What about one for the objects MAN, GIRL, COW, BOY, WOMAN, BULL?

The EPAM program uses a discrimination tree to simulate the learning of "paired associates", i.e. pairs of nonsense syllables, where the subject has to learn that when given DAX he has to reply LOM, and so on. By the very nature of the program's learning process it exhibits the phenomena of

    stimulus and response generalisation

    retroactive interference

    forgetting as a failure of *accessing* (rather than *storage*)

and thus provides a non-probabilistic model of paired-associate learning. Compared to Winston's program, EPAM is cruder but it does its learning more gradually.

5.2.4   General Comments on Learning

Paradigms and Contrasts.

(a) statistical *vs* structural learning, e.g. height of man *vs* number of hands.

    Statistical: summarise wide experience in numbers

                     implicit descriptions (e.g. Samuel's program)

    Structural: reflect characteristics of individual cases

                    explicit descriptions (e.g. Winston, EPAM)

                    significant learning from single instances

(b) Improving an existing program (cf. tuning an engine) *vs* writing a new program (cf. building a bridge). In the case of improving an existing program, we already have a program that does the job, and the task is to make it perform better. Such programs usually have two distinct parts, the part that does the job and another part that fiddles with the first part.

Trivial Kinds of Change.
(a) Adding new procedures, new data: is this "learning"? For example, LOGO doesn't know how TO LAUGH, but if we "teach" it, then afterwards it does? Or, we might have a program that stores titles of books and the names of their authors. But it can't tell us who the author of *Waverley* is until it has learned it?

(b) The issue of "store *vs* recompute". This is essentially a matter of trading off space against time: should the program remember all the results it produces? If we are selective enough in what gets remembered, we may get an improvement of performance (e.g. MEMO functions).

No Attempt to Define "Learning"
(a) Learning as a possible aspect of the answer in the "what is intelligence?" game. A feeling that a program is not intelligent if it is "merely programmed" to do some task, but it *is* "if it learns to do it by itself".

(b) The slipperiness of learning programs when looked at hard. A program that *learns* to do task T can usually be thought of as simply *doing* a related task T', e.g. Samuel's program *learns* to play better checkers, or it *optimises* its performance. (Cf. "the computer just does what its programmer tells it to".)

(c) Informal, everyday use of learning as an "explanation" — as an *alternative* to "mechanism"? For example, how does one ride a bicycle? You can't be *told* how to do it, you have to "learn by experience". For the period c.1920-1950, experimental psychology (especially in the U.S.) was dominated by the "behaviourist" view, which saw learning as *the* problem of psychology.

The objection to doing this is the need to have a sufficient mechanism to accomplish the task. Look at the device/organism at a particular moment in time: you can ask valid questions about the mechanisms it's using, irrespective of how they were acquired.
(BUT ALSO: a deeper sense in which this formulation may be valid?)

5.2.5 References
J.S. Bruner (1960) *The Process of Learning.* Vintage Books.

J.S. Bruner (1966) *Toward a Theory of Instruction.* Harvard U.P.

J.S. Bruner, J.J. Goodnow, & G.A. Austin (1956) *A Study of Thinking.* Wiley.

E.A. Feigenbaum (1961) The simulation of verbal learning behaviour, reprinted in *Computers and Thought* (eds E.A. Feigenbaum & J. Feldman), McGraw-Hill.

P.H. Winston (1970). Learning structural descriptions from examples. Ph.D. thesis, AI Technical Report 231, MIT. (especially chapters 5 and 6).

5.3 PERCEPTRONS

5.3.1 Background

One of the many striking facts about the human brain is that it contains more than 10^{10} neurons, each of which is a sophisticated little computing device in its own right. In the search for the "mechanisms of intelligence", many people have tried to confront this fact, and to ask what kind of organisational principle could enable this vast mass of information-processing units to exhibit intelligent behaviour. This approach is usually loosely called "neural net" studies (at least by workers in Artificial Intelligence).

Underlying much of this research is the widespread notion ". . . of the brain itself as a rather loosely organised, randomly interconnected network of relatively simple devices". Several key ideas that arose during the 1940s and '50s had an important influence on this line of thought, for instance:
(a) the basic idea that *lots* (but lots!) of simple elements suitably put together can yield interesting, complex behaviour;
(b) the theoretical demonstration in the mid-1940s that networks of simple neuron-like elements can be constructed to compute any logical function;
(c) results that were starting to appear from neurophysiological studies of the way that information is processed in the visual systems of various animals;
(d) proposals from the newly-emerging field of Artificial Intelligence as to how pattern recognition can be done by using a large number of independent little decision-making units, working simultaneously, "organised" in a rather unstructured way.

So far in this course we have examined ways of generating intelligent behaviour by *imposing an organisation* on a sequential process — that is what programming is all about. By contrast, the emphasis in the neural net studies is largely on *self-organising* systems. The extreme case is the idea of a system with initially random connections that become selectively strengthened or weakened by learning.

At one time these ideas were very popular, and much research — both experimental and mathematical — was done on devices of this kind. Sometimes over-ambitious claims were made, for example that such devices would be able to play master chess by learning to "recognise"

181

good board situations. Nowadays it is felt (at least by workers in Artificial Intelligence) that this approach has severe limitations. There is a need for greater *structure*, for an appropriate match between the mechanism and the task to be done.

One class of device to emerge from this work has a particularly interesting history, and we look at it more closely.

5.3.2   Perceptrons

The idea is to have a machine that recognises a class of objects by a *simple combining of the evidence* obtained from lots of *small experiments* performed independently. Thus the perceptron provides a paradigm for the intuitive notion of simple decision-making carried out by a richly parallel mechanism.

Presented with an object X, a perceptron computes the values of various features $f_i(X)$, then combines them in aa weighted vote:

$$\Sigma \ w_i f_i = w_1 f_1 + w_2 f_2 + w_3 f_3 + ... + w_n f_n$$

This value is compared to a threshold θ. If $\Sigma \ w_i f_i > \theta$, we say the perceptron *responds positively*. We want it to respond positively if X is an object of a certain type, and negatively if not, e.g. if X is-a-circle; if X is-a-convex-figure; or if X is-a-single-connected-figure.

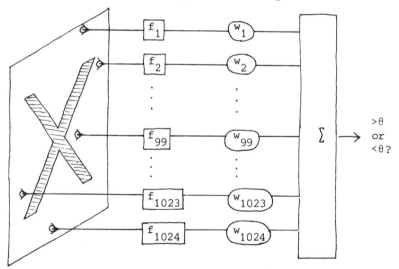

We can imagine some figure projected onto a two-dimensional "retina", which is "looked at" by a large number of little "demons", each computing one of the f_i. The outputs of these demons are then multiplied by their respective weights and added together.

How can this device be used to classify objects? Consider two examples:
Example 1. Take the simple case where we want the perceptron to recognise just *one particular figure*, at a fixed place on the retina. (Perhaps

182

a block capital letter X, as shown in the diagram above.) Let each f_i look at just one small spot on the retina. For each f_i that is looking at a spot that should be *black* if the object is in fact the one we are interested in, suppose it produces output 0 if its spot *is* black, and output −1 if its spot is white. For each f_i looking at a spot that should be *white* for the correct object, suppose it produces output 0 if the spot *is* white and −1 if it is black.

Now consider the perceptron with all weights = 1 and a threshold of −1, so that we expect $\Sigma\ f_i > -1$ for the correct object. If we show this perceptron our desired object, then all the f_i will have value zero, the whole sum will be zero, and therefore the inequality will be true. But if the object differs in any way from the intended one, *then at least one* of the f_i will have value −1, so the whole sum will be ≤ -1, and the inequality will be broken. So this simple perceptron discriminates between our desired figure and all others.

Example 2. Consider next a case where we want to recognise not just a single object, but a broad class of objects. Suppose we want it to recognise whether the black area forms a single, *convex* object.

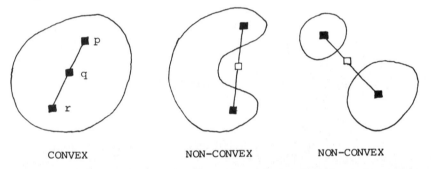

CONVEX   NON−CONVEX   NON−CONVEX

One way of testing for convexity — or even for defining it ! — is to consider collections of three collinear points, p, q, r. In a *convex* figure, if two points p and r are black, then all points q on the line between them must also be black. In a *non-convex* figure, however, there will always be some black points p and r that have a white point q between them.

Suppose each f_i looks at three collinear spots. If the two outer spots are black and the middle one is white, let the f_i produce output −1. Otherwise the output is 0. Suppose now there are enough f_i to "cover" the whole retina, in some sense. Again consider the inequality $\Sigma\ f_i > -1$. The argument proceeds as before. If the object is convex, then all the f_i will be zero and the inequality will hold true. But if the figure is non-convex, at least one of the f_i will have value −1, and the inequality will be broken. So this perceptron discriminates between convex and non-convex objects.

5.3.3 Learning in Perceptrons

Not surprisingly, given the neural-net background to the perceptron research, much of the interest with perceptrons lies in the question of whether a perceptron can *learn* to recognise objects. As with Samuel's draughts program, learning is a matter of finding an appropriate set of weights, w_i. To get the perceptron to learn to recognise a class C, we present it with a sequence of examples, some in C and some not. Each time, depending on right or wrong, we take appropriate reinforcing or correcting action.

We can make an intuitive argument for the form the correction should take, analogous to the argument made in discussing Samuel's program. If the weighted vote $\Sigma\ w_i f_i$ is below threshold for a figure belonging to C, then clearly the weights of the positive terms should be increased, and those of the negative terms decreased. And conversely, if $\Sigma\ w_i f_i > \theta$ for a figure *not* in C, then vice versa. One easy way to think about this is to suppose all the f_i have value either 1 or 0. Then the correction procedure takes the form of adding (or subtracting) 1 to (from) the weights of all the features that have value 1.

It was possible to prove a remarkable theorem which says, in effect, that if a perceptron is inherently capable of recognising a class of objects, Ehen it can *learn* to recognise them, by means of a simple learning procedure, in a finite number of steps:

Perceptron Training Theorem. Given a class C, suppose that there do exist weights $w_i{}^*$ such that
$$D^* = \Sigma\ w_i{}^* f_i(X)$$
is > 0 for objects in C, and < 0 for objects not in C. Start with any set of weights $D_i = \Sigma\ w_i f_i$, and try the perceptron on a sequence of examples, X:
(a) If X is classified correctly, fine;
(b) If $D < 0$ for an X in C, then replace each w_i by $(w_i + f_i(X))$. Conversely, if $D > 0$ for an X not in C, then replace each w_i by $(w_i - f_i(X))$.
Then step (b) will be taken only a finite number of times. In other words, the perceptron will learn to recognise the class correctly after only a finite number of errors. Notice how the description of the class C is *implicit*, and *distributed* over the final w_i (or $w_i{}^*$).

5.3.4 Capabilities of Perceptrons

In 1969, Minsky and Papert published an influential book on perceptrons. Their highly original contribution was to by-pass the question of learning, and to ask instead about the fundamental abilities and limitations of perceptrons. They point out that it is not sufficient to know merely that if a perceptron can do a task, then it can also *learn* to do it. We need also to understand *what* tasks perceptrons can and cannot do *in principle*.

The important point about a perceptron is that it makes a *global* decision about a figure by weighing only *local* evidence. We distinguish two senses of "local evidence":

(a) Order-limited: each f_i depends on at most k points
(b) Diameter-limited: each f_i sees points in only a small area

It turns out that order-limited perceptrons are the deeper and more interesting, but similar results hold for both, and as the diameter-limited case is easier to deal with we concentrate on it here.

Diameter-limited perceptrons can recognise, e.g. a scene consisting only of rectangles. If all f_i output zero for any of

and -1 for anything else, then we can set all $w_i = 1$ and have
$$(\Sigma f_i(X) > -1) \text{ if and only if [scene consists of rectangles]}$$
But a perceptron cannot recognise, e.g., a scene consisting of a single dot. Consider the figures:

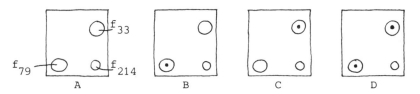

For (A), we need $\Sigma\ w_i f_i < \Theta$. For (B), we need $\Sigma\ w_i f_i > \Theta$, so some $w_i f_i$ (e.g. $w_{79}f_{79}$) must have increased. Similarly, for (C), some other $w_i f_i$ (e.g. $w_{33}f_{33}$) must have increased. For (D) we need $\Sigma\ w_i f_i < \Theta$, but this is *impossible* since *both* groups (like f_{79} and f_{33}) will have increased.

Neither can it recognise whether a figure is *connected*. Consider

and divide the f_i into three groups: (a) those that can "see" the left-hand end of the figure; (b) those than can "see" the right-hand end of the figure; and (c) those that can see neither end. Then we can make the same argument as for the single dot. The point is that we are trying to get the perceptron to make a global judgement — about connectivity — on the basis of local evidence. But the trouble is that B, which is connected, looks *locally* just like A or D, which are disconnected. (But is it quite easy to write programs for a serial machine, e.g. in LOGO, to determine whether a figure is connected, and they use very little storage.)

Various other interesting figures cannot be recognised, e.g. objects that contain other objects, a rectangle embedded in context, etc.

185

5.3.5 Discussion

There is a general moral to be drawn from the analysis. There is no point in discussing elaborate schemes for "teaching" a machine to do something it inherently cannot be made to do. Most of the early proposed schemes lacked careful analysis of

> their inherent limitations
> the *rates* of learning
> the sizes of the weights w_i.

Consider for example, the inability of the diameter-limited perceptron to recognise the scene consisting of a single dot.

Notice, however, that Minsky and Papert's analysis applies only to the very simplest kind of perceptron, called "single-layered". Real perceptron enthusiasts play with far more complicated varieties, called "multi-layered", and "cross-coupled", etc. It is not at all clear whether limitations analogous to those of Minsky and Papert apply to these more complex perceptrons. (If you are interested, see the careful review of the *Perceptron* book by Block.)

5.3.6 References

M. Minsky & S. Papert (1969) *Perceptrons: An Introduction to Computational Geometry*. MIT Press.

H.D. Block (1970) A review of *Perceptrons*: . . ., in *Information and Control, 17*, 501-522.

5.4 INDUCTION

5.4.1 Introduction

Inductive tasks require detection of a pattern, or *regularity*, in the information presented, such as spotting a trend, seeing similarities, finding the odd-man-out, etc. Examples are:

(a) Geometric analogy tasks. These were discussed extensively at the beginning of the course (see chapter 1).

(b) Letter analogies. Fill in the blanks:
IJ JI   PO OP   ED --

(c) Letter grouping. Pick out the one that doesn't belong:
AABC ACAD ACFH AACG

(d) Number groups. State what is common:
35   110   75

(e) Number relations. Pick the one that doesn't belong:
2 6   3 9   4 12   6 15

(f) Number series. State the rule:
15   18   21   24   27   30

(g) Number correction. State the one in error:
1   2   3   4   5   7

(h) Seeing trends. What is the trend?:
ANGER BACTERIA CAMEL DEAD EXCITE
(i) Word groups. What is common?:
MAIM TEST GANG LABEL
(j) Word relations. Fill in the blanks:
REAL SEAL   MEAT NEAT   BORE ----
(k) Series completion. Write the correct letter in the blanks:
(i)   C D C D C D —
(ii)   A A A B B B C C C D D —
(iii) A T B A T A A T B A T —
(iv)   A B M C D M E F M G H M —
(v)   D E F G E F G H F G H I —
(vi)   Q X A P X B Q X A —
(vii) A D U A C U A E U A B U A F U A —
(viii) M A B M B C M C D M —
(ix)   U R T U S T U T T U —
(x)   A B Y A B X A B W A B —
(xi)   R S C D S T D E T U E F —
(xii) N P A O Q A P R A Q S A —
(xiii) W X A X Y B Y Z C Z A D A B —
(xiv) J K Q R K L R S L M S T —
(xv)   P O N O N M N M L M L K —

Compared to more "deductive" problems, these tasks have a certain "openness". Finding the solution is a genuine "creative act" and involves going *beyond* the evidence given (cf. a scientific theory). The answer is not *in* the sequence itself: the problem solver himself has to bring something to the task.

What defines a right answer? Mathematically speaking, there is an indefinite number of sequences that begin 1 2 3 4 ...

5.4.2 Letter Sequences
See problem (k) in the examples above. Notice how the problems vary in difficulty (e.g. as measured by time taken to solve, or the number of people failing). Some seem especially difficult: (v), (vii), (ix), (xv), ... (Why?) By and large, different people tend to agree about which ones are easier and which ones are harder. (Why?)

Notice how it is important to find the periodicity of the sequence. People usually start by doing this.

Simon and Kotovsky (1963) created a descriptive language for this class of sequences. All that is needed is:
the idea of a repeating *pattern*, in square brackets []
the idea of *pointers* into the alphabet
the operations of NEXT and BACKWARD NEXT on the pointers

For example, using the problems from (k) above:

(iv) A B M C D M E F M G H M —

    is: x ◄—A/ALPH, [x nx x nx M]

and is interpreted as follows: The sequence uses a pointer, x, which is initialised to the letter A in the ALPHabet. The sequence is generated by saying the letter that x currently points to ("x"), then stepping x to point to the next letter in sequence ("nx"), saying the letter that x now points to ("x"), stepping x again ("nx"), and then saying the letter M. The sequence is repeated over and over again. Similarly:

(ix) U R T U S T U T T U —

    is: x ◄—R/ALPH, [U x nx T]

(xv) P O N O N M N M L M L K —

    is: x ◄—y ◄—P/ALPH, [x bx x bx x by x ◄—y]

Simon & Kotovsky find that the harder problems have more complex descriptions. In particular, the sequences that require *two* pointers impose a bigger memory load and are almost always harder than the *one*-pointer sequences. (Why?) (A more detailed analysis, based on thinking-aloud protocols and eye movements is given in Kotovsky and Simon 1973.)

5.4.3 Induction Program

Simon & Kotovsky wrote various versions of a program to derive the pattern description from the given sequences. This led to the idea of a "natural" ordering of the difficulty of the problems, since a "stronger" version of the program (i.e. one that solved more problems than a "weaker" one) tended to solve all the problems the weaker one did. Indeed, it would be hard to write a program that solved the harder problems and failed on the easier ones.

We look at a "rational reconstruction" of Simon & Kotovsky's program, presented by Newell (1973). The idea is to start with a broad class of hypotheses (e.g. "all sequences of period 3") and then make successive refinements by repeated comparison with the given sequence. The trick is to allow for a large number of possibilities by using variables (α β γ), but then deducing what the variables *must* be in order to generate the sequence correctly. In comparing the pattern against the sequence, there are six different situations that can occur, each of which leads to an appropriate action:

Case 1. Pattern has a variable α , sequence has a letter which is pointed to by some pointer x. *Action*: replace α by "x".

Case 2. Pattern has a variable α , sequence has a letter which is "next" after some pointer x. *Action*: Replace α by "nx x".

Case 3. Pattern has a variable α , sequence has a letter L. *Action*: Replace α by a new pointer "y", and add "y ◄—L/ALPH".

Case 4. Pattern has a pointer x, sequence has the letter pointed to by x. *Action*: That's fine, do nothing.

188

Case 5. Pattern has a pointer x, sequence has the letter next after x.
        Action: Replace "x" by "nx x".
Case 6. Otherwise fail.

Let us see how this works out on problem (viii),
i.e. given M A B M B C M C D M ...:

1.   Guess [α β γ], i.e. a sequence of period 3. (See exercise below).
     Generate: α ... compared to: M ...
     Case 3: α must be pointer x, initialised to M.
2.   Now have: x ← M/ALPH, [x β γ]
     Generate: M β ... compared to: M A ...
     Case 3: β must be pointer y, initialised to A.
3.   Now have: x ← M/ALPH, y ← A/ALPH, [x y γ]
     Generate: M A γ ... compared to: M A B ...
     Case 2: γ must be "ny y".
4.   Now have: x ← M/ALPH, y ← A/ALPH, [x y ny y]
     Generate: M A B M B C M C D ...
     OK: we're there!

Unlike the Simon and Kotovsky program, this one does not begin by finding the periodicity of the sequence. But it has no need to, since the hypotheses that it has period one ([α]) or two ([α β]) quickly come to grief.

Exercise. Show this.

5.4.4   Discussion

By working with symbolic descriptions of sequences instead of with the sequences themselves, we have managed to cast the induction problem into the same form as earlier problems we have looked at. As in the Missionaries and Cannibals problem, for example, we have *an initial* state, e.g. [α β γ], which has to be transformed into a *goal state* (i.e. a fully-specified pattern that generates the given sequence) by means of a series of *operators*, e.g. replace " α " by "nx x".

Notice that in this case, for each kind of difference between the pattern and the given sequence there is a *single* kind of change to be made to the pattern, so we never have to undo a decision we made earlier. This means that we can use the powerful *matching* technique instead of the comparatively weaker tree-search.

The traditional distinction between "deduction" and "induction" leads to a certain mystique attached to the latter. I hope to have dispelled some of this by showing how an "inductive" problem can be solved by the same means as were used for "deductive" problems, i.e. (a) use of symbolic descriptions, and (b) application of operators to reduce the difference between the current state and the goal state.

Some interesting questions have to do with the hypotheses, e.g., where do they come from? Consider:
(a) O T T F F S S E . . . ?
(b) S M T W T F . . . ?
(c) B C D G J O P Q R S . . . ?

5.4.5   References
A. Newell (1973) Artificial intelligence and the concept of mind, in *Computer Models of Thought and Language* (eds R.C. Schank & K.M. Colby) pp.1-60. W.H. Freeman.

H.A. Simon & K. Kotovsky (1963) Human acquisition of concepts for sequential patterns. *Psychological Review 70*, 534-46.

K. Kotovsky & H.A. Simon (1973) Empirical tests of a theory of human acquisition of concepts for sequential patterns. *Cognitive Psychology 4*, 399-424.

5.5   PRODUCTION SYSTEMS

5.5.1   The Need for a Constrained Language
In the programs we have looked at so far, the "learning" has consisted of the building up of some *data* structure distinct from the learning program itself, e.g. Winston's descriptive networks, EPAM discrimination tree, Samuel's weighted evaluation score, and Simon & Kotovsky's letter sequence pattern. However, in order to get a wider range and greater flexibility of learning, and to write programs that acquire the ability to do something they could not do before, it will clearly be necessary to have programs that modify and add to their existing *program*. For example, we might want to write a robot program that, the first few times it is asked to assemble a toy car, does so slowly and painfully from first principles; but after a while, we would want it to have acquired a new *procedure* for that particular task.

Unfortunately, LOGO and other "ordinary" programming languages are not really suitable for this kind of automatic manipulation. The difficulty is rather like trying to understand someone else's LOGO program, where all the procedures are called just P1,P2,P3, etc., and the arguments and variables are all called X,Y,Z! In order to modify someone else's program, you have to know the significance of each of the procedures, arguments, variables, etc.; to understand the purpose of each line in a procedure; to know enough about the context to be able to make the modification without introducing new bugs; to be able to use the EDITor effectively to change the old procedure or define a new one.

Needless to say, it is very hard to automate this process. What we do instead is to simplify and restrict the programming language drastically, and to write programs in this more primitive language in a systematic way. We will suggest a way of doing this by considering how to write LOGO programs that have the desired properties.

5.5.2 Production Systems

First suggestion. Suppose we write our program in the form:

```
TO MYPROGRAM
    1 IF ⟨ condition 1 ⟩ THEN ⟨ DO action 1 ⟩ AND GO 1
    2 IF ⟨ condition 2 ⟩ THEN ⟨ DO action 2 ⟩ AND GO 1
    3 IF ⟨ condition 3 ⟩ THEN ⟨ DO action 3 ⟩ AND GO 1
    . . .
    999 IF ⟨ condition 999 ⟩ THEN ⟨ DO action 999 ⟩ AND GO 1
END
```

Notice that this is a special kind of program. Its execution takes place in a sequence of *cycles*. During each cycle, just one line gets fully obeyed. LOGO looks at the lines 1,2,3,. . . in turn, and finds which one has a true ⟨condition⟩. The ⟨action⟩ on that line is obeyed, and then LOGO jumps back to line 1 and the next cycle begins.

This kind of program has some of the properties we want, for we are now stating explicitly what the conditions are for each possible action to occur. However, this is not yet enough, because we have said nothing about what the conditions and actions are allowed to be. And if we allow arbitrary LOGO code to be written there, then all the old problems come back. So:

Second suggestion. Suppose that we have a *working memory*, called WM, that is used to hold all the changing information in the system. In other words, there are to be no other variables, lists, etc., to hold data other than those in WM. By analogy with the INFERENCE system (see section 2.2), we can think of WM as a database, and we are saying that all data must be stored in the database.

We are now in a position to place interesting restrictions on the conditions and actions. We will say:

(a) All ⟨conditions⟩ consist of a pattern match against the information in WM, rather like the ISO pattern match in the INFERENCE system. Call this operation MATCHES. Note that this is the *only* way of retrieving information from WM: we allow no FIRSTs, BUTFIRSTs, etc.

(b) All ⟨actions⟩ consist of an addition to, or modification of, the information in WM, analogous to ASSERT.

Then our program will look like:

191

```
TO MYPROGRAM
    1 IF MATCHES ⟨pattern 1⟩ THEN ⟨WM-action 1⟩ AND GO 1
    2 IF MATCHES ⟨pattern 2⟩ THEN ⟨WM-action 2⟩ AND GO 1
    3 IF MATCHES ⟨pattern 3⟩ THEN ⟨WM-action 3⟩ AND GO 1
    ...
999 IF MATCHES ⟨pattern 999⟩ THEN ⟨WM-action 999⟩
        AND GO 1
END
```

This kind of program is usually written in the following notation:

```
RULE    1 :   ⟨pattern    1⟩   ⟹ ⟨WM-action 1⟩
RULE    2 :   ⟨pattern    2⟩   ⟹ ⟨WM-action 2⟩
RULE    3 :   ⟨pattern    3⟩   ⟹ ⟨WM-action 3⟩
    ...
RULE 999 :    ⟨pattern 999⟩    ⟹ ⟨WM-action 999⟩
```

This is called a *production system*. The individual rules are called *productions* or *production rules*.

5.5.3 An Example: ANIMAL Program Revisited

Remember the ANIMAL program, which guesses what animal you are thinking of by asking a series of questions about its properties? The diagram below shows the state of the program after it has learned about MOUSE, ELEPHANT, EMU, STORK, DALMATION and LEOPARD:

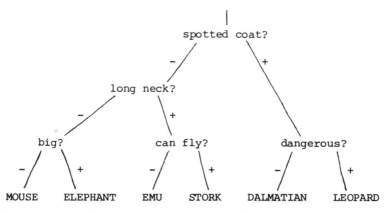

Table 1 is a production system to find which of these animals you have in mind. The notation is similar to that used for the INFERENCE system. The easiest way to understand how the system works is to watch it stepping through an example. Suppose we think of EMU, and suppose that the WM is initially empty.

Cycle 1. The patterns of neither Rule A nor Rule B match the WM, nor do Anim1, Ques1, or Anim2. But the pattern of Ques2 does match (since there is no item [ASKED SPOTTED-COAT] in WM), so the system obeys the actions of Ques2:

(a) It asks: SPOTTED-COAT?

(b) It puts into WM the item [ASKED SPOTTED-COAT]

(c) It attends to the answer: we type in [ANSWER NO], which gets automatically ASSERTed.

Table 1.   A production system for the ANIMAL program

Rule A: [GUESS 'ANIMAL] [NOT [RESPONSE 'RIGHTORWRONG]]
    ⇒ [SAY :ANIMAL!] [ATTEND-TO RESPONSE]
Rule B: [ANSWER YES] [ASKED 'PROP]
    ⇒ [DELETE [ANSWER YES]] [ASSERT [PROPERTY :PROP]]
Anim1: [PROPERTY SPOTTED-COAT] [PROPERTY DANGEROUS]
    ⇒ [ASSERT [GUESS LEOPARD]]
Ques1: [PROPERTY SPOTTED-COAT] [NOT [ASKED DANGEROUS]]
    ⇒ [SAY DANGEROUS ?] [ASSERT [ASKED DANGEROUS]]
    [ATTEND-TO ANSWER]
Anim2: [PROPERTY SPOTTED-COAT]
    ⇒ [ASSERT [GUESS [DALMATIAN]]]
Ques2: [NOT [ASKED SPOTTED-COAT]]
    ⇒ [SAY SPOTTED-COAT?] [ASSERT [ASKED SPOTTED-
    COAT]] [ATTEND-TO ANSWER]
Anim3: [PROPERTY LONG-NECK] [PROPERTY CAN-FLY]
    ⇒ [ASSERT [GUESS STORK]]
Ques3: [PROPERTY LONG-NECK] [NOT [ASKED CAN-FLY]]
    ⇒ [SAY CAN-FLY ?] [ASSERT [ASKED CAN-FLY]]
    [ATTEND-TO ANSWER]
Anim4: [PROPERTY LONG-NECK] ⇒ [ASSERT [GUESS EMU]]
Ques4: [NOT [ASKED LONG-NECK]]
    ⇒ [SAY LONG-NECK ?] [ASSERT [ASKED LONG-NECK]]
    [ATTEND-TO ANSWER]
Anim5: [PROPERTY BIG] ⇒ [ASSERT [GUESS ELEPHANT]]
Ques5: [NOT [ASKED BIG]]
    ⇒ [SAY BIG ?] [ASSERT [ASKED BIG]] [ATTEND-TO
    ANSWER]
Anim6: ⇒ [ASSERT [GUESS MOUSE]]

Cycle 2. This time Ques2 does not match, since there now *is* an item [ASKED SPOTTED-COAT] in the WM. The first rule to match is Ques4, so as in Cycle 1:

(a) It asks: LONG NECK?

(b) It puts into WM the item [ASKED LONG-NECK]

(c) It attends to, and ASSERTs, our answer: [ANSWER YES].

Cycle 3. This time Rule B matches, since the items [ANSWER YES] and [ASKED LONG-NECK] are both in WM. So, taking the actions of Rule B, the system deletes the item [ANSWER YES], and adds the item [PROPERTY LONG-NECK].

193

Cycle 4. Ques3 is the first rule which matches. As before, it asks about "CAN-FLY", and gets our [ANSWER NO].

Cycle 5. This time Anim4 is the first rule that matches. Obeying the action, the system adds to WM the item [GUESS EMU].

Cycle 6. Finally, Rule A can apply, since the item [GUESS EMU] is in WM. It guesses "EMU!", asks us for the response, and records our typed-in [RESPONSE RIGHT].

5.5.4 Properties of Production Systems

1. Notice how the "facts" that have been learned are of the same kind as the original "program" — Rule A, Rule B, and perhaps Anim6. Rule Anim3, for example, is just as much part of the present program as is Rule A, and it is treated in the same way.

2. Notice how "modular" the production system is. Each rule states a self-contained part of the knowledge embedded in the total system. Rule Anim3, for example, states that if the animal is known to have a long neck and be able to fly, then STORK should be guessed. Similarly, Ques1 states that if the animal is known to have a spotted coat, but it is not yet known whether it is dangerous, then that should be the next thing to be found out. If we look at the corresponding nodes in the tree, we can see how "reasonable" these rules are.

3. Largely because of this modularity, the production system is highly amenable to automatic learning — which is why we were interested in it in the first place. To see how this automatic learning might happen, again it is best to follow an example. Suppose that we think of OSTRICH instead of EMU. The answers to all the questions will be the same, so the system will still guess "EMU!", but this time we tell it: [RESPONSE WRONG]. What needs to happen?

(a) Clearly the system must ask us for a distinguishing property of the new animal, i.e. it does an [ATTEND-TO DISTINGUISHING-PROPERTY], and we tell it: [DISTINGUISHING-PROPERTY HEAD-IN-SAND].

(b) The system now has in hand all the information it needs in order to build the new rules. If it takes all the [PROPERTY . . .]s that it has in WM, these are what specify the incorrect guess that was made. If it adds to these the distinguishing property we have just given it, then those are all the features relevant to the new animal. So the system forms two new rules:

Anim3.5: [PROPERTY LONG-NECK] [PROPERTY HEAD-IN-SAND]
      ⇒ [ASSERT [GUESS OSTRICH]]
Ques3.5: [PROPERTY LONG-NECK] [NOT [ASKED HEAD-IN-SAND]]
      ⇒ [SAY HEAD-IN-SAND ?] [ASSERT [ASKED HEAD-IN-SAND]] [ATTEND-TO ANSWER]

and puts them just before the rule responsible for the wrong guess, i.e. between Ques3 and Anim4.

Actually to implement these steps as part of the original production system requires only a few extra rules, and one then has a fully-fledged system capable of learning about new animals. For details of how this is done, see the paper by Waterman.

In fact, production systems of this kind were originally developed for the purpose of modelling human problem-solving behaviour. We will have some more to say about this next time.

5.5.5 Reference

D.A. Waterman (1975) Adaptive production systems. *Proc. Fourth IJCAI*, pp.296-303.

5.6 SCHEMATA

5.6.1 Production Systems as Psychological Models
(a) In *origin*, production systems (PSs) of the kind we looked at last time were developed by Newell and Simon for representing human problem solving behaviour. The data typically consist of thinking-aloud protocols on tasks such as chess and symbolic logic — much the same sort of material as GPS was applied to. PSs turn out to provide a convenient and appropriate form to express the models of problem solving.

(b) A typical *later application* of Newell and Simon's ideas is the use of PSs to investigate cognitive development in children. This work capitalises on the suitability of the PSs for modelling learning, and the ease of adding new rules.

(c) As a *psychological model*, the WM (see last section) can be more-or-less identified with the psychologist's "short-term memory", and the PS itself with "long-term memory", i.e. our knowledge, abilities and memories.

(d) *Parallel evocation*. Although we described PSs last time as a serial process, in terms of a special kind of LOGO program that tests the rules one by one until it finds one whose " ⟨condition⟩ " is satisfied, there is a psychologically more interesting way of regarding them. By analogy with the Perceptron, we can think of each rule as a little "demon", each on the look out for its own ⟨condition⟩ . As with the Perceptron, all the demons are active at once. The first one whose ⟨condition⟩ is satisfied yells loudly, and the system obeys the corresponding ⟨action⟩ .

(e) Thus we get the prototype for the idea of a system working on a *recognise-act* cycle. More on this below. We can think of the Perceptron-like aspects of the system as "recognising" what to do next, while the LOGO-like aspects actually perform the "acts".

5.6.2 Schemata

The idea of a schema as a representation of skill and knowledge, i.e. as information about something and about how to do things with it, derives from:

(a) Work of Bartlett (1932: *Remembering*). Schema as the essence of a story: outline features remembered, plus any unusual characteristics — but distorted in a normalising direction.

(b) Piaget. Two aspects of adaptation: (i) Assimilation — incorporation of new experience into existing structure; (ii) Accommodation — modification of existing structure (or building of new structure); e.g. children's fantasy-play *vs* imitation.

(c) Wertheimer (1945, 1959: *Productive Thinking*). Role of naive, everyday schemata in understanding formal material, such as geometry or algebra. Hence an emphasis on difference between "rote learning" and "real understanding".

Then in AI:

(d) J.D. Becker: a concrete suggestion for learning and use of simple schemata, but not a working program. Schema is:

$$[\underbrace{k_1 \longrightarrow k_2 \longrightarrow k_3}_{\text{event}} \Rightarrow \underbrace{k_4}_{\text{event}}],$$

i.e. "if k_1, then if k_2 and k_3, then k_4". There are weights attached to indicate the confidence of the schema (i.e. the probability of the regularity holding) and criteriality of each of its components. The schema can be used, e.g. to achieve k_4, given k_1.

(e) Minsky: "frames" — already discussed, particularly in Vision. High-level guidelines, but no program.

5.6.3 What does this Buy?

(a) Can represent knowledge ranging from general to specific. Lots of specialised schemata in an area where you are "expert".

(b) Place to attach items of information where they are likely to be found when needed.

(c) Provides the all-important *context* for perception triggered by a feature.

(d) Model of cognitive *skills*: what you can *do*, as well as what you *know*.

(e) (Again:) Idea of a cognitive system functioning on a "recognise-act" cycle. "Recognition" means the evocation of a schema, "act" means its use. The "act" part in humans is serial, quite slow, and depends heavily on symbolic description. The "recognise" part seems parallel and rapid, and is poorly understood.

5.6.4 Discussion

(a) Statistical and structural learning: the need for both, e.g. to learn significantly from a single example and also to continue improving during extended practice.

(b) Deeper sense of "learning by experience". Our abilities are structured in terms of things that are "familiar" to us, and the actions they lead to. Thus our past experience, captured in schemata, serves to guide our present behaviour.

5.6.5   References

J.D. Becker (1973) A model for the encoding of experiential information, in *Computer Models of Thought and Language* (eds R.C. Schank & K.M. Colby) pp.396-434. W.H. Freeman

H. Ginsburg & S. Opper (1969) *Piaget's Theory of Intellectual Development: An Introduction.* Prentice-Hall.

A. Newell & H.A. Simon (1972) *Human Problem Solving.* Prentice-Hall.

6. PROGRAMMING

6.1 HOW TO USE A COMPUTER

6.1.1 Introduction

The best way to learn about programming is to hold a series of conversations with a computer via a terminal. For this you will need:

(a) Access to a computer terminal
(b) An interactive (conversational) programming language, like LOGO, mounted on the computer.
(c) A reference manual for the programming language, containing precise and concise descriptions of the facilities available.
(d) A primer for the programming language which is a guide to help you explore the language. It should contain elementary explanations and graded exercises.

Unfortunately we cannot help you with a-c. Either your teacher or you will have to make these available. The notes that follow attempt to satisfy need d, a primer for LOGO. People come to programming with different backgrounds and no one primer can suit everybody. Some of our students have used an alternative primer, which we can thoroughly recommend for those requiring a less intensive introduction: *How to Work the LOGO Machine*, by Benedict du Boulay and Tim O'Shea, Occasional Paper No.4, Department of Artificial Intelligence, University of Edinburgh.

6.1.2 The Terminal

The terminal you will use to communicate with the computer will probably be either a teletype or a visual display unit. The teletype is like an electric typewriter on a stand. The visual display unit is similar except that instead of a roll of paper to type on the symbols will appear on a television screen.

The main part of the keyboard is laid out like an ordinary typewriter. Notice the 'shift' key at the left side of the keyboard, which you must use to type some of the special characters, e.g.

SHIFT and 2 results in ''
SHIFT and 7 results in '

Notice also that there is a complete row of numerals across the top of the keyboard. Be careful to distinguish between the *letter* 'oh' and the *digit* 'zero', between the *letter* 'ell' and the *digit* 'one' — be sure always to type the one you really mean.

Locate the keys; for returning the carriage to the start of a new line; for deleting characters and lines and for interrupting the computer. Ask your teacher to help with this and to show you how they work.

6.1.3   Logging On and Off

To get in contact with the computer you will need to switch on the terminal and *log on*. Logging on entails telling the computer who you are, what you want and possibly giving a password. This information is given in a stylised 'log on' sequence. This sequence differs from computer to computer. Your teacher will tell you what the sequence is for your particular computer. Similarly when you want to finish your programming session you will have to *log off*. You tell the computer you are finished and it gives you a log off message.

People who design these logging sequences are predisposed to have the computer give you masses of esoteric information, e.g. precisely which computer system you are using, what time of day it is. You are best to ignore all this information at this stage. One day you might be interested in it.

6.1.4   Bugs

A *bug* is a computing term for a mistake in your program. If this is your first programming experience you are going to be surprised at the number of mistakes you will make — everybody is. Do not worry about them, because:

(a) Nothing you can do will damage the computer, and you will need at least a small hammer to damage the terminal. If you hear people talking about the computer 'crashing' this refers to psychological not physical breakdown. Smoke pours out of computers only in bad science fiction films.

(b) Bugs are good for you. They help you to learn. If you do not get bugs you are not stretching yourself.

(c) If you get in a mess ask your teacher for help. That is what he is there for.

6.1.5   Terminal Listing

The piece of paper with typewriting on it that comes from a teletype is called a 'listing'. It is solely for your benefit. The computer keeps its own record. You will normally throw it away except for bits on which you have:

(a) The final record of your program

(b) The results of the program

(c) Some particular sequence (e.g. logging on) that you want to remember.

(d) The record of an unsolved bug.

Keep your records tidy or you will be swamped. Do not leave the listing hanging from the terminal — it is a fire hazard.

6.2   PROCEDURES

6.2.1   Introduction

In the LOGO programming language there are two kinds of beast:

(a) *Objects*, which can be numbers (like 2,13, 105), words (like CAT, or TRIANGLE2) or lists (like [ON THE MAT] or [ON [THE MAT]]).

(b) *Procedures*, which are instructions or recipes that allow us to manipulate objects, e.g.

　　　PRINT 4

causes 4 to be printed on the terminal.

Synonyms. Not everybody uses the same notation as we do. Objects are sometimes called datastructures, data or items. Procedures are sometimes called programs, functions, routines, operations, commands or predicates. A process is a procedure that is running.

What is Provided? Numbers must be whole numbers. Words can be any string of letters or digits, containing a letter. Lists are any sequence of objects (i.e. numbers, words or sublists) separated by spaces and surrounded by brackets. Lists can be as nested as you like, e.g.

　　　[THIS [IS [A]] [[VERY NESTED] LIST]]

Quite a lot of procedures are provided by LOGO, e.g.

　　　PRINT, FIRST, FIRSTPUT, COUNT, SUM, DIFF, NL, VALUE, etc.

A complete list and definitions can be found in the reference manual.

You can also define your own procedures and add them to the ones already provided. For the mechanics of doing this, see section 6.3.

Exercise 6.2.1. PRINT TYPE and SAY are very similar procedures. Find out how they differ by experimenting at the terminal.

6.2.2　Quotes

Each procedure has a name, which must be a word. To distinguish words as objects from procedure names, words intended as objects have a quote sign ' in front of them, e.g.

　　　PRINT 'HI

where PRINT is a procedure name, 'HI is an object. PRINT HI would cause an error, unless HI was the name of a procedure.

Exceptions to this rule are words in lists, since these could not possibly be intended as procedure names: e.g. PRINT [HI THERE] will work.

6.2.3　Procedure Calls

We communicate with the computer by typing in *procedure calls*, e.g.

　　　PRINT 4 is a procedure call.

The procedure PRINT prints one LOGO object (number, word or list) on the terminal listing. This LOGO object is called its *argument*:

　　　4 is the argument of PRINT in PRINT 4.

Some procedures, like SUM, take two arguments. Some, like GOODBYE, take none. Some take three or more. The number of arguments a procedure takes is fixed. Arguments are always LOGO objects.

Sometimes arguments are not given explicitly but are the result of some other procedure call, e.g.

   PRINT SUM 2 3

   the arguments of SUM are 2 and 3.

   the argument of PRINT is 5, the result of SUM 2 3.

This nesting of procedure calls can get arbitrarily deep, e.g.

   1: PRINT FIRST BUTFIRST BUTFIRST [A B C D]

   C

The decisions about which procedure calls provide the arguments to which procedures, are called the *calling pattern* of the procedure call. In the above examples the calling patterns are obvious. In some examples it can be non-obvious, e.g.

   PRINT SUM COUNT [A B C] FIRST [2 4 5]

When we write a procedure call we can try to make the calling pattern clearer by putting brackets around sub-procedure calls and using new lines and indentation for the second and consecutive arguments of a procedure, e.g.

   PRINT (SUM (COUNT [A B C])
             (FIRST [2 4 5]))

In fact these are not strictly necessary for the computer. Because:

(a) The procedure name comes first, followed by its arguments;

(b) The computer knows how many arguments each procedure takes;

(c) The computer can distinguish between procedure names and objects; it can always fix the calling pattern in a unique way. Can you do it?

Exercise 6.2.2. What will the computer type out if you type in each of the following commands?

   PRINT FIRST [A B C]

   PRINT COUNT FIRST [[UP DOWN] [NORTH SOUTH EAST WEST]]

   PRINT BUTFIRST FIRST BUTFIRST [[X] [Y Z] [U V W]]

   PRINT SUM COUNT [1 2 3] FIRST [1 2 3]

   PRINT SUM LAST FIRST [[2 1] [4 3]] FIRST LAST [[3 4] [1 2]]

   PRINT DIFF FIRST BUTFIRST [10 9 8 7] COUNT BUTFIRST BUTFIRST [1 2 3 4 5 6]

Now log on to LOGO and check your answers.

6.2.4   Evaluation

We communicate with the computer by typing procedure calls at the terminal. Each procedure call is *evaluated* by the computer, which causes LOGO procedures to be *run* on LOGO objects. The evaluation process is as follows:

1.   The computer works along the line from left to right.

2.   When it sees an unquoted word it knows this must be a procedure name. The definition of this procedure is recovered from the com-

puter's *memory*. It decides how many arguments the procedure takes, and looks further along the line to find out what these are. The procedure is then run on these arguments and the result is stored in memory.

3.   When it sees a number, list or quoted word, it knows that these must be the arguments of some procedure. These LOGO objects are stored in a special place where the procedure can find them when it runs.

6.2.5   Simple Procedures

Suppose we have a longish message that we often want to have typed out on the terminal. We can define a procedure to do this, e.g.

```
TO HELP
10 PRINT [TO LOGOFF TYPE]
20 PRINT 'GOODBYE
30 PRINT [THEN TYPE]
40 PRINT 'STOP
END
```

The words TO and END mark the beginning and end of the procedure definition. The first line — TO HELP — is the *title line*. It consists of TO followed by the procedure name, HELP. The middle four lines are the *body* of the procedure. Each line starts with a number. When the procedure is called, the lines are executed in *numerical* order. If they have bugs in, procedures can be *edited* by inserting, changing or deleting lines. A line can be inserted between lines 20 and 30 by giving it a number between 20 and 30, e.g.

```
25 PRINT [WAIT FOR THE PROMPT COMMAND]
```

Exercise 6.2.3. Write a procedure called HELLO, which will type out
```
HELLO
[HOW ARE YOU]
```

6.2.6   Procedures with Arguments

Procedures like HELP and HELLO always behave in an identical way each time they are called. We would like to be able to write procedures, like PRINT and SUM, which are given as arguments objects that they manipulate. Such procedures behave differently according to the object they are given. Procedures with arguments are defined in a similar way to simple procedures except that they involve words (called *parameters* or input variables) which *stand for* the arguments, e.g.

```
TO PRINTENDS 'LIST
10 PRINT FIRST (VALUE 'LIST)
20 PRINT LAST (VALUE 'LIST)
END
```

LIST is a parameter in the above example. In the title line we put all the parameters just after the procedure name, so the computer knows how many parameters there are and what their names are. VALUE 'LIST will give the particular object that has been input. The effect of typing

202

            PRINTENDS [SUNDAY MONDAY . . . SATURDAY]
will be that
        SUNDAY
        SATURDAY
is printed on the terminal. Typing VALUE 'LIST gives the list
        [SUNDAY . . . SATURDAY].
Here is another example
        TO PRINTTOTAL 'NUM1 'NUM2
        10 PRINT (SUM (VALUE 'NUM1) (VALUE 'NUM2))
        END

Exercises
6.2.4. What would be the effect of typing
(a) PRINTTOTAL 2 3
(b) PRINTTOTAL (SUM 2 3) 1
In (b), what are VALUE 'NUM2 and VALUE 'NUM1?

6.2.5. Write a procedure that takes a list as argument and prints the
number of elements in it (use COUNT).

6.2.7 Results and Effects
In LOGO there is a sharp distinction between two different aspects of a
procedure's behaviour, namely its *result* (or output) and its *effect* (or side-
effect). To understand the difference consider the LOGO line
        PRINT FIRST [A B C]
The job of FIRST is to take one LOGO object, [A B C], and calculate
another, A, which is the *result* of this application of FIRST. It is stored
away in a special place, where it is later collected to be the VALUE of the
parameter of PRINT. LOGO procedures always produce exactly one result,
and this must be a LOGO object. Some procedures, like PRINT, are
executed mainly for their *effect*, which in this case is to cause the terminal
to work and start printing characters. Other effects might be to cause the
computer to read some characters from the teletype or to log you off
LOGO (e.g. GOODBYE).

LOGO procedures that are executed mainly for their effect (like PRINT) we
will call *commands*. LOGO procedures that are executed mainly for their
result (like FIRST), we will call *functions*. Note that the leftmost procedure
in a line will usually be a command and that the rest will be functions.

Exercise 6.2.6. Classify the following procedures into commands and
functions: SAY; LAST; COUNT; SUM; DIFF; NL; VALUE; FIRSTPUT.

6.2.8 Little Men
It is sometimes useful to think of each call of a procedure as a "little man".

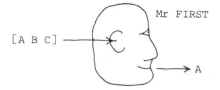

Mr FIRST

[A B C]

A

Arguments to the little man go in through his ears. Results come from his mouth. Other things he does, like effects, are achieved by other organs. We can use this analogy to visualize what happens when, say, PRINT (SUM 2 3) is evaluated.

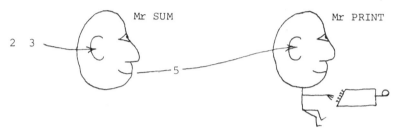

Mr SUM

2   3

5

Mr PRINT

6.2.8   Procedures that Produce Results

So far all the procedures we have defined (HELP, PRINTENDS, etc.) have been commands. By using the command RESULT we can also define functions. RESULT takes one argument and stores it in the special place. For instance, suppose we wanted to write a procedure to find the second element of a list, we could write

```
TO SECOND 'LIST
10 RESULT FIRST BUTFIRST VALUE 'LIST
END
```

Exercises

6.2.7. Define a procedure, FOURTH, for finding the fourth element of a list.

6.2.8. Define a procedure SUM3, which takes three numbers and returns their sum as result.

6.2.9   Sub-Procedures

We have seen plenty of examples in procedure definitions where one procedure calls another, e.g.

```
TO THIRD 'LIST
10 RESULT FIRST BUTFIRST BUTFIRST VALUE 'LIST
END
```

RESULT, FIRST, BUTFIRST and VALUE are called *sub-procedures* of THIRD. We can use user-defined procedures as sub-procedures, e.g.

```
10 RESULT SECOND BUTFIRST VALUE 'LIST
```

where SECOND is a user-defined procedure.

204

6.2.10 Variables and Assignment

It is often useful to have variables in addition to the parameters, e.g. as place holders for partial results. Consider the following arthmetic procedure, DIFFSQ, for calculating the difference of two squares:

```
TO DIFFSQ 'N1 'N2
10 NEW [S D]
20 MAKE 'S (SUM VALUE 'N1 VALUE 'N2)
30 MAKE 'D (DIFF VALUE 'N1 VALUE 'N2)
40 RESULT (PROD VALUE 'S VALUE 'D)
END
```

Line 10 *declares* that S and D are to be new *local-variables* within the procedure DIFFSQ. S and D are very similar to the parameters N1 and N2 except that they are not *assigned* VALUE's when the procedure is entered. The VALUES of S and D are assigned (we say S and D are *bound*) in lines 20 and 30 by the command MAKE. MAKE takes two arguments, a word and an object, and assigns the object to be the VALUE of the word, e.g.

```
MAKE 'S 3
PRINT VALUE 'S
```

causes 3 to be printed.

Of course we could have written DIFFSQ without using local variables, but it would have been a little difficult to read. We will soon meet examples where they are not so easy to dispense with.

The *variable declaration* (e.g. NEW [N1 N2]) and the *assignment statement* (e.g. MAKE 'N1 8) are not required for parameters (e.g. N1 and N2). They are implicitly made when the procedure is *entered*.

When the procedure is *exited* (i.e. when it is finished) the assignments of the parameters and local variables are cancelled, e.g. outside of DIFFSQ the VALUES of N1, N2, S and D are undefined. This is important, because it allows the same variable name to be used in different procedures that call each other. Consider the procedure THIRD:

```
TO THIRD 'LIST
10 RESULT FIRST BUTFIRST BUTFIRST VALUE 'LIST
END
```

It is vital that the two different versions of BUTFIRST have different ideas about the VALUE's of their parameter (called, say, L).Consider the following "little man" diagram:

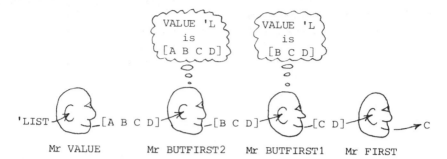

'LIST ... [A B C D] ... [B C D] ... [C D] ... C

Mr VALUE   Mr BUTFIRST2   Mr BUTFIRST1   Mr FIRST

What each little man thinks are the VALUE's of his parameters and local variables is called his *conceptual cloud*.

Principle of Reincarnation. Each time we call a procedure we get a new little man with his own conceptual cloud.

6.2.11 Abbreviations

Some of the LOGO procedure names are a bit long-winded, e.g. BUTFIRST, FIRSTPUT. We want to minimise typing as much as possible, so each of the LOGO procedure names has an abbreviation, e.g.

FIRST is F
BUTFIRST is BF
FIRSTPUT is FPUT

For a complete list see the reference manual.

There is also a facility for creating new abbreviations of LOGO or user-defined procedures. The command ABBREV is used. It takes as argument, the old procedure name and the new abbreviation. For example, calling

ABBREV 'LONGPROCEDURENAME 'LPN

will make LPN the abbreviation for LONGPROCEDURENAME

There is a special kind of abbreviation for VALUE. If VALUE is being called on some quoted word, VALUE is omitted and the quote is replaced by a colon, e.g. :FRED is an abbreviation for VALUE 'FRED

6.2.12 Infix Procedures

Some mathematical function names are usually written between the arguments rather than in front of them, e.g. we usually write 2 + 3 rather than SUM 2 3. + is called an *infix function*. Many LOGO functions have an equivalent infix form:

Function	Abbreviation	Infix Form
SUM	SUM	+
DIFFERENCE	DIFF	−
PRODUCT	PROD	*
QUOTIENT	QUOT	/
LESSQ	LQ	<
LESSEQUALQ	LEQ	<=

GRTRQ	GQ	$>$
GRTREQUALQ	GEQ	$>=$
EQUALQ	EQ	$=$

Take care when you use infix functions because the calling pattern can be ambiguous, e.g.

FIRST :LIST1 = FIRST :LIST2

will be interpreted (parsed) by LOGO as

FIRST (:LIST1 = (FIRST :LIST2))

which will result in an error. When using the infix form always use plenty of brackets and this will remove the ambiguity, e.g.

(FIRST :LIST1) = (FIRST :LIST2)

will be parsed correctly. For similar reasons always put brackets around negative numbers, e.g. (−23).

Exercise 6.2.9. The following is an uncompleted table of LOGO functions. Fill in the rest of the table by performing experiments at the terminal.

Name of function	Number of arguments	Type of argument: Number	Word	List	Result
FIRST	1	$\times$	$\times$	$\checkmark$	First element of list
BUTFIRST					
LAST					
BUTLAST					
SUM					
DIFF					
PROD					
QUOT					
WORD					
EQUALQ					
WORDQ					
NUMBERQ					
LISTQ					
EMPTYQ					
JOIN					

Example of experiment:

```
1:PRINT FIRST 87
FIRST MUST HAVE A LIST AS ARGUMENT — 87
1:PRINT FIRST 'WORD
FIRST MUST HAVE A LIST AS ARGUMENT — WORD
1:PRINT FIRST [THIS IS A LIST]
THIS
```

6.3   HOW TO DEFINE A PROCEDURE

6.3.1   The Procedure

To define a procedure
10 design the procedure and write it on paper
20 type it into the computer
30 show it
40 save it
50 test it
60 If procedure works perfectly then stop
70 debug it
80 edit it
90 go back to line 30
End

6.3.2   Designing Procedures

Analyse the problem and break it into parts, then analyse these parts.
Continue this process until all the problems are trivial. You should now
have a tree-structured plan:

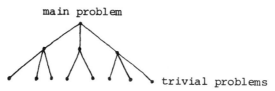

Always work from the top down. You will gradually develop intuitions
about what is trivial at the lower levels and about how to break problems
down.

Write the top level procedure first and its subprocedures next. The top
level procedure can be tested before the subprocedures are written, by
using the CALLUSER facility. For instance, suppose you needed a
subprocedure ISITANENGLISHWORDQ, which checked whether words
were in a dictionary. This would obviously be time-consuming to write.
However, we can define it as follows:

TO ISITANENGLISHWORDQ 'WORD
10 CALLUSER
END

When this procedure is called processing is temporarily halted and you get
a message and the prompt "RESULT:". You now type in the result you
think the procedure should return, this is evaluated and processing will
continue.

Find a procedure that does a similar task to the one you want done, and
use it as a model.

Keep your procedures short i.e. less than 9 lines long.

Use mnemonics for procedure names and variables. ABBREViate them afterwards if necessary.

6.3.3   Typing in the Procedure

Log on to LOGO and type the title line of your procedure, e.g.

TO SECOND 'LIST

After this, the "prompt" that LOGO gives you at the beginning of each line changes from its usual "1:" to a "&:". This reminds you that you are defining a procedure. If there is a mistake in the format of the title line you will get an error message. Try again.

Each line of the procedure must begin with a line number. Lines can be typed-in in any order, and will be stored not necessarily in the order you type them but in the order of their line numbers. If you forget the line number you will get an error message. Try again.

In order to change a line already typed, merely type a new line with the same line number. To remove a line, say line 30, type

&: DELETE 30

To type in a command that is longer than a single physical line, towards the end of the first line type @ CR. LOGO will respond with "C:" and you can then type in the continuation.

When you have finished defining the procedure, type

&: END

and the prompt will then revert to "1:", e.g.

1: <u>TO SECOND 'LIST</u>
&: <u>10 RESULT FIRST BUTFIRST :LIST</u>
&: <u>END</u>
1: <u>PRINT SECOND [A B C]</u>
B
1:

When you are defining (or editing) procedures the lines you type in are *not* run, they are merely stored away in the computer's memory for future reference.

6.3.4   Saving Procedures

If you are writing a program, you do not want to have to retype all your procedures every time you use LOGO. So there is a way to get LOGO to remember your procedures at one session, so that you can use them again at a later session. Procedures can be stored in a "file", by analogy with storing objects in a file drawer. You can have several different files — one for each program you are writing.

The procedure GETFILE is used for creating a new file or getting an old one. It takes as argument the name of your file and makes this the currently active file, e.g.

GETFILE 'JIM

The procedure SAVE is used to save procedures on the currently active file, e.g.

> SAVE 'SECOND

stores the procedure SECOND on file JIM.

> SAVE [SECOND PRINTENDS HELP]

stores all three named procedures.

There is also a useful command

> 1: SAVENEW

which saves all procedures which have been typed in or EDITed, and not yet SAVEd.

FORGET can be used to remove procedures from a file, e.g.

> 1: FORGET 'PRINTENDS, or
> 1: FORGET [SECOND HELP]

To recover the procedures at a later session, we first GETFILE the relevant file, and then use LOAD, e.g.

> 1: LOAD 'SECOND
> 1: LOAD [PRINTENDS HELP]

or more simply

> 1: LOADSAVED

which loads *all* the procedures in the current file.

6.3.5 Showing Procedures

To get a procedure typed on the terminal use the procedure SHOW, e.g.

> SHOW 'SECOND will type procedure SECOND
> SHOW [SECOND PRINTENDS HELP] will type all three
> SHOWALL will type all procedures currently loaded
> SHOWTITLES will type just the titles

6.3.6 Testing Procedures

If you are an inexperienced programmer your procedures are much more likely to be wrong than right. To test a procedure, call it on some of the arguments you expect it to be receiving in practice. Try a wide range of types of arguments. Do not forget "awkward" cases like the empty list, especially long lists, negative numbers, etc.

You will notice a bug because either the procedure does not produce the result you expected or you get an error message.

6.3.7 Debugging Procedures

There are two types of bug: syntax errors and run-time errors. Syntax errors are ungrammatical LOGO procedure calls. They always result in error messages, either when the procedure is typed in, or when it is run. Run-time errors come from procedures that do not do what you expected them to. These can sometimes give error messages if they cause a procedure to receive an argument it is not equipped to deal with.

If you get an error message, make sure you understand what it means, and what typical kinds of bug cause it. Ask the demonstrator if necessary. If the error message tells you the line in error examine this line and possibly one or two lines before.

Make sure you have a listing of the most recent version of the procedure at fault. Follow the execution of the procedure through with your finger, pretending to be the computer. Execute each line of the procedure in turn. Does it work as expected? Make sure lines containing infix procedures are being interpreted properly.

Sometimes the error will leave you in the middle of executing the procedure which failed. You can now PRINT the current VALUES of the local variables and parameters. Are they what you expected? You can cause execution of your own procedures to be suspended by inserting the command BREAK into them. CONTINUE will cause the processing to continue, QUIT will cause it to be abandoned.

If you want a record of which procedures are called and by whom, before the error, call the command TRACE on each procedure you want recorded, and then call your procedure, e.g.

>   TRACE [SECOND HELP]

Using FULLTRACE instead will give the VALUEs of parameters on entry, and result on exit. To stop procedures being TRACEd call UNTRACE on them. Do not TRACE too many procedures, or you will be swamped.

To see whether a procedure reaches a certain point edit a PRINT or BREAK command into that point.

For further advice see the reference manual or ask a demonstrator.

6.3.8   Editing Procedures

To change a procedure that has already been defined call the command EDIT on that procedure. You will get the prompt "&:", and will be back in the mode in which you defined the procedure, e.g.

>   EDIT 'SECOND
> &: 5 PRINT 'ENTER
> &: 15 PRINT [TOO FAR]
> &: END
> 1:

6.3.9   Exercises

6.3.1. Type in definitions of HELP, SECOND and PRINTENDS; and then try them out.

6.3.2. Make sure you understand the procedure FIRSTPUT. Use it to define a procedure BACKTOFRONT which outputs a list with the last element moved to the front, e.g.

>   BACKTOFRONT [A B C D] is [D A B C].

211

6.3.3. Write a procedure, QUERY, that switches the first two elements of a list, so that

    PRINT QUERY [BILL CAN FIX IT]

gives

    [CAN BILL FIX IT].

(Hints: What gives the list [FIX IT]? What gives the list [BILL FIX IT]?)
What is QUERY [DOGS LIKE CHEESE]? Or QUERY [THE CAT
CHASED THE SQUIRREL]? How would you set about improving the
procedure QUERY?

6.4   CONTROL STRUCTURES

6.4.1   Introduction

So far all our procedures have consisted of a simple sequence of
instructions, to be obeyed in order. Sometimes we will want the order to
be variable according to the circumstances, or we will want some
instructions to be repeated several times.

6.4.2   Conditionals

Suppose we wanted to amend the procedure SECOND so that it produced
an error message it its argument was not a list. We can do this with the
conditional IF . . . THEN . . . ELSE . . ., e.g.

    TO SECOND 'LIST
    10 IF LISTQ :LIST THEN RESULT FIRST BUTFIRST :LIST
       ELSE SECERR :LIST
    END

    TO SECERR 'ARG
    10 SAY [NON LIST ARGUMENT FOR SECOND]
    20 PRINT :ARG
    END

The general form of the conditional is

    IF condition THEN instruction1 ELSE instruction2

It is a funny kind of procedure. Its name is split into three parts, IF, THEN
and ELSE, and distributed between the three arguments. The first
argument must return as result either the word TRUE or the word FALSE.
Procedures like this are called *predicates*. Examples are:

    EQUALQ :A :B tests whether :A and :B are equal
    ZEROQ :NUMBER tests whether the :NUMBER is zero
    EMPTYQ :LIST tests whether the :LIST is empty
    LIST :THING tests whether the :THING is a list
    WORDQ :THING tests whether the :THING is a word
    NUMBERQ :THING tests whether the :THING is a number

We will adopt the convention that predicate names, even user-defined
ones, end in a Q (for Question).

Normally procedures evaluate all their arguments before they are called themselves. However, when

> IF condition THEN instruction1 ELSE instruction2

is called only "condition" is evaluated. If "condition" returns TRUE "instruction1" is evaluated. If "condition" returns FALSE, "instruction2" is evaluated, otherwise an error message is called. There is a shortened version, i.e.

> IF condition THEN instruction

RESULT not only causes its argument to be stored in the special place for results, it also causes the current procedure to be exited. So an alternative form for SECOND would be

```
TO SECOND 'LIST
10 IF LISTQ :LIST THEN RESULT FIRST BUTFIRST :LIST
20 SECERR :LIST
END
```

Exercises

6.4.1. Write a version of SECOND that does not check that its argument is a list, but does check that it is at least two elements long.

6.4.2. Write a version of SECOND that performs both checks.

6.4.3 Linking Procedure Calls Together

The arguments of IF-THEN-ELSE-, like the arguments of any other procedure, must be a LOGO object or a single procedure call. However, if a conditional test succeeds we often want to do a sequence of instructions, e.g.

```
IF SUNNY :DAY THEN HANGOUT :WASHING
                  WEED :FLOWERBEDS
                  SUNBATHE
```

As it stands this is illegal LOGO syntax. What we need is a way of linking together the last three LOGO procedure calls into one procedure call. This is provided by the *infix command* AND. AND causes the procedure calls it links to be evaluated simply by having them as arguments, but it does nothing further to them. The following *is* legal LOGO syntax:

```
IF SUNNY :DAY THEN HANGOUT :WASHING
              AND WEED :FLOWERBEDS
              AND SUNBATHE
```

Exercise 6.4.3. Write a version of SECOND that prints out a message "SECOND CALLED SUCCESSFULLY" whenever it is called successfully.

6.4.4 Repetition

Suppose we wanted to repeat an instruction several times. It would be tedious to have to write the instruction several times. Instead we can use the command REPEAT, e.g.

```
TO LOVE
10 REPEAT 3 SAY [I LOVE YOU]
END
```
This will print "I LOVE YOU" three times.

We can REPEAT things a variable number of times by having the first argument of REPEAT be a procedure call or variable, e.g.
```
TO MUCHLOVE 'NUM
10 REPEAT :NUM SAY [I LOVE YOU]
END
```
MUCHLOVE 1000 will now print "I LOVE YOU" a thousand times.

Exercises

6.4.4. Write a procedure, PRIDE, which prints
COMPUTERS NEVER MAKE
MISTAKES
MISTAKES
MISTAKES
. . .
MISTAKES

6.4.5. Write a procedure that prints three times
I LOVE YOU
VERY MUCH

Warning. You now have the facility to define procedures that may go on for a long time. Before running one, make sure you understand how to interrupt and QUIT. Otherwise it will be very boring for you waiting for the procedure to finish and you will needlessly use computer time. There is a facility to prevent this kind of accident, called the EVALIMIT. This will prevent you doing too much processing, by setting a limit on the depth to which you can have sub-procedures calling each other. EVALIMIT is currently 500. You can increase or decrease this with the command SETELIM, which takes one argument, the new limit.

6.4.5   Running Down Lists
We will sometimes want to do something to each member of a list in turn, e.g. PRINT each member of the list on a new line. The easiest way to do this is with the command APPLIST, e.g.
```
1: APPLIST [SUNDAY MONDAY . . . SATURDAY] 'PRINT
SUNDAY
MONDAY

. . .
SATURDAY
```
APPLIST applies the command PRINT to each member of the list in turn. Since PRINT always prints its arguments and then does a new line, a new line is inserted between every member.

The second argument of APPLIST can be the name of any system or user-defined, one-argument procedure (though it is usually a command). Sometimes we do not have the appropriate command already defined, and we do not need it except for this APPLIST. In this case the definition can be made implicitly in the second argument to APPLIST. For instance, suppose we wanted a procedure that printed TRUE for each word in a list and FALSE for each list or number. It could be done as follows:

```
1: APPLIST [JOHN 23 MALE] [PRINT WORDQ EACH]
TRUE
FALSE
TRUE
```

For each member of the list, [JOHN 23 MALE], EACH finds the VALUE of that member, WORDQ works on that VALUE returning as result TRUE or FALSE, and PRINT prints that result.

[PRINT WORDQ EACH] is an alternative to some procedure name, say 'FOO, where FOO is defined by

```
TO FOO 'ARG
10 PRINT WORDQ :ARG
END
```

Corresponding to the command APPLIST there is a function MAPLIST. This takes a list and a function name and produces as a result the new list obtained from applying the function to each member of the old list, e.g.

```
1: PRINT MAPLIST [JOHN 23 MALE] 'WORDQ
[TRUE FALSE TRUE]
```

As in APPLIST the second argument of MAPLIST can be a procedure call in the form of a list, e.g.

```
1: PRINT MAPLIST [1 2 3] [SUM 1 EACH]
[2 3 4]
```

Exercises

6.4.6. What would be the effect of typing

```
1: PRINT MAPLIST [1 0 3] ZEROQ
1: APPLIST [JOHN 23 MALE] [PRINT NUMBERQ EACH]
1: PRINT MAPLIST [1 2 3] [PROD 2 EACH]
```

6.4.7. Write a function, DOUBLELIST, which takes a list of numbers and returns a list with each member doubled.

6.4.6   Conditional Loops

Sometimes we cannot say in advance how often we would like to repeat a command, we just want to go on repeating it until some goal has been achieved (like hitting a nail repeatedly until it has sunk right into the wood). This facility is provided in LOGO by the construction "WHILE condition THEN instruction", e.g.

WHILE OUT :NAIL THEN HIT :NAIL

WHILE combines the ideas of conditionals and repetition. As in IF-THEN-, the condition is evaluated. If it returns TRUE the instruction is evaluated. Then the process is repeated until the condition returns FALSE. Clearly, evaluating the instruction should have some effect upon whatever the condition is testing or this process will never stop.

We can use the WHILE-THEN- procedure to define a procedure SUMFROM1TON, which adds up all the numbers from 1 to some number N, say.

```
1: PRINT SUMFROM1TON 2
3 (i.e., 1+2)
1: PRINT SUMFROM1TON 5
15 (i.e., 1+2+3+4+5)
```

```
TO SUMFROM1TON 'N
10 NEW [TALLY TOTAL]
20 MAKE 'TALLY 1
30 MAKE 'TOTAL 1
40 WHILE NOT EQUALQ :TALLY :N
   THEN MAKE 'TALLY SUM :TALLY 1
   AND MAKE 'TOTAL SUM :TOTAL :TALLY
50 RESULT :TOTAL
END
```

Note the use of local variables (a) to keep a running score (TOTAL), and (b) to count how many times something was done (TALLY). Note also the use of AND to enable us both to do something and to record we did it, each time round the loop. It is nearly always necessary to use AND in WHILE loops.

Exercise 6.4.8. Write a procedure, SUMOFLIST, which adds up all the numbers in a list of numbers, e.g.

```
1: PRINT SUMOFLIST [5 7 3]
15
```

(a) using APPLIST, and (b) using WHILE- THEN-.

6.5   RECURSION

6.5.1   Breaking problems into parts

So far most of the problems we have tackled have been fairly easy. It has been possible to break the problem down into a short sequence of instructions, each of which can be written with the LOGO procedures currrently available. Sometimes these instructions cannot be written using existing procedures. Then writing these instructions becomes a new problem and we begin to build up a hierarchical structure of procedures, e.g.

```
TO SINGSONG
10 SINGVERSE1
20 SINGCHORUS
30 SINGVERSE2
40 SINGCHORUS
etc.
END

TO SINGVERSE1
10 SAY [RICH GIRL WEARS A . . .]
20 SAY [POOR GIRL . . .]
etc.
END

TO SINGCHORUS
10 SAY [DINAH DINAH . . .]
etc.
END
```

This device of "divide and conquer", the breaking of a problem into parts, is one of the main weapons of program writing. We will be developing it further in our "little man methods".

Until now the break down of the task has been strictly hierarchical, e.g.

In fact there is nothing in LOGO to stop one of the sub-procedures or sub-sub-procedures being the same as the main procedures. When this happens it is called *recursion*, e.g.

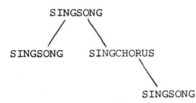

In the rest of this section we will be exploring this possibility; seeing how it is possible and when it is useful.

Many of the examples we will be using could also be done using REPEAT, APPLIST, MAPLIST or WHILE. For expository purposes we will be ignoring these alternatives in this section. When designing your own procedures you should choose the alternative that reflects the way you naturally break down the task. Recursion is a very powerful programming device. It can always replace REPEAT, APPLIST, MAPLIST and WHILE, but not vice versa.

6.5.2 Indefinite Repetition

Using REPEAT we can repeat an instruction a finite number of times, but suppose we want to go on repeating something indefinitely? We can do this using recursion. Consider, if we tell LOGO how to LAUGH:

```
TO LAUGH
10 PRINT 'HAHAHA
20 PRINT 'HOHOHO
END
```

If we use this procedure, "1: LAUGH", then LOGO will laugh just once;

```
HAHAHA
HOHOHO
1:
```

But suppose we want LOGO to laugh again and again and again? We could try

```
TO LAUGHALOT
10 LAUGH
20 LAUGH
30 LAUGH
etc.
END
```

but these do not look promising because (a) it's a nuisance to have to write out all these LAUGHs, and (b) it still doesn't make LOGO laugh indefinitely. Instead, try this:

```
TO KEEPLAUGHING
10 LAUGH
20 KEEPLAUGHING
END
```

KEEPLAUGHING calls itself, and this has the desired effect:

```
1: KEEPLAUGHING
HAHAHA
HOHOHO
HAHAHA
HOHOHO
etc. (indefinitely)
```

The "Little Man" Method. We give two ways of understanding how KEEPLAUGHING works. We have simplified the task from the one large problem given, to a small problem we can solve plus another large problem. We were asked to produce:

218

```
HAHAHA
HOHOHO
HAHAHA
HOHOHO
```

an indefinite number of times. We tackle the problem by breaking it into two parts: (a) produce a single laugh, and (b) produce the rest of the laughs (an indefinite number). But now we can easily write the procedure KEEPLAUGHING, since task (a) is what LAUGH is designed to do, and task (b) is identical to what KEEPLAUGHING is meant to do! So these become lines 10 and 20 of the procedure.

The second way is to think about the "little men" involved. We have only two *kinds* of little man here, LAUGH and KEEPLAUGHING, but there may be many of each kind:

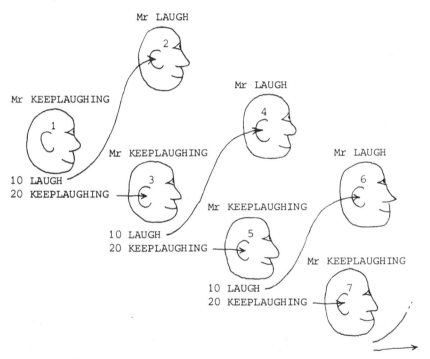

When we type KEEPLAUGHING we create l.m.1, who in turn creates (line 10) l.m.2 and asks him to "do his thing", then (line 20) creates l.m.3 and asks him to "do *his* thing". So l.m.3 first creates l.m.4 etc.

We have here a powerful method of tackling problems involving repetition. We'll see soon that it is only half of an even more powerful method, so let's say:

(Second Half of) Little Man Method

B.   Can I break the task I'm given into two (or more) parts, such that

(i) I can cope with one of the parts myself, and

(ii) I can give the other part(s) to someone else to deal with?

Be sure to understand how this applies to the case of KEEPLAUGHING.

Exercises

6.5.1. Write a procedure, STORY, which prints out the following monologue:

```
IT WAS A DARK AND STORMY NIGHT
AND THE CAPTAIN SAID TO THE MATE
TELL US A STORY
AND THE MATE BEGAN
IT WAS A DARK AND STORMY NIGHT
etc.
```

6.5.2. Suppose you have procedures SING and DANCE. Define a procedure SINGANDDANCEFOREVER, which will SING, then DANCE, then SING, then DANCE, etc. Define appropriate procedures for SING and DANCE, and try them out.

Another Example: COUNTUPFROM. Suppose we want to write a procedure that behaves as follows:

```
1: COUNTUPFROM 10    or    1: COUNTUPFROM 127
10                         127
11                         128
12                         129
13                         130
14                         131
etc.                       etc.
```

We can start with

TO COUNTUPFROM 'GIVENNUMBER

Try the same method as before. Break up the whole task into two parts:

```
1: COUNTUPFROM 127
127        (this line produced by PRINT 127)

128 ⎫
129 ⎪
130 ⎬  (The rest of the lines produced by COUNTUPFROM 128)
131 ⎪
etc. ⎭
```

So, in terms of the little man method:

(a) The subtask we can do ourselves is to print the given number

10 PRINT :GIVENNUMBER

(b) the rest of the task is given to someone else to do

20 COUNTUPFROM SUM :GIVENNUMBER 1

i.e. one greater than the given number. So:

220

```
TO COUNTUPFROM 'GIVENNUMBER
10 PRINT :GIVENNUMBER
20 COUNTUPFROM SUM :GIVEN NUMBER 1
END
```

Notice that each COUNTUPFROM little man has his own conceptual cloud:

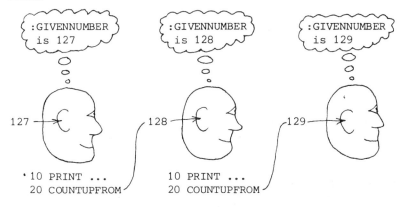

Repeated Warning. Before trying these procedures on LOGO, make sure you understand about Interrupts.

6.5.3 Terminated Recursion: COUNTDOWN

Try an example similar to the earlier procedure COUTUPFROM but with an important difference:

```
1: COUNTDOWN 10
10
9
8
7
6
5
4
3
2
1
0
BLASTOFF
1: SHOW COUNTDOWN
```

How can we write COUNTDOWN using recursion? Most of it is easy, analogous to COUNTUPFROM. Applying the (second half of the) little man method, we break the task into two parts, and realise that in the call of COUNTDOWN 10 above, the "10" in the typeout is printed directly by the COUNTDOWN little man, whereas the rest (9,8,7, etc.) are printed by a recursive call on COUNTDOWN 9. This gives us our first approximation:

```
TO COUNTDOWN 'NUMBER
10 PRINT :NUMBER
20 COUNTDOWN DIFF :NUMBER 1
END
```

But when we try this we get

```
1: COUNTDOWN 3
3
2
1
0
−1
−2
etc.
```

Clearly, there is nothing to stop COUNTDOWN continuing indefinitely. After printing zero, it will not print BLASTOFF and stop because we have not asked it to. It is easy to correct this omission:

```
    TO COUNTDOWN 'NUMBER
    10 PRINT :NUMBER
⟶ 15 IF ZEROQ :NUMBER THEN PRINT 'BLASTOFF AND STOP
    20 COUNTDOWN DIFF :NUMBER 1
    END
```

This will now work correctly. ZEROQ is a predicate that tests whether or not a number is zero. Make sure you understand the little man structure of a call on COUNTDOWN. Here is a complete diagram of the little men for COUNTDOWN 2. This time we have added explicitly a line to represent each l.m. saying "done":

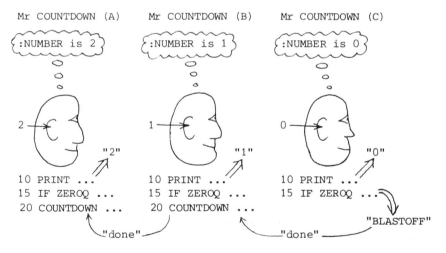

l.m.A prints "2" (line 10), which is not zero (line 15), so calls l.m.B, who similarly prints "1" and calls l.m.C, l.m.C prints "0", which *is* zero so (line 15) he prints "BLASTOFF" and STOPs, i.e. tells l.m.B that he is done.

l.m.B has already executed his last instruction (line 20), so he too is done, and so similarly is l.m.A.

6.5.4 Full Little Man Method

We have just used an application of our very powerful little man method, which looks like this:

Little Man Method

A.   Is (are) there any special or simple case(s) that I can take care of myself?
B.   Otherwise, can I break the task into two (or more) parts, such that
     (i) I can cope with one of the parts myself, and
     (ii) I can give the other part(s) to someone else?

In the case of COUNTDOWN, the special case (A) is when the number is zero, the part the little man can do himself (B(i)) is to print the given number, and the part (B(ii)) that he gives to someone else is to COUNTDOWN one less than the given number.

It follows that the structure of a procedure written by this method is somewhat as follows:

1.   Test for the special case; if so, take care of it, and stop.
2.   Deal with the part to be handled directly.
3.   Ask someone else to deal with the rest.

(Sometimes, as in COUNTDOWN, step 2 may precede step 1).

Another example: LAUGHNTIMES. Try the Little Man Method on another example. Remember the procedure LAUGH? How about a procedure LAUGH7TIMES, which will laugh exactly seven times? We *could* have

```
TO  LAUGH7TIMES
10 LAUGH
20 LAUGH
30 LAUGH
40 LAUGH
50 LAUGH
60 LAUGH
70 LAUGH
END
```

but this doesn't look too good, and is obviously hopeless for LAUGHing 2719 times. It's actually easier to write the more general procedure that can laugh *any* number of times, and then tell it how many times we want. So let's try writing

```
TO  LAUGHNTIMES 'HOWMANY
```

We could follow the same argument as for COUNTDOWN, so that we first have a procedure that laughs indefinitely (cf. KEEPLAUGHING) and then we worry about how to stop it. Instead, apply the little man method and try to get the procedure right directly. So, *is there any special case the l.m.*

can take care of himself? Yes of course, if he is asked to laugh zero times then he simply stops:

      10 IF ZEROQ :HOWMANY THEN STOP

Otherwise, *can the l.m. break the task into two parts such that . . .?* Yes; for example if he is asked to laugh 19 times, he can laugh once himself and ask someone to laugh the other 18 times:

      TO LAUGHNTIMES 'HOWMANY
      10 IF ZEROQ :HOWMANY THEN STOP
⟶ 20 LAUGH
⟶ 30 LAUGHNTIMES DIFF :HOWMANY 1
      END

Simple!

Exercises

6.5.3. Draw the little men diagram for LAUGHNTIMES 3.

6.5.4. Write a procedure to sing a simplified version of a well-known song, e.g.

      1: SIMPLEMOW 23
      23 MEN WENT TO MOW
      22 MEN WENT TO MOW
      21 MEN WENT TO MOW
      etc.

6.5.5 Recursion along a list

In both COUNTDOWN and LAUGHNTIMES, we have determined when to stop by *counting*. There is another important class of procedures where we control the recursion by *doing something to each item on a list.* The two kinds of procedures correspond directly:

For a *counting* recursion, where we do something N times,
(a) we ask if N is zero, if so we stop;
(b) we do it once;
(c) someone else does it (N-1) times.

For a *list* recursion, where we do something with each item on a list,
(a) we ask if the list is empty, if so we stop;
(b) we do it with the FIRST item of the list;
(c) someone else does it with the rest (i.e. BUTFIRST) of the list.

An example: PRINTLIST. Most of our examples could be done with APPLIST or WHILE, but this will not always be possible. In order that we can explore recursion along a list in some simple cases we will suppress the APPLIST and WHILE solutions. Let us again try to write the procedure PRINTLIST, which prints each element of a list on a separate line. Assume we have

      TO PRINTLIST 'ANYLIST

and apply the little man method. *Is there any special case the l.m. can take care of himself?* Yes, if the list is empty, then he has nothing to do:

    10 IF EMPTYQ :ANYLIST THEN STOP

Otherwise, *can he break the task into two parts . . .?* Yes, he himself can print the first item

    20 PRINT FIRST :ANYLIST

and ask another l.m. to look after the rest of the list:

    30 PRINTLIST BUTFIRST :ANYLIST

So we have:

```
TO PRINTLIST 'ANYLIST
10 IF EMPTYQ :ANYLIST THEN STOP
20 PRINT FIRST :ANYLIST
30 PRINTLIST BUTFIRST :ANYLIST
END
```

Here is the l.m. diagram for PRINTLIST [PENCIL PEN]:

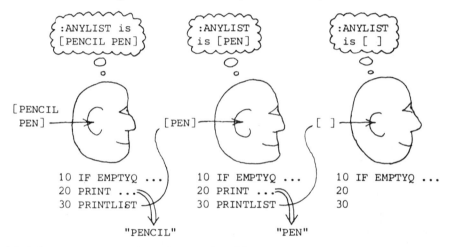

6.5.6   **Exegesis of the Little Man Method**

Try summarising our experience with the kind of procedures discussed above, as a commentary to help in the use of the method:

For *counting* recursion, we often have:

    Special case (A) consists of equality between two numbers
        (with zero as a particular instance).

    Step B(i) consists of doing what was asked just once.

    Step B(ii) consists of doing what was asked "N-1" times.

For *list* recursion, we often have:

    Special case (A) consists of the empty list.

    Step B(i) consists of doing something to the FIRST of the list.

    Step B(ii) consists of recursing on the BUTFIRST of the list.

AMONGQ. We are now in a position to write the procedure AMONGQ:

    TO AMONGQ 'ITEM 'LIST

Clearly, this involves some kind of a recursion down the list, though we may not have to go to the very end. What we have to "do" with each element of the list is to check whether it is the same as the given item. Apply the little man method: *Is there any special case . . .?* The commentary recommends checking for the empty list. If we *have* the empty list, then clearly the given item is not contained in it, so the result of the procedure must be FALSE:

    10 IF EMPTYQ :LIST THEN RESULT FALSE

Break into two tasks . . .? The commentary recommends dealing with the first element of the list. If it is the same as the given item, then the result of the procedure must be TRUE:

    20 IF EQUALQ :ITEM FIRST :LIST THEN RESULT TRUE

Otherwise we need to go searching down the rest of the list:

    30 RESULT AMONGQ :ITEM BUTFIRST :LIST

So we have:

    TO AMONGQ 'ITEM 'LIST
    10 IF EMPTYQ :LIST THEN RESULT FALSE
    20 IF EQUALQ :ITEM FIRST :LIST THEN RESULT TRUE
    30 RESULT AMONGQ :ITEM BUTFIRST :LIST
    END

Exercise 6.5.5. Draw little man diagrams for AMONGQ 'HOUSE [DOG CAT COW] and AMONGQ 'CAT [DOG CAT COW].

6.5.6 Understanding recursion: TRIANGLE

Consider the procedure TRIANGLE

    1: TRIANGLE [V W X Y Z]
    [V W X Y Z]
    [W X Y Z]
    [X Y Z]
    [Y Z]
    [Z]
    []
    1:

Writing this should now be a simple exercise:

    TO TRIANGLE 'LIST
    10 PRINT :LIST   part B(i)
    20 IF EMPTYQ :LIST THEN STOP   special case (A)
    30 TRIANGLE BUTFIRST :LIST   the rest, B(ii)
    END

But what happens if we add a new line?

    40 PRINT :LIST

Try it and see! Is the effect surprising? Try understanding it in terms of the little men involved:

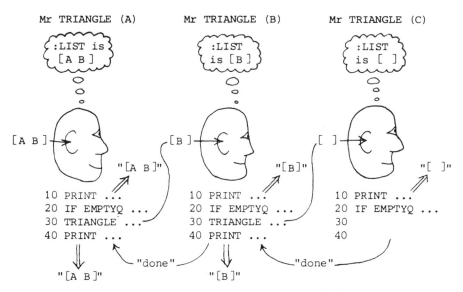

When l.m.C stops (line 20), l.m.B resumes with his next instruction (line 40) and prints "[B]", then *he* is finished so l.m.A resumes and prints "[A B]".

Exercises

6.5.6. What happens if we swap lines 10 and 15 of COUNTDOWN? Or lines 10 and 20 of TRIANGLE?

6.5.7. Define the procedure COUNTUP, which counts up from one number to another:

```
1: COUNTUP 8 11
8
9
10
11
```

6.5.8. Define the procedure NTH, which returns the Nth element of a list:

```
1: PRINT NTH 2 [COW DOG HORSE]
DOG
1: PRINT NTH 3 [ON CIRCLE SQUARE]
SQUARE
1: PRINT NTH 2 [PINK]
LIST TOO SHORT
```

6.5.9. The procedure RANDOM returns a random number between 0 and the number it is given as argument, e.g. RANDOM 3 returns one of the numbers 0, 1, 2, or 3 with equal likelihood. Use RANDOM and NTH to write a procedure RANDOMSELECT, which returns a randomly chosen element of the list it is given:

227

1: PRINT RANDOMSELECT [BLUE GREEN RED YELLOW]
RED
1: PRINT RANDOMSELECT [BLUE GREEN RED YELLOW]
BLUE

6.5.7 Constructing Recursive Objects

Just as we have used the little man method to deal with tasks that have a
recursive structure, so also we can use it to *construct objects* with a
recursive structure. Adapt the wording of the l.m.m. appropriately, i.e. we
ask if there is a special case where we can construct the entire object
immediately, otherwise we ask other little men to build parts of the object
and then we put them together, etc.

In LOGO the "objects" we are constructing are usually numbers or lists,
e.g. in COUNTDOWN we *analysed* the task of doing something ten times
as: doing it once, then doing it the remaining nine times:

$10 \rightarrow 1 + 9$ (recursive)

Similarly, to construct an object of ten parts, we get someone else to build
the object with nine parts and then we add the tenth part, an act of
synthesis:

$1 + 9$ (recursive) $\rightarrow 10$

SUMOFLIST. We want a procedure whose argument is a list of numbers,
and which returns the sum of all the numbers as result.

1: PRINT SUMOFLIST [5 7 9 11 13]
45

As usual, we break the list into its FIRST and BUTFIRST components:

[5 7 9 11 13]$\rightarrow$ 5 & [7 9 11 13]

There is a corresponding *synthesis* of the total sum we are seeking:

5 + SUMOFLIST [7 9 11 13]$\rightarrow$ 45

All we need now to apply the l.m.m. is the specially easy case, which as
usual comes from the empty list. Notice that SUMOFLIST [] is 0. So we
get

```
TO SUMOFLIST 'NUMBERLIST
10 IF EMPTYQ :NUMBERLIST THEN RESULT 0
20 RESULT SUM FIRST :NUMBERLIST
                 SUMOFLIST BUTFIRST :NUMBERLIST
END
```

Exercise 6.5.10. Draw the l.m. diagram for SUMOFLIST [10 17 23].

COUNT. This is of course a built-in procedure, but how could we write it if
it weren't already provided, e.g. COUNT [A B C D E]? Apply the usual
l.m. analysis of the list, and there is a corresponding synthesis of the
number we want:

1 + COUNT [B C D E]$\rightarrow$ COUNT [A B C D E]

And of course, COUNT [] is 0.

228

```
TO COUNT 'LIST
10 IF EMPTYQ :LIST THEN RESULT 0
20 RESULT SUM 1 COUNT BUTFIRST :LIST
END
```

Exercise 6.5.11. The procedure NUMBEROF, e.g.
    NUMBEROF 'COW [HORSE COW DOG COW SHEEP] is 2.
What are the analysis/synthesis rules?
(a) NUMBEROF 'COW [HORSE COW DOG COW SHEEP] ←
                    0 + NUMBEROF 'COW [COW DOG COW SHEEP]
(b) NUMBEROF 'COW [COW DOG COW SHEEP] ←
                    1 + NUMBEROF 'COW [DOG COW SHEEP]
(c) NUMBEROF 'COW [ ] ← 0
Can you write the procedure?

6.5.8   Constructing Lists
To get the parts of a list, we have used the analysis
    LIST $\xrightarrow{\text{F,BF}}$ F :LIST & BF :LIST
To build up a list, we can use FIRSTPUT
    :ITEM & :LIST $\xrightarrow{\text{FPUT}}$ FPUT :ITEM :LIST
e.g. FPUT 'A [B C D] is [A B C D].

Notice these relationships that hold for all lists:
    FIRST FIRSTPUT :X :Y is :X
    BUTFIRST FIRSTPUT :X :Y is :Y

ADD1LIST. Given a list of numbers, write a procedure to return the list
with one added to each of the numbers, e.g.
    ADD1LIST [100 200 300] is [101 201 301].
ADD1LIST could be easily written using MAPLIST, but this is not true of
the next two examples, so we ignore the MAPLIST solution and
concentrate on the recursive one. We analyse the argument list as follows:
    [100 200 300] → 100 & [200 300]
The corresponding synthesis of the result list is
    ADD1LIST [100 200 300] ← (100 + 1) & ADD1LIST [200 300]
unless this is the null list, in which case the synthesis is
    ADD1LIST [ ] ← [ ]
So we have
```
TO ADD1LIST 'LIST
10 IF EMPTYQ :LIST THEN RESULT [ ]
20 RESULT FPUT SUM 1 FIRST :LIST
                ADD1LIST BF :LIST
END
```

Exercise 6.5.12. Write a procedure, NEGSUBLIST, which returns a list of
those numbers on its argument list that are negative, e.g.
    NEGSUBLIST [1 −2 3 −4 5] is [−2 −4].

Example: WITHOUT. In the M & C program we will need the procedure WITHOUT for changing one state description into another, i.e.

    MAKE 'LEFTBANK WITHOUT :MOVELIST :LEFTBANK

where WITHOUT is a procedure that removes a sublist from a list, e.g.

    1: <u>PRINT WITHOUT [M C BOAT] [M M C C BOAT]</u>
    [M C]

We now tackle the problem of writing this procedure. Remember that the heart of programming is breaking tasks up into easier sub-tasks, so we first tackle the easier problem of removing just a single item from a list, e.g.

    WITHOUT1 'M [C M C BOAT] is [C C BOAT]

What are the synthesis rules? It must depend on whether or not the first of the list is the item we are trying to remove, e.g.

(a) WITHOUT1 'M [C M C BOAT] ←

                                  'C & WITHOUT1 'M [M C BOAT]

(b) WITHOUT1 'M [M C BOAT] ← [C BOAT]

(c) The empty list this time is a bit weird: if we can reach it it means that we haven't been able to find the item we're looking for. This may indicate an error.

So we have

    TO WITHOUT1 'ITEM 'LIST

(c) 10 IF EMPTYQ :LIST THEN BREAK ERROR

(b) 20 IF EQ :ITEM FIRST :LIST THEN RESULT BF :LIST

(a) 30 RESULT FPUT FIRST :LIST WITHOUT1 :ITEM BF :LIST
    END

Exercise 6.5.13. Write WITHOUT, making use of the sub-procedure WITHOUT1.

6.6   MISCELLANEOUS EXERCISES

6.6.1.   What is the result of the following LOGO commands:
    (a) COUNT [DESK [TABLE CHAIR] CARPET]
    (b) FIRST [CIRCLE SQUARE TRIANGLE]
    (c) FIRST [[COLOUR RED] [SIZE BIG]]
    (d) BUTFIRST [CIRCLE SQUARE TRIANGLE]
    (e) BUTFIRST [[COLOUR RED] [SIZE BIG]]
    (f) BUTFIRST [MAN WOMAN]
    (g) SUM COUNT BUTFIRST [A B C] 7

6.6.2.   Define a procedure, CENSOR, which checks on the public acceptability of lists. More precisely, the procedure CENSOR takes a list as argument, and if the word "SEX" occurs in the list it prints out the word "CENSORED", and if not it prints out the word "PASSED", e.g.

```
1: CENSOR [A PORNOGRAPHIC FILM]
PASSED
1: CENSOR [REPRESENTATIVE OF THE FAIR SEX]
CENSORED
```
Hint: Use the predicate AMONGQ — see previous sections.

6.6.3. Suppose that we keep student records in the form of lists, containing the name, age, and department of each student, e.g.
```
[BLOGGS 23 ASTROLOGY]
[MCFINLAY 95 GERIATRICS]
```
Write a procedure, NICEPRINT, that will type out one of these lists in a readable format, e.g.
```
1: NICEPRINT [BLOGGS 23 ASTROLOGY]
NAME BLOGGS
AGE 23
DEPT ASTROLOGY
```

6.6.4. Define a predicate, VOWELQ, which decides whether a given letter is one of A, E, I, O, or U, e.g.
```
1: PRINT VOWELQ 'E
TRUE
1: PRINT VOWELQ 'F
FALSE
```

6.6.5. Define a predicate, CONSONANTQ, which tests for consonants.

6.7   BEHIND THE SCENES

6.7.1   Introduction
One of the joys of programming with an advanced programming language like LOGO is that you do not have to concern yourself with the details of how the computer works, how your programs are actually stored etc. You need only think about the LOGO machine, i.e. what LOGO will do with the message you type. Nevertheless you may still be curious about what is going on behind the scenes, and it is sometimes useful to know for sorting out difficult bugs. This note is intended to give a brief glimpse behind LOGO.

6.7.2   The Physical Set-Up
You may have been surprised to be able to communicate with the computer without having to touch it. Nowadays it is normal to talk to computers via a terminal linked to it by a telephone line. The computer may actually be situated thousands of miles from the terminal.

231

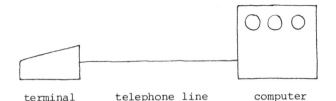

terminal   telephone line   computer

If you do your computing in a room with several other terminals then it is unlikely that each terminal has a separate telephone line to the computer. Telephone lines are expensive to buy or rent, so several terminals are made to share the same line. To make this possible the different messages are interleaved by a mini-computer (the concentrator) at your end; sent down the line as one message, and decoded by another mini-computer (the front end processor) at the computer end.

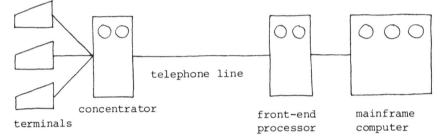

terminals   concentrator   front-end   mainframe
                                    processor   computer

The mainframe computer you use will be simultaneously handling several users at once. To manage this it is running a main program called the *operating system*. This program divides the effort of the computer between the users on a "round robin" basis. It also keeps each user's program isolated from everyone else's in the computer working memory. In case your message should come in at a time when the computer is dealing with someone else, all messages are temporarily stored in a special place called a *buffer* until they can be processed. All this is done in such a way that it should appear to you that you have the computer all to yourself.

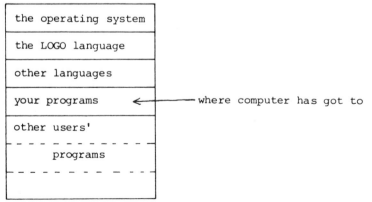

232

6.7.3   How Computers Work

Computers can be conveniently divided into four components: the *control unit*; the *arithmetic unit*; the *store* and the *input/output*.

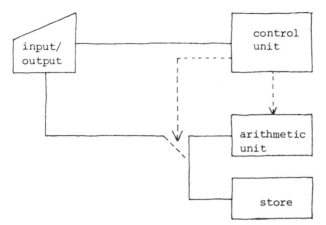

The Arithmetic Unit is where the basic arithmetic operations, like adding two numbers, are performed. The store is where your programs and data are stored. Input/output covers a wide range of *peripheral* devices, like teletypes, line printers, card readers. disc files, and even other computers. The control unit is the thing that decides what to do next, e.g. whether to add two numbers, get something from store, or output to the line printer. It knows what to do because it feeds itself *your program* in a suitably coded form.

Machine Code. The suitably coded form is called *machine code*. This is the only programming language that the control unit understands. All other languages (LOGO, IMP, FORTRAN, ALGOL, etc.) have first to be translated into machine code. The computer does this for itself by using either a *compiler* or an *interpreter*. These are programs that operate on your program as if it were a piece of data and produce a machine code translation. A compiler does this once, giving you the machine code in a form in which you can ask for it to be run. An interpreter translates your program as it is run.

Interpretation is much slower and more expensive than running an already compiled, machine code program. However, interpretation is much more convenient when a program is being developed interactively, because you do not have to recompile after every change. Compiling is best when a program has been completely developed and is now to be used for several "production runs".

Machine code is actually a sequence of binary numbers like:

233

```
0 1 1 0 0 0 1 1 1 1 1
0 0 1 1 1 0 0 0 0 1 1
0 1 0 0 0 1 1 1 0 0 0
```
etc.

The control unit will break this into parts according to its own conventions. One part will tell it the instruction to be performed, and one part will tell it where, in store, to find the thing to perform the instruction on. For example, the first number might be broken into

0 1 1 0 and 0 0 1 1 1 1 1

The number 0 1 1 0 tells us this is a "fetch from store" instruction, and the number 0 0 1 1 1 1 1 is the *address* of some location in store. Whatever is currently in that location is copied into a special place (the *accumulator*) in the arithmetic unit. The next number is broken down into

0 0 1 1 and 1 0 0 0 0 1 1

The number 0 0 1 1 tells us this is an "addition" instruction. The number 1 0 0 0 0 1 1 is the address of some place in store. The contents of that place are added to the number in the accumulator and the result is stored in the accumulator. The next instruction would be to store the result in some place in store.

For more information see the Open University introduction to computing or read S.H. Hollingdale & G.C. Toothill (1965) *Electronic Computers*, Penguin Books.

6.7.4 The Computer's Memory

So far we have discussed only one part of the computer's memory, the store (sometimes called core store). This is where the computer keeps the things it is currently working on. Information in core store can be accessed fast, but core store is expensive. Therefore the computer has a hierarchy of cheaper but slower memories. These are, in order of decreasing cost and speed: the paging drum; the disc files; the archives.

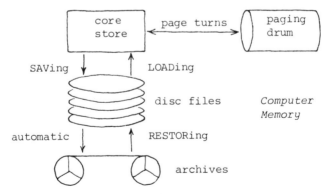

All these extension memories are based on magnetic recording, like your home tape recorder. The archive store is in fact just that: a tape recorder. The disc files are a stack of magnetic discs, like a juke box for LPs. The

234

paging drum is a revolving magnetic drum, and is an (optional) extension to the computer's core store. Users who are logged on but who are waiting to be worked on, will probably have their programs stored there. Even parts of a program that is being worked on may be there. You should not notice your program being put out to or brought in from the drum, except that the number of "page turns", i.e. the number of times bits (or pages) of your program are moved in and out, is recorded in your logoff message.

The disc files are where your programs are remembered when you are logged off. Procedures you want to be remembered are put onto the disc by the LOGO command SAVE. They are copied from the disc into the core store by the LOGO command LOAD.

7. APPENDIXES

7.1 TEACHING AND ASSESSMENT METHODS

This appendix records the methods used to teach the course and assess the students. For opinions on the success of these methods see Appendix 6 on the student questionnaire.

7.1.1 Formal Lectures

The course ran for three terms (of 9, 9 and 6 weeks) and there were three lecture slots per week. Because of the difficulty of finding appropriate background reading, the lectures were accompanied by the extensive handouts bound in this volume. Not all the lecture slots were used for formal lectures. Some were used for class discussions, problem classes, student presentations and an introductory teletype session. These are explained below.

Class Discussions. Three of the slots were used for holding general discussions on: Can machines think? Why is understanding natural language so hard? The scope and limitations of AI.

Problem Classes. Because some of the skills we were trying to impart were too new to some of the students for them to make much initial progress, unassisted, we set aside some of the lecture time for them to do exercises, with the lecturer on hand to give assistance if needed.

Student Presentations. Each student was required to give a 25-minute talk on an AI topic of his choice, usually his project, to the whole class.

Introductory Teletype Session. The whole class was assembled in the terminal room for the second slot and nursed onto the computer by a large number of staff. A series of games and simple copied commands were devised for this.

7.1.2 General Notes on Teaching

Audio Visual Aids. The overhead projector was universally used with prepared transparencies. Various films were shown including Winograd's "Dialog with a Robot", the MIT vision film "The Eye of a Robot", SHAKEY and the Edinburgh Car/Ship assembly film.

Tutorials. Weekly tutorials were held in the first two terms with small (i.e. 2-5 students), mixed ability groups. Exercises were set and marked by the lecturers, and were used by tutors as a basis in a variety of ways according to their style. These tutorials were replaced by individual project supervisions in the third term.

Teletype Sessions. Students were expected to put in about three hours a week at the terminal in interactive computing. This computing often involved preparation for tutorials. The terminal room was shared with the Computer Science Department. It could be used at any time, but the students were encouraged to use it during the four hours when an AI demonstrator was present.

Assigned Reading. This was kept to a minimum (approximately one hour a week), because of the lack of suitable material and the pressure of other assigned work. The general reading list is given in section 7.3. Specific reading is included in the text, usually at the end of each section.

Reading Fortnight. At the end of the first term in 1975/76 it became apparent that there were wide discrepancies in the progress being made by different students. It was decided to suspend all lectures and tutorials for a fortnight and run individual supervisions geared to each student's needs. The reading fortnight was not required in subsequent years.

7.1.3   Assessment
Assessment was by one three-hour written examination and a project. The marks were split on a 60 (examination)-40 (project) basis. Sample examination papers can be found in section 7.4. Projects could be of three types: a programming project, the design of a program, or a survey of a small set of AI programs. Students were expected to spend about 30-40 hours on them and write a report of 3-5000 words (some students spent much more time than this). The list of project titles for 1974/75, 1975/76 and 1976/77 is given in section 7.5.

7.2   A ROUGH TIMETABLE

No. of Lectures:	Subject
1st term	
9 + 6	Problem Solving (9 lectures) and Programming (6 lectures) in parallel.
7	Introductions to: Natural Language (2); Vision (3) and Learning (2).
1	Class Discussion "Can Machines be Intelligent?".
4	Natural Language
2nd Term	
2 weeks	Reading Fortnight (no lectures)
11	Natural Language (including 3 guest lectures by Yorick Wilks, and class discussion on Natural Language).
5	Representation of Knowledge
4 + 1	Vision (4) and a Programming lecture.
3rd Term	
3	Vision
5	Learning
9	Student Presentations
1	Concluding Class Discussion.

7.3   GENERAL READING LIST

In addition to the recommended reading on specific topics (to be found in the lecture notes), the students were required to read the following general references.

M. Minsky & S. Papert (1972) *Artificial Intelligence Progress Report*. AI Memo No. 252, MIT.

J.N. Nilsson (1974) *Artificial Intelligence*. IFIP Congress, August 1974.

A.M. Turing (1963) *Computing Machinery and Intelligence* in *Computers and Thought* (eds F.A. Feigenbaum & J. Feldman) pp.11-35. McGraw Hill.

F.A. Feigenbaum (1969) Themes in the second decade, in *Information Processing 68*, vol.2 (ed. A.J.H. Morell), pp.1008-22. North Holland.

C. Longuet-Higgins (1972) Artificial Intelligence. *Br. Med. Bull, 27*, no.3, 218-21.

7.4   EXAMINATION QUESTIONS

Here are the papers set for the class examination 1974-75 and the degree examinations 1974-75, 1975-76, and 1976-77. (There were no class examinations after 1974-75.)

Instructions to candidates were: Answer any FOUR questions. All questions carry equal weight.

7.4.1   Class Examination 1974-75
Question 1.

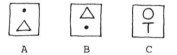

(a) Give a symbolic description of figures A, B and C and a description of the similarities between corresponding objects in A and B.

(b) Give a symbolic description of the rule which would change figure A into figure B.

(c) If the description of the rule were applied to the description of figure C what would be the description of the resulting answer figure?

(d) Suppose figure C had been

D

What goes wrong when we try to apply the description of the rule to the description of figure D? How might we amend the rule description so that it applies to the description of D and produces a description of figure E?

E

Question 2.
(a) What tests does Roberts' program use in order to select a picture fragment for matching to a model?

(b) Show one possible decomposition of the scene depicted below and one of the intermediate stages which would result from applying Roberts' program.

(c) What are the principle virtues of Roberts' approach compared to the way other programs you know do scene analysis?

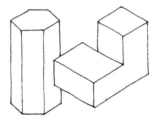

Question 3. Times of day are expressed by phrases such as: twelve fifteen, three o'clock, five thirty-seven, a quarter to three, half past ten.

(a) Make a context-free grammar to describe such sentences.

(b) Give the parse trees for the above phrases.

(c) Indicate by writing typical procedures how you would write a LOGO program to take a list of words and return YES or NO according to whether it is described by your grammar. (You may assume procedures CHECK and TRY are provided.)

Question 4. Discuss what is meant by:
(a) A Look-Ahead tree.
(b) A weighted sum of feature scores.
(c) Mini-Maxing.
Illustrate your answer with reference to any board game of your choice except draughts (checkers).

Question 5. Explain how a syntactic production rule may have a semantic rule attached to it to compute the meaning of the phrases generated. Illustrate your answer by referring to the meanings of various kinds of phrase in the blocks world program described in the course.

239

Question 6. Discuss Guzman's use of picture junctions and linking rules to decompose a picture of a polyhedral scene. What are the limitations of such an approach?

Question 7.

(a) Using the LOGO inference system translate each of the following sentences into a procedure call corresponding to its meaning:

> The Pope is good
> John Wayne is good
> John Wayne is courageous
> Anyone who is good and courageous is a hero
> ──
> Who is a hero?

(b) Suppose the translations of the sentences above the line were used to set up a database and the translation of the sentence below the line were used to interrogate that database. Draw the search tree of that interrogation.

7.4.2   Degree Examination 1974–75
Question 1.

Using the LOGO INFERENCE system:

(a) Give a partial symbolic description of the above drawing of a face sufficient to answer "yes" to the following questions, by direct data-base lookup:

> Is the mouth in the lower portion of the face?
> Is the left eye in the upper portion of the face?
> Is the nose in the centre of the face?

(b) In addition represent the laws that:

> Anything in the centre of the face is also in the middle portion.
> Anything in the middle portion of something is always above anything in the lower portion.
> Anything in the upper portion of something is always above anything in the middle portion.

(c) Represent the question:

> Is the nose above the mouth?
> Draw the complete search tree of its interrogation of the database.

(d) In addition represent the law:

> To infer that x is above y show that x is above z and z is above y.

240

and the question:

Is the mouth above the nose?

Draw some of the search tree of this interrogation. What problem arises? How might it be overcome?

Does your solution involve changing the LOGO INFERENCE system?

Question 2. Suppose that a computer program is to be written to take in simple directions such as the ones below and check their correctness from a street map from a given starting place.

'To get to the school, take the first road on the left, then the first road on the right after the bridge'

'To get to the hospital, take the second road on the left, then the first road on the right'

'To get to the station, take the fourth road on the left'

'To get to the bridge, take the first road on the right after the school'

(a) Write a context-free grammar to generate directions such as these, using the vocabulary in the above sentences.

(b) Explain how the following simple street map might be represented in LOGO so as to be usable as a semantic model for such a checking program. (Hint: recall the list structure representations of the state of the blocks world described in the course.)

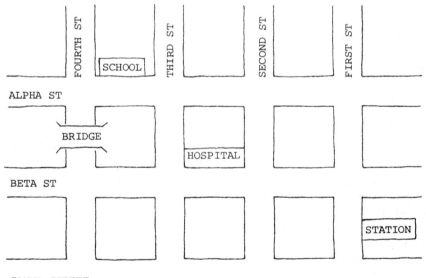

Question 3. The "Eight-Puzzle" is played on the 3 x 3 tray illustrated below:

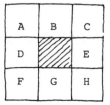

Mounted in the tray are eight 1 x 1 square pieces, which are free to slide left, right, up or down into an empty square. The standard position is illustrated in which the centre square is empty and the letters are arranged in alphabetic order. The puzzle is played by initializing the pieces in some other order and then trying to get them back into the standard position.

(a) Explain how a course of play can be represented as a search through a tree or graph.

(b) How would this representation help you to design a computer program to solve eight-puzzle problems?

(c) Suppose you were writing such a program. How could you represent in LOGO: states of the tray and moves. Explain in English (or LOGO) how you would apply moves to states to produce new states.

Question 4. "The correspondence between 2D features and 3D concepts is central to the design of any program for interpreting pictures of scenes." Discuss, giving a critical account of relevant aspects of vision programs you know of.

Question 5. What difficulties arise in attempting to write a computer program to understand children's stories? Describe some mechanisms which have been proposed to tackle them.

Question 6. Explain briefly (one paragraph each) each of the following:
(a) credit assignment problem
(b) hill climbing
(c) near miss
(d) Winston's notion of "appropriate generalization"
(e) discrimination tree
(f) diameter-limited perceptron

Question 7. Discuss *up to four* of the following statements. You may write at length on one of them or more briefly on two or more.
(a) Representing the effects of operators by add and delete lists solves the frame problem.
(b) Line-verifying is better than line-finding.
(c) Alpha-beta pruning is a way to obtain a gain in efficiency in exchange for an increased danger of overlooking the best choice.

(d) Since a program can now do analogy problems it makes no sense to use them on human intelligence tests.

(e) Attempts to model human intelligence on a computer are doomed to failure since the human brain and the digital computer are based on different hardware.

7.4.3   Degree Examination 1975-76

Question 1. The following context-free grammar generates linguistic descriptions of chess pieces in terms of their colour and board position. (Terminal symbols are quoted.)

> Piecename ⟶ pawn
>
> . . .
>
> Piecename ⟶ 'king
> Colour ⟶ 'black
> Colour ⟶ 'white
> Piece ⟶ Piecename
> Piece ⟶ Colour Piecename
> Nth ⟶ 'first
>
> . . .
>
> Nth ⟶ 'eight
> Position ⟶ Nth 'rank
> Position ⟶ Nth 'file
> Position ⟶ Nth 'rank 'and Nth 'file
> Description ⟶ 'the Piece
> Description ⟶ 'the Piece 'on 'the Position

(i) Write out five descriptions generated by grammar.

The current state of a chess board can be represented, e.g. in LOGO, by a list of quadruples, where each quadruple represents a piece by a list of four elements, namely

> PIECEKIND which is 'PAWN or . . . or 'KING
> BLAWHI which is 'BLACK or 'WHITE
> RANKNO which is 1 or . . . or 8
> FILENO which is 1 or . . . or 8

A chess playing program accepts linguistic descriptions of the above form and needs to find their meaning relative to the current state. For example, in the current state "The pawn on the first rank" might refer to [PAWN BLACK 1 8].

(ii) What LOGO or other data structures could you use as the meaning of each of the six kinds of phrase: Piecename, Colour, . . ., Description?

(iii) How could you write procedures to calculate the meaning of each phrase from the meaning of its components and (if necessary) the current state? (Say what these procedures would have to do; you need not write them.)

Question 2. "*Deduction* is a formal, logical procedure with well-defined rules and can be carried out by a computer program. *Induction*, on the other hand, by its very nature involves a creative component and cannot even in principle be done by a machine."
Discuss, with reference to computer programs you know of that claim to do induction.

Question 3. Below is a typical "Geometric Analogy Problem".

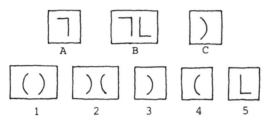

"Find the rule by which figure A has been changed to make figure B. Apply the rule to figure C. Select the resulting figure from figures 1-5."

(a) Explain, briefly, how Evans' computer program, ANALOGY, could solve such problems.
(b) Give an example of a geometric analogy problem which Evans' program would be unable to solve and explain why.

Question 4.
(i) Explain the distinction between forward inference and backward inference, giving as an example some AI tasks for which they might be used.

(ii) What problems arise with the use of (a) forward inference and (b) backward inference? Illustrate your answer with examples. Suggest ways in which these problems might be overcome.

Question 5. Consider the task defined by the following diagrams.

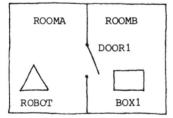 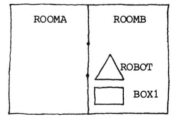

    Initial State   *Goal State*

The initial state is described by:
    [IN ROBOT ROOMA] [IN BOX1 ROOMB] [OPEN DOOR]
    [IN DOOR1 ROOMA] [IN DOOR1 ROOMB] [CONNECTS
    DOOR1 ROOMA ROOMB]

The goal is described by:

    [NEXTTO ROBOT BOX1] [CLOSED DOOR]

The Robot has three operators, described by:

    [GOTO ?OBJ] Puts the ROBOT next to the OBJ, and not next to anything else. (Represent this latter by putting [NEXTTO ROBOT *] in the delete list). It is applicable if the ROBOT and OBJ are in the same room.

    [GOTHRU ?DOOR] Puts the ROBOT in the room which the DOOR connects to his present room. Initially the ROBOT must be next to the open DOOR.

    [CLOSE ?DOOR] Closes the open DOOR. The ROBOT must be next to the DOOR.

(a) Describe the three operators by drawing an Operator Table giving their preconditions, delete and add lists.

(b) Describe a plan for achieving the goal, and draw a diagram giving symbolic descriptions of the sequence of states which would be achieved if the plan were executed.

(c) What is subgoal protection? Why is subgoal protection sometimes needed by planning programs? If a robot plan formation program, which used subgoal protection, was given the above task, what difficulty would it encounter? How might this difficulty be overcome?

Question 6. "A stimulus fragment takes its meaning from a consideration of its neighbouring fragments; i.e. from the context in which it occurs." Discuss possible mechanisms for achieving this principle of context-sensitive analysis, drawing examples from AI *VISION* programs with which you are familiar.

Question 7. Can computer programs be used to model human intelligence? At what level can they be compared? Illustrate your answer with reference to GPS or some other program designed to simulate human behaviour.

Question 8. Discuss the relevance of AI programs to either philosophy, psychology or linguistics.

7.4.4   Degree Resit Examination 1975-76

Question 1.
(a) What follows is a description of the behaviour of a hungry monkey. Explain how a computer program could build a plan, which if executed, would model the behaviour of the monkey.

245

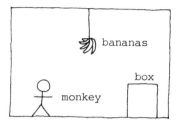

"A hungry monkey is sitting in a cage. Suspended from the roof, just out of his reach is a bunch of bananas. In the corner of the cage is a box. After several unsuccessful attempts to reach the bananas the monkey walks to the box, pushes it under the bananas, climbs on it, picks the bananas and eats them."

(b) Discuss the plausibility of the program as an explanation of the thought processes of a real monkey.

Question 2.
(a) Explain how the meanings of noun phrases and adjectives in conversations about a simple world of blocks could be adequately represented in a computer program.

(b) Discuss a proposal for representing meanings of verbs (e.g. Schank's).

Question 3.

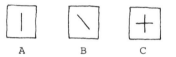

(a) How might a program for describing the similarities and differences between figures A, B and C describe each of them? How might it describe the similarities between A and B?

(b) Give a symbolic description of a rule which would change figure A into figure B and explain how this rule could have been formed automatically from the descriptions given in part (a).

(c) Apply your rule to your description of figure C. What is the resulting description? Draw the figure this describes. Describe the similarities between this figure and figure C.

(d) Alter the description of figure C so that your rule still applies to it but gives a different result. [Hint: consider the following possible resultant figures].

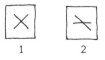

Question 4. "*Deduction* is a formal, logical procedure with well-defined rules and can be carried out by a computer program. *Induction*, on the other hand, by its very nature involves a creative component and cannot even in principle be done by a machine."
Discuss with reference to computer programs you know of that claim to do induction.

Question 5. Explain how you might use a system like the LOGO inference system to represent information about the countries of Western Europe, their capital cities, flights between the cities and which countries have a common land frontier. Explain how this could be used to answer questions about travelling by car or by plane from one country to another, e.g. how to get from Spain to Sweden. Point out difficulties (if any) from which your proposed method would suffer.

Question 6. "Perception is an interpretative constructive activity involving the interaction between stimulus patterns and stored internal descriptions."
Discuss how Roberts' program embodies such an idea.

Question 7. Discuss two of the following statements.
(a) Evans' ANALOGY program has shown that, given descriptions of the figures in geometric analogy problems, the process of finding a rule and applying it is purely mechanical. Therefore the only intelligence required to do these problems is in choosing the original descriptions.

(b) "The method of Samuel's checkers [draughts] program's learning was no different in principle from that of the human being who learns to play checkers" — Norbert Wiener.

(c) Since programs dictate a preordered, inviolable sequence of steps a computer's attention cannot be drawn by "fringe consciousness" to those unusual elements of a scene that are so telling in human experience.

(d) "The Analytical Engine [a very early digital computer] has no pretensions to originate anything. It can only do whatever we know how to order it to perform" — Lady Lovelace.

Question 8. Discuss the relevance of AI programs to either philosophy, psychology or linguistics.

7.4.5 Degree Examination 1976-77

Question 1. The European Economic Community has decided to pay farmers a subsidy of one pound per leg for every animal on their farm. Farmers must send in returns, in English, of the form
　　Six chickens and four cows and seventy seven pigs, or
　　One hundred and twenty seven hens and one horse.

(i) Write a suitable context-free grammar for these returns.

(ii) Sketch briefly how you would write a LOGO program to calculate the subsidy, giving some typical procedures with input and output and what they would do. (The answers for the returns above are 6*2 + 4*4 + 77*4 and 127*2 + 1*4 respectively.)

Question 2.
(i) Discuss briefly the design of a computer program which could search for a solution to the missionaries and cannibals puzzle.

(ii) Design an evaluation function for the states of this puzzle.

(iii) Discuss methods of guiding the program's search with special reference to the use of your evaluation function.

Question 3. What is means/ends analysis? Compare the ways in which means/ends analysis is implemented in GPS and STRIPS, with particular reference to the following points.
(i) How are differences represented in GPS and STRIPS?

(ii) How are differences found in GPS and STRIPS?

(iii) How are relevant operators found in GPS and STRIPS?

(iv) In STRIPS what corresponds to the three GPS goal types of: Transforming one object into another; Reducing a difference and Applying an Operator?

Question 4.
(i) Explain what is meant by 'deep case' as opposed to 'surface case'.

(ii) Explain eight possible deep cases which may be distinguished in English sentences.

(iii) Analyse the following sentences showing which cases are used
    (a) Mary sent John a parcel by rail
    (b) The airship burst into flames
    (c) I bought it for my wife

(iv) How would you represent the case structure of (a) as a series of assertions to the LOGO inference system?

Question 5. "Perception is an interpretative constructive activity involving the interaction between stimulus patterns and stored internal descriptions".
Discuss how Roberts' program embodies such an idea.

Question 6. Both Evans' Geometric Analogy program and Winston's Concept Formation program worked by forming symbolic descriptions of line drawings and compairing these descriptions. Compare and contrast the methods used and discuss the thesis that the formation and comparison of symbolic descriptions is a basic element in intelligent activity.

Question 7. Discuss in detail two of the following topics:
(i) The local-global problem in perceptron "learning".

(ii) Discrimination nets (or trees) such as EPAM. Construct a simple example.

(iii) Simon & Kotovsky's "induction" program for the completion of series. In what sense can machines perform inductions?

Question 8. Discuss two of the following statements.
(i) The design of programs to solve puzzles, like the missionaries and cannibals, throws no light on human problem solving.

(ii) Attempts to model human intelligence on a computer are doomed to failure since the human brain and the digital computer are based on different hardware.

(iii) A computer could never exercise judgement.

(iv) "In order for a program to be capable of learning something it must first be capable of being told it" (John McCarthy).

7.5   STUDENT PROJECT TITLES

1974-75

Student	Title
N.Conliffe	GRIP: Graphics Routines with Interpretive Parsing
C.Davie	Relation of work in AI and Psychology in Visual Perception
A.Fletcher	A Bidding Program in LOGO
T.Gayle	BUILD: A Lesson on Anarchism in the Blocks World
S.Holtzman	A Program for Key Determination*
I.Malcolm	Maze Traversing
D.Paterson	The Imitation Game: An Anti-Behaviourist Approach
P.Reddish	Approaching Perception
K.Schroeder	Models of Linguistic Description and Implications for Computer Programs involving Natural Language

*Also available as DAI Research Report No.20

1975-76

Student	Title
R.Aikman	Generating English Sentences
M.Bennett	SUBSTITUTOR — CAI error analysis
M.Bottomley	Machine Translation reviewed: evaluation of selected programs
K.Chisholm	DRAFT4 — A Draughts program
A.Coldham	Date (and time) Translation Quizzing Machine

249

P.Dunne	Two Move Chess Problems
E.Doe	Fox and Hounds
D.Giles	Natural Language Analysis Using Case
J.Kennaway	Geometry theorem proving
E.Lawson	A Puzzle Solving System
G.Morris	P.A. Learning Models
M.Schairer	Word into sentence: parsing an agglutinative language
S.Wrigglesworth	A program to play Backgammon

1976–77

Student	Title
G.Connelly	Variations on a theme, a computer program
M.Lineberry	A Program to play backgammon
K.McLelland	Variations on theme, a musical program
R.Omond	A spelling correction system (the speller)
A.Pauson	ELIZA
M.Philip	Assembling a jigsaw
P.Turcan	Mastermind
I.Wershofen	Numbers into numerals

The project reports are kept in the Library, Department of Artificial Intelligence, Forrest Hill.

7.6 STUDENT QUESTIONNAIRE RETURNS 1975-76

In order to get feedback to help us improve the course we issued a questionnaire at the end of each year. The questions asked in 1975-76, together with a brief summary of the replies, are given below. All 21 students who started the course were circulated: we received 12 replies.

Student Questionnaire

In order to get feedback to enable us to plan next year's course, we should be grateful if you would complete this questionnaire and give us your comments on any aspect of the course. Please be completely frank.

1. How did you find out about the course?
    Original source: Director of Studies, 2; Faculty programme, 5; a friend, 2; noticeboard, 1; lecture in Computer Science on AI, 2.

2. What factors influenced your decision to enrol in the course?
    Most frequently mentioned factors were: looked interesting; previous interest in AI; general interest in computers; relevance to some other subject.

3. What do you think the objective of the course was? Did it succeed?
    Most answers centred on the "Introduction to AI" idea, mentioning some aspect like past achievements, current developments, or scope and limitations. A few answers mentioned our specific aims of teaching the methodology or establishing the relevance with soft

sciences. Three gave no answer at all. Nearly everyone thought it succeeded.

4. Did you find the subject matter of the course: (i) Interesting?
   Nearly everyone found it interesting, some said "very".

(ii) Demanding?
   Reaction was mixed, from a non programmer's "I still found myself completely out of my depth" through "Some of the programs, particularly in Natural Language (parsing), were difficult to follow", to an experienced programmer's "Most of the work I did was fun rather than 'real' work". Most people found it time consuming (too many exercises) whether or not they also found it demanding.

(iii) Relevant to other subjects you are studying (please specify)?
   People also doing computer science or linguistics found AI relevant to those subjects. Otherwise a fairly negative response (e.g. not much — but should it be?), apart from one reference to psychology.

5. How do you think the teaching and assessment could be improved?
As an aid to thought we have listed the teaching and assessment methods below.

(i) Formal Lectures
(ii) Handouts
   Much appreciation expressed. They found lectures well prepared and were able to give full attention to following them: "Handouts were better than those I got in any other course so far — complete and readable — and most of the lectures appeared to be well prepared".

(iii) Problem Classes
(iv) Class Discussions
   More of both wanted. Several criticisms levelled at class discussions as being too infrequent, too general and class too large.

(v) Student Presentations
   Welcomed, but too late in term for feedback to be incorporated in projects.

(vi) Audio Visual Aids
   Compliments expressed on films, videos, overheads, etc.

(vii) Tutorials
(x) Other Assigned Work
   Strong feeling that these should continue into second term. A suggestion that they should be streamed by programming ability.

(viii) Teletype Sessions
   Too much programming in course. More personal tuition wanted.

(ix) Assigned Reading
   Several suggestions for improving the method of access.

(xi) Informal contact with members of the department
   Better than most departments but could be better. More information wanted about research work of department.

(xii) Examinations

(xiii) Project

Two requests for an extra class examination, balanced by one request for continuous assessment and one for exemptions for deserving cases. Opportunity to do project much appreciated but not enough time in course to do it justice (e.g. "why give 30-40 hours as a guide-line and then show previous examples which must have taken their authors about twice as long?").

6. (i) Was this your first opportunity to program a computer? (ii) If so, how hard did you find it? (iii) Did any particular aspect of learning to program give you trouble, e.g., a particular concept, a misconception you harboured, a particular type of bug? (please specify).

People with no previous experience found programming very hard (typical comments were "very, very hard"; "bad", etc.). Unfortunately (and significantly) they were unable to identify particular areas of difficulty, but just said "all of it (except the very early programming)" or "everything".

7. Please record any other comments you wish.

Mainly used to expand on above points. General mood was that course was good (e.g. "10/10 for effort put into 5(ii,vi,vii,viii, ix, xiii) etc."), but we had gone overboard with the imparting of specific skills (e.g. programming), to the detriment of general philosophical discussion (e.g. "more a series of intellectual exercises"; "even after deciding to drop the course it was stressed to me that AI was not a mathematical-type subject — but it is!"; "lack of spontaneous class discussion"). Some pointed out that the proper balance was difficult to strike while the class continued to contain a mixture of soft and hard scientists (e.g. "I don't think the same course should apply for people who have done computer science and also for people who have done nothing of this sort before"; "more places should be allocated to Psychologists, Philosophers, Linguists and other non-mathematicians").

7.7 AFTERNOTE

We received our most adverse criticism in 1975-76, especially as regards the teaching of programming to non-scientists. To answer this criticism we took the following steps.

(i) Plans were made to replace the existing one-year course with two consecutive one-year courses. The first was designed as an elementary introduction, and the second was skill and project oriented. These plans cannot take full effect until 1979-80.

(ii) In 1976-77 the class was divided into two groups for programming tuition: beginners and those with previous experience. The beginners' tuition was based on that developed in the highly successful Edinburgh LOGO project, using the primer *How to Work the LOGO Machine* by B. du Boulay and T. O'Shea. This method was a great improvement on the previous one, but it remains true that a great deal of time is needed to teach programming to students with a poor mathematical background.

(iii) In 1976-77, the number of exercises, which had been excessive, was reduced.

(iv) In 1976-77, tutorials were continued into the second term and grouped by programming ability.